MADE IN THE U.S.A.

The History of American Business

THOMAS V. DIBACCO

PERENNIAL LIBRARY

HARPER & ROW, PUBLISHERS, New York
Cambridge, Philadelphia, San Francisco
Washington, London, Mexico City
São Paulo, Singapore, Sydney

A hardcover edition of this book is published by Harper & Row, Publishers, Inc.

MADE IN THE U.S.A. Copyright © 1987 by Thomas V. DiBacco. All rights reserved. Printed in the United States of America. No part of this book may be used or reproduced in any manner whatsoever without written permission except in the case of brief quotations embodied in critical articles and reviews. For information address Harper & Row, Publishers, Inc., 10 East 53rd Street, New York, N.Y. 10022. Published simultaneously in Canada by Fitzhenry & Whiteside Limited, Toronto.

First PERENNIAL LIBRARY edition published 1988.

Designer: C. Linda Dingler
Copy editor: Libby Kessman

Library of Congress Cataloging-in-Publication Data

DiBacco, Thomas V.
    Made in the U.S.A.

    "Perennial Library."
    Includes index.
    1. United States—Industries—History.   2. Business enterprises—United States—History.   3. Capitalists and financiers—United States—History.   4. Entrepreneur—History.   I. Title.   II. Title: Made in the USA.
    HC103.D46   1988   338.0973   86-45652
    ISBN 0-06-091466-1(pbk.)

---

88 89 90 91 92 MPC 10 9 8 7 6 5 4 3 2 1

For Mallie

CONTENTS

CONTENTS

PREFACE

Contemporary Americans know the history of their nation in political terms: the era of the Founding Fathers, the rise of American democracy, the struggle of the Civil War and Reconstruction, the emergence of modern America. Largely neglected in this chronicle is the role of business, even though economic activities, unlike the political ones under a long string of weak Presidents and Congresses, are scarcely unimportant to the nation's development and stability. To be sure, by the late nineteenth century business would draw the attention of historians, but mostly to its negative side, such as the era of the "Robber Barons." For the same reason, there would be focus on the business contribution to the coming of the Great Depression of the 1930s, the formation of the military-industrial complex, the spread of American imperialism, and similar untoward events of recent times.

The tragedy of this one-sided interpretation is that the good that business people have done over the years has been interred with their bones. America was the world's first and most successful capitalistic nation. From its earliest days, business theory and practice were evident, although often camouflaged by intellectual and political matters that took center stage. What is more, the growth of America's capitalistic system was seldom easy, and usually an enormous challenge. At first, the challenge was a wilderness environment, then it was a system of religious values that attempted to put significant restraints on the accumulation of wealth. By the mid-eighteenth century the challenge was whether to accept a stable, slow-growth economic environment that British mercantilism illustrated, or to chart an independent and, perhaps, perilous economic course as a new nation.

The challenges multiplied by the turn of the nineteenth century with the acquisition of new territory, the arrival of numerous immigrants and, most of all, the expansion of democracy. When applied to politics, democracy meant that virtually anyone could vote and hold office; when applied to business, it meant too many businessmen, some able, some not, thereby providing the ecstasy of boom times and quick growth and the agony of sharp collapses and lengthy recovery periods. The challenge to stabilize this frantic situation was met not by government, which preferred a predominantly laissez-faire approach to economic matters, but by businessmen such as Andrew Carnegie, John D. Rockefeller, and Henry Ford. And when government did enter the scene in the twentieth century, the challenge to businessmen was to continue America's economic growth while ensuring that government regulations under new predicaments—including entry into major wars—would be honored.

Much of the story of *Made in the U.S.A.* is positive because Americans have viewed business positively from the perspective of their times. Increasingly, it was the business system that Americans turned to in solving their economic problems —even the first roads and canals, usually thought to be public projects, were the products of private individuals extolled for their enterprising genius. Foreign visitors flocked to the United States for a glimpse of America's state-of-the-art technology, and even circumspect British observers on rare occasions were forced to exude a bit of emotion over the expert ways of businessmen "in the colonies." Although many of the thirty million immigrants who came to America in the nineteenth century became farmers, more entered the industrial labor force with the aspiration of moving onward and upward in the business community. Not a few became inventors and businessmen whose products transformed American life—and for the better. In sum, "made in the U.S.A." was a term of endearment over much of the nation's history. And that past has created a contemporary business system—what I call a mature business civilization—that still has enormous strength and attractiveness.

This book is a distillation of my insights about American business history after a quarter century of teaching and writing about the subject. The narrative is designed for the general reader without sacrificing accuracy or meaningful detail. I am especially grateful to the editors of the *Christian Science Monitor* and the *Wall Street Journal,* in whose newspapers much of my work has appeared, for their encouragement of my brand of history. William H. Jones, formerly business editor of the *Washington Post*'s "Washington Business" section, gave me the opportunity to begin my career on a regular basis with my "Business of History" column. And my many students over the years, who often heard and critiqued the first drafts of my writings, deserve a special note of thanks for their always candid appraisals.

Although I take full responsibility for the book's contents, several individuals encouraged and assisted in this undertaking, most especially senior editor Harriet Rubin of Harper & Row. To my brother Arch and the late Wilbur Dorsett, professor of English at Rollins College, I owe special thanks for their constructive critiques of my writing. And to my academic colleague Herbert E. Striner, I am indebted for his provision of an appointment in a business college where I have found new perspectives about America's capitalistic system. To my wife of twenty-eight years, Mallie—a loving and supportive partner—I dedicate this book.

THOMAS V. DIBACCO

Bethesda, Maryland

1

THE
BEGINNINGS

It was a bitterly cold day—so cold that the sea spray froze on the coats of the ship's passengers. But this was minor in comparison to the other problems they had encountered since leaving Europe. Their ship, for example, was a wine carrier that had been poorly converted to passenger use. It was much too small for 102 people in addition to the crew and forced the mingling of individuals who had little in common with each other. Most passengers were hell-bent on making money in the New World, while a minority, "the Saints" as they would be called, hoped to build a religious community unimpeded by the arbitrary actions of political bodies. During the long voyage the Saints sang hymns, while the other passengers chimed in boos. Then there was the fact that both groups had been witnesses not only to jeering and similar improprieties but also to suicide. To be sure, many had signed an agreement on board ship setting up a new form of government in their new country, but there was squabbling over the matter, especially regarding the election of their first governor, John Carver. And as the groups moved on shore with the frozen sea spray on their coats, a reminder of the inhospitable quality of their journey, little did they realize that the worst was yet to come. It was the beginning, nevertheless, of a business civilization. Its leading figures would be William Bradford, who succeeded Carver as governor of what came to be known as the Pilgrim colony, and John Winthrop, the governor who molded the nearby Massachusetts Bay settlement. Both men and their environments, strongly religious, appeared at first glance to be unlikely individuals and settings for the drama of American capitalism to unfold.

This first settlement by the Pilgrims in New England in 1620 was indeed a business civilization, although not immediately. The first winter was spent in caves and shoddy wooden shelters; starvation threatened even though the Atlantic's waters were filled with codfish; and the Pilgrims were scarcely prepared to conduct diplomatic relations with the Indians of the area. But they were hardy souls, and after John Carver's untimely death in the spring, they would elect a governor who would forge America's first business civilization. William Bradford would serve thirty-three years as the chief executive officer of Plymouth and largely escape historic notice, in part because his modus operandi was low-key and hardly comparable to that of most political figures in early America. Born in Austerfield, Yorkshire, in 1590, Bradford was only thirty-one when he assumed the governorship of Plymouth for the first time. As a boy, he proved to be a maverick, deserting his family's church for a Separatist sect. The consternation that his move brought to his family was exceeded only by Bradford's absolute confidence in the rectitude of his choice. "Were I to endanger my life or consume my estate by any ungodly courses, your counsels to me were very seasonable," he wrote as a teenager to his relatives. "But you know that I have been diligent and provident in my calling, and not only desirous to augment what I have, but to enjoy it in your company; to part from which will be as great a cross as can befall me. Nevertheless, to keep a good conscience, and walk in such way as God has prescribed in his

Word, is a thing which I must prefer before all, and above life itself. . . ."

Along with other Separatists, Bradford ventured to Holland in 1608 when the English government began to prosecute religious dissidents. Why Holland? Because Bradford and his colleagues always tried to blend their religious beliefs with prudent material objectives. Holland was the center of Europe's cloth industry, with much money to be made by those with the requisite skills. Although Bradford received a family inheritance when he was twenty-one, he was not content to rest on such wealth. He learned much about the silk business in Holland and even became a fustian weaver. He made money and learned to invest it. In addition, he recognized that a successful artisan needed an education. So he learned to speak Dutch, French, Latin, and Greek. Leyden was an especially attractive Dutch city to Bradford because of its fine university and "learned men." Nevertheless, Bradford and the other Separatists recognized that Holland's bustling commercial life was too worldly. Sunday, for instance, was given over to much beer drinking and general frolicking, and while the present-day generation of Separatists could maintain their religious zeal, they worried about their children. "But that which was more lamentable," wrote Bradford, "and of all sorrows most heavy to be borne, was that many of their children, by these occasions, and the great licentiousness of youth in that country, and the manifold temptations of the place, were drawn away by evil examples into extravagance & dangerous courses, getting the reins off their necks, & departing from their parents." In spite of this dire prospect, there was something even worse for the 500 or so Separatists living in Holland: "the grim and grisley face of poverty." Little wonder, then, that materialism prevailed over religious purity, and only about forty Separatists along with Bradford decided to establish their own society in America.

The Separatists were not so financially secure, however, as to underwrite the entire cost of the American venture. A London merchant backed the enterprise, on the assumption that emigrants would establish a settlement just north of the Virginia Company's grant and location of 1607. Save for his diarylike account of the religious group's movement, Bradford doesn't emerge as the architect of a sound business society until many years into his governorship. The reason is largely attributable to historians' fascination with the dramatic aspects of Plymouth and their ignoring of the mundane ones. Every American schoolchild is familiar with the *Mayflower, Mayflower Compact*, the hard times of the Pilgrims in 1620, and perhaps with the fact that the name *Pilgrim* was applied to these people long after their settlement began. But once that first Thanksgiving took place in the autumn of 1621, Plymouth seems to have been a stable colony, with both historians and schoolchildren consigning it to an obscurity that it does not merit. Like corporation history in the twentieth century, the day-to-day annals of Plymouth after 1621 suggest a chronicle every bit as important, although not as dramatic, as America's later political disputes with Great Britain.

First and foremost, Bradford espoused capitalist principles. The London merchant who had backed the Pilgrims' removal required that all economic activity be communally owned. This meant that wives did the laundry of men other than their husbands and that economic innovation and resourcefulness, because of the lack of individual rewards, were dulled. This collectivistic society, given another kind of leadership, might well have continued, but Bradford found it offensive. Thus the Pilgrims became private entrepreneurs in 1627 when the agreement with their London backer was terminated and arrangements were made to pay off their debt to him. Although this took until 1643 (and at interest rates as high as 45 percent), every penny was repaid, and Plymouth would be dependent on no outside individual for its economic direction. More importantly, the Pilgrims under Bradford's management attempted to engage in economic activities that would bring them wealth. Farming, of course, was pursued but mostly to meet their immediate needs. The terrain of New England, rocky and occasionally broken by hills, mountains, lakes, and rivers, was rarely possessed of those valleys where fertile lands would sustain an agricultural society that was more than mere subsistence. Although the Pilgrims caught only one fish during their first winter in 1620–21—and found one other washed ashore—they began to master that trade, which would bring enormous economic activity for New Englanders for many generations. They also turned to fur trading, establishing posts as far north as Maine and as far south as Long Island. And Bradford himself formed a fur-trading company that was big business for a time, shipping in one six-year period some 10,000 pounds sterling of beaver furs.

No doubt these business activities were overshadowed by the religious ones for the reason that the latter were more difficult to achieve. Fish and furs were easier to garner than sinners. And sin was more likely to be divisive than hard times, when people stuck together. In 1642, the Pilgrims really seemed to let loose with their excessess, with Bradford complaining of a virtual crime wave. There was something for everyone: drunkenness, adultery, profanity, and sodomy. "Marvelous it may be to see and consider," wrote Bradford of that year, "how some kind of wickedness did grow and break forth here, in a land where the same was so much witnessed against, and so narrowly looked unto, and severely punished when it was known. . . ." Earlier, in 1627, the Pilgrims had gone after the sinfulness of an adjacent settlement, conducted by one Thomas Morton, who also dabbled in the fur trade. To be sure, competition in business matters was insufficient reason to make war on the settlement—until Morton erected a huge Maypole replete with a titillating poem about Indian maidens:

Lasses in beaver coats come away,
Yee shall be welcome to us night and day . . .
Then drink and be merry, merry, merry boyes;
Let all your delight be in Hymens joyes.

Needless to say, Morton's settlement was soon history.

In addition to forging a small but solid capitalistic base in the New World, the Pilgrims illustrated the stresses and strains that would accompany subsequent businessmen on the economic make. On the one hand, they tried to avoid the excesses of good living; on the other hand, they were not so austere as to look the drab part with which they've been popularly identified. They bought fine English goods, including lace scarfs, handkerchiefs, cushioned chairs, and the latest fashions. Bradford's clothes, for example, were often brightly colored, and other Pilgrims reveled in violet and even bright green fashions.

The basic dilemma of Plymouth was that it was small and isolated. It looked inward, essentially to matters involving only the area's saints and sinners. When, after more than seventy years of independent existence, it was absorbed by the larger Massachusetts Bay colony, it would appear that the nation's first capitalistic experiment was a mere footnote to history. But not really, for Massachusetts Bay was Plymouth writ large and would demonstrate that capitalism baptized in religious creeds was still capitalism—and that it was in America to stay.

Like Plymouth, the Massachusetts Bay settlement has been discussed in tones other than economic. Even the word *Puritan,* used to describe the particular brand of religious dissidence employed by early Massachusetts residents, seems the antithesis of the capitalistic world of American business. Yet it should be noted that poor people rarely have a monopoly on religion. In fact, among Protestant nations including the United States, religion thrives in good times rather than bad. Also like the Pilgrims, the Puritan migration to America was largely motivated by a sense of loss that adherents experienced—not because of hard times but because their economic affairs were such that contemplation about their larger place in the world was their luxury and frustration.

John Winthrop, who, like William Bradford, would assume

a critical role in the early history of the colony, is a case in point. He came from a solid family that would provide him with an ample inheritance. He would study law, become a lawyer and justice of the peace, and move up to higher legal positions in London. He also became utterly bored. The one excitement in his life was his religious creed, which shared little in common with the prevailing Anglican mentality. Puritanism stressed man's quest for perfection, even though that was unlikely ever to come about on earth. It emphasized continual activity in man's economic and religious life. Idleness, the plague of the well-to-do in England, was sinful. Puritanism mandated an economic calling that was respectful and successful, yet was wary of man's enjoying too much of the fruits of his success. And it attempted to serve as a model to the rest of the indulgent and lazy world that good people could indeed prevail. Massachusetts would be a city upon a hill. "The eyes of all people are upon us," said Winthrop, "so that if we shall deal falsely with our God in this work we have undertaken and so cause him to withdraw his present help from us, we shall be made a story and a by-word through the world, we shall open the mouths of enemies to speak evil of the ways of God and all professors for God's sake."

Expectedly, the Puritans did not master the art of sinless living, although they had high hopes when they left England for the New World in April 1630. Their initial settlement was not unlike Plymouth's: several hundred lived a hand-to-mouth existence for some months, which made sheer survival take precedence over the accounting of the sins they were committing. But by 1635 the colony was firmly established, and attention was given to rooting out each and every sin in their community. At first, the sins were obvious: unmarried men were lusting after the few women; children weren't being taught by parents to read the Bible; attendees at church services did not demonstrate the required attentiveness. As time went on, the line between sin and proper activity became harder to identify and even harder to follow. In order to sustain the religious group's adequate numbers for the future, compromises were inevitably made with regard to the qualifications for church membership. Such compromises, combined with the fact that second and third generations had little of the zeal of their parents and grandparents, ensured that Puritanism as a religion would come far short of its objectives.

Not so, however, with Puritanism's economic foundations. The Puritans were a leg up on the Pilgrims in this area. They were better off economically, often bringing their furniture and servants to the New World. They had no debts to any London investor. Winthrop was a manager who "fell to work with his own hands, and thereby so encouraged the rest that there was not an idle person then to be found in the whole Plantation. . . ." Instead of concentrating on furs and fish, the Puritans recognized the wisdom of attracting people to Massachusetts. For the area's biggest resource—land—was also its major problem. A society long on land and short on people would have a difficult time achieving economic stability. Immigration, helped considerably by the English government's restrictive religious policies, provided an enormous economic opportunity: English ships were loaded not only with immigrants but goods that could not be made in Massachusetts. Old settlers could afford to buy these imports because they produced goods that the new immigrants needed: corn, cattle, and lumber. The ripple effect of this expanding economy worried Winthrop and other leaders who feared that 20,000 immigrants in less than two decades would bring about ruinous inflation. So price and wage legislation was enacted.

To be sure, such regulation put some kinks into the developing capitalistic system. And it was burdensome to individual shopkeepers, such as Robert Keayne, a Boston merchant. Keayne appears to have been a God-fearing, Bible-carrying member of the community, but he was censured for selling tenpenny nails for more than what authorities believed to be a just price. Keayne never got over the social stigma from this experience, as reflected by his will of 1653: "These were the great matters in which I had offended, when myself have often seen and heard offenses, complaints, and crimes of a high nature, against God and men, such as filthy uncleanness, fornications, drunkenness, fearful oaths, quarreling, mutinies, sabbath breakings, thefts, forgeries, and such like, which have passed with fines and censures so small or easy as have not been worth the naming or regarding, which I cannot think upon but with sad thoughts of [the] inequality of such proceedings, which have been the very cause of tying up my heart and hands from doing such general and public good acts as in my heart I both desired and intended."

The price and wage regulations would ease, however, in large part because gains from a developing economy were too great to be ignored. Puritanism committed its adherents to hard work; success from working hard may well have been an outward and visible sign of the individual's religious worth. What is more, the New England terrain induced more than a reliance on farming: agriculture led to the construction of mills and canals and the first significant use of the area's great water power; inventiveness followed, as illustrated by a tide-mill constructed in Boston in 1643 for the grinding of corn; cattle meant not only milk and meat, but hides that led to the making of leather and shoes. The Puritan emphasis on literacy would give rise to a printing industry separate from London facilities, and while hymnbooks would be its first products, it was only a matter of time before newspapers and secular books would be published. In fact, the first newspaper arose in Boston by the end of the seventeenth century because of the demands of merchants for news that could affect their business. And, of course, all the supplies coming from England needed middlemen to direct their course to the buyer.

Massachusetts ingenuity would also be directed to the resources *in* the land. Iron ore was abundant in eastern Massachusetts, and by 1650 foundries were evident, producing pots, pans, and even a metal wagon to put out fires in Boston. John Winthrop's eldest son was an entrepreneur in the industry, establishing in 1641 a formal "Company of Undertakers for the Iron-Works" located near the town of Lynn. Copper mines were also established early on, and so successful was the growth of extractive industries that within a century Parliament passed legislation to protect England's iron industry from American competition. The Iron Act of 1750 forbade establishment of any "mill or other engine for splitting and rolling of iron, or any plating forge to work with a tilt hammer, or any furnace for making steel." But the legislation didn't work, for by the time of the American Revolution the colonies produced one seventh of the world's iron supply, having more mills than England. Parliament did the same thing with respect to American hats and woolens, but like the Iron Act, such legislation was difficult to enforce.

Much of the early business activity of Massachusetts Bay was camouflaged, although not intentionally. When individuals entered business as merchants or artisans, they also kept their ties to the land as farmers. These businessmen-farmers are less apparent today, but they were excellent adaptations to the social environment of colonial America. For land possessed that one quality that was perenially attractive to businessmen: it would always appreciate, whereas other business activities might fluctuate radically, especially in instances when the Atlantic Ocean would send ships laden with goods to its bottom. Moreover, land ownership brought farmers and businessmen closer together, preventing the rise of discord that in other countries would become bitter and debilitating in terms of economic development. The jack-of-all-trades characteristic of the Massachusetts businessman is illustrated by Samuel Sewall (1652–1730). A minister by profession and a graduate of Harvard, Sewall was a merchant, public official, and landowner, as recorded in a diary that mixes religion, personal matters, and business:

Oct. 27, 1687. Mr. Joseph Eliot preached the Lecture from 1 Cor. 2.2 parallels the diseases of New England with Corinth;

among others mentions itching ears, hearkening after false Teachers, and consequently sucking in false Principles, and despising, sitting loose from the true Teachers. . . .

Friday, Jan. 13. Betty Lane falls sick of the Measles. Get Mehetabel Thirston to help us. Sabbath only Mother and self at Meeting: Betty vomits up a long worm: Mehetabel goes home sick.

Ap. 2, 1688. Mr. Robert Sanderson rides with me to Neponset and gives me Livery and Seisin of his 8th of the powder-mill Stream, Dwelling-House and Land on each side of the River, Mr. Jn. Fayerwether, Desire Clap, and Walter Everenden, witnesses, the deed there and exhibiting it, when he gave me Turf, Twigg, and Splinter. Mr. Thacher's Son, Tho., dies this morn. Lodge at Unkle Quinsey's with Cous. Dan. Gookin, who has a son born last Saturday.

The biggest economic problem that faced the early Puritan society was social and demographic change. In 1640 the emigration from the Old World that had given the colony a new lease on life came to an end; the industries that had grown to supply new immigrants could have gone the way of the wind. Unlike the colony's unsuccessful battle with sin, this economic problem would be solved, specifically by finding new outlets for farm produce. Massachusetts had forests so dense and so tall as to defy comparison with contemporary counterparts. The white pine, for example, could tower to 250 feet, with trunks six feet in diameter. Oak trees were only slightly less impressive. In an age when handsome ships were as treasured as contemporary luxury cars and yachts and when wars among European powers were more prevalent than peace, New England forests became the basis for a mighty shipbuilding industry. Leading Boston merchants often invested in this lucrative area, with Andrew Belcher, a tavern owner who rose to a merchant, owning shares in more than 130 ships in the early eighteenth century. What is more, Massachusetts built ships for her own carrying trade, as well as the British navy, moving the area's farm and fish exports to the West Indies where molasses was purchased from the islands' sugar industries. Back home, rum was made, sold throughout the colonies, and exported, particularly to Africa in return for slaves, which, in turn, were exchanged in the Caribbean for molasses. This triangular trade that stretched from the African coast to the French West Indies to Massachusetts would sustain the New England economy for over a hundred years and lead the British, in the Sugar Act of 1773, to attempt unsuccessfully to restrict it. Then, too, Massachusetts ships would haul southern tobacco to Europe, adding one other dimension to its varied economy.

The individuals in the Massachusetts business civilization were also varied. There were shopkeepers and artisans who usually combined their home and shop in selling goods or making them and relied upon all members of their family for a labor force. In Boston in 1687, there were well over 500 artisans out of a total town population of 7,000. Shopkeepers and merchants accounted for another 500 persons, and there were still other businessmen—ship captains, the first managers in America—who played a critical part in the area's economy as well as politics. Of the nine selectmen in Boston in 1687, five were sea captains. Of course, the businessmen who stood out were individuals who, like Bradford and Winthrop, exercised colonywide political authority or catapulted to enormous wealth, such as John Hull. Brought to the New World by his father in 1634, Hull became an apprentice goldsmith and silversmith by the time he was eighteen. He mastered his craft, so much so that he designed the coins for the colony and became master of the mint. What is more, he trained numerous other youngsters in the two areas. By the time he was middle-aged, Hull had invested in land, ships, and a fine house in Boston—all possible from the income from his craft.

The Burrill family of Lynn, Masachusetts, went from landed wealth to investments in crafts, just the opposite of the Hull model. Led by George Burrill, who purchased about 200 acres of land in 1638, the children ventured into such trades as sailmakers, coopers, tanners, and shoemakers, first starting as apprentices and working themselves up to the position of master

craftsmen. And then there was a third way to business wealth
—namely, marriage—as illustrated by the life of William Phips.
A ship's carpenter in Boston for years, Phips married the
widow of craftsman John Hull, who provided him with the
money to venture into shipping and shipbuilding. Stirred by the
vision of raising Spanish galleons filled with gold and nestled
deep in ocean waters, Phips was so charismatic in his claim to
be successful that he got King Charles II to back his enterprise.
Sure enough, Phips salvaged a Spanish treasure ship off Haiti
and took in enough gold to become one of the colony's richest
men. The king made him a knight in 1687 and later the royal
governor of Massachusetts. Of course, such enormous wealth
resulted in both agony and ecstasy for the Puritans. It may have
prompted Reverend John Higginson's widely referenced sermon of 1663, which concluded with the words, "My Fathers
and Brethren, this is never to be forgotten, that New-England
is originally a plantation of Religion, not a Plantation of Trade.
Let Merchants and such as are increasing Cent per Cent remember this, Let others that have come over since at several
times understand this, that worldly gain was not the end and
designe of the people of New-England, but Religion. And if any
man amongst us make Religion as twelve, and the world as
thirteen, let such a one know he hath neither the spirit of a true
New-England man, nor yet of a sincere Christian." On the
other hand, Reverend Cotton Mather, who wrote a magnificent
history of the Puritans in 1702, concluded that Phips's "heroic
virtues" must surely have been a sign of God's blessings on him.

By the time of the deaths of New England's first leaders—
John Winthrop in 1649 and William Bradford in 1657—a business society had been forged in America. It would still pale in
comparison to the English economy, and subsequent economic
analysts would minimize it even more by using the term "petty
capitalism" to describe its modest characteristics. Boston, for
example, was still a village in 1650 and would reach a popula-

tion of only about 12,000 by 1722, nearly a century after the exodus to New England began. The entire colony of Plymouth could boast only 3,000 souls in 1660, forty years after its initial settlement. Had both colonies merely survived in a wilderness environment, such would have been sufficient to merit praise; that they rose to deal with other levels of the problems of civilization tends to maximize their failures, such as in religion, and minimize their accomplishments, such as in business theory, practice, and development. And it tends to ignore the personal side of the colonies' individuals, who wept and laughed and hated and loved. John Winthrop described his wife Margaret as "a very gracious woman," and in his many letters often poured out his heart, ending with an array of "kisses" that would make some modern readers blush.

So Plymouth and Massachusetts Bay appear insignificant by comparison to subsequent American history. No matter. For they should be seen, most of all, as representing and providing that elusive, if not mysterious, challenge that was missing from the lives of so many Englishmen. Not one Pilgrim opted to return to the Old World, and only a few Puritans. The Pilgrims said of themselves: "It was not with them as with other men, whom small things could discourage, or small discontents cause to wish themselves home again." And John Winthrop wrote his wife shortly after arriving in America, "I thank God. I like so well to be here, as I do not repent my coming: and if I were to come again, I would not have altered my course, though I had foreseen all these Afflictions: I never fared better in my life, never slept better, never had more content of mind."

2

BEN FRANKLIN: THE FIRST SUCCESS STORY

Benjamin Franklin was an unlikely candidate for America's first business success story. His father, who sired seventeen children, was a candlemaker content more with the stature of a secure trade than with increasing his wealth. Born near the sea in 1706 in Boston, Ben longed for a youthful career on waters that were likely to provide him more with seasickness than a personal treasury that runneth over. And his apprenticeship with his brother James, a printer, was scarcely a good partnership because the two differed so much in talent and ill-natured temperament (Ben had the edge on the former, James on the latter). Ben was forced to run away. One final factor that was a bad omen for Ben's ultimate success in business was his first encounter with money. "When I was a child of seven years old," he would recall, "my friends, on a holiday, filled my pockets with copper. I went directly to a shop where they sold toys for children; and, being charmed with the sound of a whistle that I met by the way in the hands of another boy, I voluntarily offered and gave all my money for one. I then came home and went whistling all over the house, much pleased with my whistle, but disturbing all the family. My brothers and sisters and cousins, understanding the bargain I had made, told me I had given four times as much for it as it was worth; put me in mind what good things I might have bought with the rest of the money; and laughed at me so much for my folly that I cried with vexation; and the reflection gave me more chagrin than the whistle gave me pleasure." That was Franklin's first and last serious capital loss. Most of all, however, his life embodied the unique elements that came to be identified with the American business success story—ambition, creative enterprise, self-education, research and invention, community service, and philanthropy.

Venturing first to New York and then Philadelphia, Franklin was a mere teenage runaway in a man's world. He liked the printer's trade by this time but recognized that his talent as a tradesman and writer was superior to the men he would work for. But Philadelphia was a great city for an ambitious young person. Ingrained in Massachusetts with the Puritan values of building a solid religious community, Franklin fit in readily in the city dominated by Quakers, who were much more liberal in their equation of capitalism with salvation. "True Godliness," wrote William Penn, "don't turn Men out of the World, but enables them to live better in it, and excites their Endeavours to mend it." Franklin's major problem in the City of Brotherly Love was that the area in the 1720s had enough printers. The only way for him to succeed was to open a shop that did something better. That would be a newspaper with a light and gossipy touch, the *Pennsylvania Gazette,* which was inaugurated in October 1729. Franklin drew upon the witty writings he had done for his brother's newspaper, the *New England Courant,* when he was an apprentice. The result was a *Gazette* filled with down-home matters on everyday life in Philadelphia: the newspaper published letters, took on controversy that was destined to sell issues, and told a lot of stories that were both entertaining and informative, such as the following on freedom of the press:

I take leave to conclude with an old fable, which some of my readers have heard before and some have not.

"A certain well-meaning man and his son were travelling toward a market town with an ass which they had to sell. The road was bad, and the old man therefore rid; but the son went a-foot. The first passenger they met asked the father if he was not ashamed to ride by himself and suffer the poor lad to wade along through the mire; this induced him to take up his son behind him. He had not travelled far when he met others, who said, they are two unmerciful lubbers to get both on the back of that poor ass, in such a deep road. Upon this the old man got off, and let his son ride alone. The next they met called the lad a graceless, rascally young jackanapes, to ride in that manner through the dirt, while his aged father trudged along on foot; and they said the old man was a fool for suffering it. He then bid his son come down and walk with him, and they traveled on leading the ass by the halter till they met another company, who called them a couple of senseless blockheads for going both on foot in such a dirty way when they had an empty ass with them which they might ride upon. The old man could bear no longer; my son, said he, it grieves me much that we cannot please all these people. Let me throw the ass over the next bridge and be no further troubled with him."

. . . I intend not to imitate him (the old man) in this last particular. I consider the variety of humors among men and despair of pleasing everybody; yet I shall not therefore leave off printing. I shall continue my business. I shall not burn my press and melt my letters.

Indeed, Franklin's commitment to put out a lively newspaper, replete with advertisements, paid off. Although his circulation was only about a hundred when he began, it ultimately reached 10,000, an enormous figure given Philadelphia's modest size at the time. But Franklin's big money-maker was not simply the *Pennsylvania Gazette*—it was *Poor Richard's Almanack,* which also illustrated the type of ingenuity that would be synonymous with American capitalism.

To be sure, the almanac was not Franklin's creation. He simply took an old idea and modeled it to the colonial environment. The main purpose of almanac writing in these early days was to provide readers with weather forecasts, tidal predictions, and astronomical tables. Franklin made it a book for every member of the family. There were recipes for the women. For children, the almanac was often the first means of learning their letters and some words, and for the writers in the family, the almanac's wide margins provided the opportunity for devising their own brand of food for thought. There was more: poetry, historical dates, conditions of highways and roads, times of court sessions, and gossip. Most of all, there were the proverbs that Franklin used to deal with the daily arrival of new immigrants often bent on speculation and shortcuts to wealth, raising the specter of a transient-dominated nation characterized by booms and busts. Franklin's adages were heavy on stabilizing virtues, such as thrift, industry, love, and marriage—and patience. And they were artfully written and hard to disagree with:

Keep your eyes wide open before marriage, half shut afterwards.

Love, cough, and a smoke can't be well hid.

A ship under sail and a big-bellied woman are the handsomest two things that can be seen common.

Let thy vices die before thee.

You may sometimes be much in the wrong in owning your being in the right.

Silks and satins put out the kitchen fire.

Cut the wings of your hens and hopes, lest they lead you a weary dance after them.

To be humble to superiors is a duty, to equals courtesy, to inferiors nobleness.

There are three things extremely hard: steel, a diamond, and to know one's self.

To err is human, to repent divine; to persist, devilish.

Fish and visitors smell in three days.

Lawyers, preachers, and tomtit's eggs, there are more of them hatched than come to perfection.

Of course, most of Poor Richard's aphorisms were taken from the pens of many European intellectuals that Franklin had read. He collected them and gave each an American flavor, and with every new edition of the almanac that appeared late in the fall each year after 1732 when the book was first published, he presented new adages skillfully sprinkled among such old favorites as "The proud hate pride—in others" and "If you know the value of money, go and borrow some." Franklin combined what in the twentieth century would become separate bestselling books in America: how-to volumes, new and updated annual editions, encyclopedias, and fiction. *Poor Richard* was second only to sales of the Bible, thanks to Franklin's ingenious methods of putting together his almanac.

Franklin's contribution to the model of the successful American businessman was more than his origin from modest means or his finding a better way to sell something. It was also his communityism, the recognition that unlike some other professions, business was forced to become involved in the affairs of communities, not only because wealth was derived from them (hence it was good business) but because public problems could benefit from private solutions. Franklin would ensure that American businessmen were utterly common, lacking in refinement and culture, in their dealings with people. His example would make it difficult for laboring men to call businessmen their enemies (in fact, AFL leader William Green would dub Franklin the Patron Saint of Labor), and the Junto that Franklin formed in 1727 was the forerunner to modern-day civic clubs dominated by businessmen that had as their goal communityism, fellowship, food and refreshments, and service.

The Junto consisted of members of disparate minds and backgrounds: a young Welsh Pennsylvanian who was "something of a reader but given to drink"; a middle-aged man who loved poetry and wrote "some that was tolerable"; a self-taught mathematician who "expected universal precision in everything said, and was for ever denying or distinguishing upon trifles, to the disturbance of all conversation"; a merchant clerk "who had the coolest, clearest head, the best heart, and the exactest morals of almost any man I ever met with." The group, like a Kiwanis or Rotary Club today, met weekly, with each member expected to hold forth on some subject every three months. The discussions were led by a presiding officer who had the authority to exact small fines for violations of propriety.

Most important, at a time when clubs were being organized in the colonies for social and prestige reasons, the Junto focused on important everyday questions, among them:

> Has any citizen in your knowledge failed in his business lately, and what have you heard of the cause?

> Have you met with any thing, in the author you last read, remarkable or suitable to be communicated to the Junto, particularly in history, morality, poetry, physics, travels, mechanic arts, or other parts of knowledge?

> Do you know of a fellow citizen who has lately done a worthy action deserving praise and imitation; or has lately committed an error, proper for us to be warned against and avoid?

> Do you know of any deserving young beginner lately set up, whom it lies in the power of the Junto any way to encourage?

Have you lately observed any encroachment on the just liberties of the people?

Is there any difficulty in matters of opinion, of justice and injustice, which you would gladly have discussed at this time?

And from Franklin's Junto came such ideas and accomplishments as the nation's first subscription library, the University of Pennsylvania, an insurance company, and a hospital. Not a bad list from what might be deemed rather average Americans.

Franklin made money from several sources in addition to his newspaper and almanac business. He permitted young boys to serve as apprentices in his shop and subsequently formed partnerships with them as they ventured out of Philadelphia to start their trades. Franklin might buy their presses and type and in a typical agreement receive a third of the profits. Or Franklin might agree to payment to him of an annual fee. His most significant partnership was made with one David Hall, who in 1748 relieved Franklin of the daily management of his printing and bookselling business, a liaison that lasted until 1766 and netted Franklin about 500 pounds per year. Franklin made money by making his printing shop a veritable department store filled with much more than books and paper: there was food (cheese, tea, coffee, codfish, mackerel, saffron, and chocolate) and a whole bunch of miscellaneous items (patent medicines, imported books, compasses, cloth, eyeglasses, even lumber). Franklin bought the contracts of indentured servants and slaves and sold them at a profit. One of his biggest and best investments was in buying linen rags that were sold to paper mills, with nearly 60,000 pounds of rags changing hands in one six-year period. Franklin became the Philadelphia postmaster in 1737 as well as the government printer for Delaware, Maryland, and New Jersey.

And although he died in 1790, the same year that the U.S.

Patent Office was founded, and thus was unable to benefit financially from his inventions and good ideas, he illustrated that progress was one of the most important legacies of an American businessman. Next to Thomas Edison, who racked up over a thousand inventions, Franklin was America's most creative act —and a hard one to follow. He dabbled in electricity, came up with a daylight-saving scheme in Paris that he figured could save Parisians some 96 million pounds of candles annually, invented a stove and clock, the harmonica, and a gadget for getting down books from the top of high bookshelves. He ground the first bifocals and even came up with a catheter. When his stove became a hit in his home colony of Pennsylvania, the governor proposed giving Franklin a monopoly on it, but the inventor refused on the grounds that "as we enjoy great advantages from the inventions of others, we should be glad of an opportunity to serve others by any invention of ours, and this we should do freely and generously." Franklin did studies on the loss of heat through evaporation, which would ultimately be the principle behind electric refrigeration, wrote extensively on the causes of the common cold, and was right on target when it came to a vexing problem for businessmen of all ages—namely, the difficult art of procuring a good night's sleep. Eat lean at dinner, counseled Franklin, keep a good flow of air into the room, use thin bedclothes, and beat your pillow and sheets occasionally. "These are the rules of the art," Franklin wrote in 1786. "But, though they will generally prove effectual in producing the end intended, there is a case in which the most punctual observance of them will be totally fruitless. I need not mention the case to you, . . . but my account of the art would be imperfect without it. The case is, when the person who desires to have pleasant dreams has not taken care to preserve, what is necessary above all things, A Good Conscience."

Perhaps Franklin's most impressive contributions to the model of the successful American businessman were public service and philanthropy. At the age of forty-two, he gave up his business enterprises, living off his investments (which included real estate) and becoming one of the nation's Founding Fathers—as a colonial agent, member of the Pennsylvania Assembly, minister abroad, member of the Continental Congress, governor of Pennsylvania, and delegate to the Constitutional Convention. In all these roles, Franklin was free of the financial worries that would plague men without incomes, which simply meant that financial gain and personal self-interest were removed from his political objectives. To be sure, he was human and sometimes offensively so: Franklin was a womanizer on two continents and early on in his life had sired an illegitimate son who, in turn, would father a bastard child. And Franklin would even write essays on associations with older women that served as another "how-to" guide of sorts. Part of the problem in Franklin's indiscretions was the nature of American religion by the mid-eighteenth century. Shorn of its ascetic and unrealistic Puritan strictures, Protestantism essentially had only one really significant difference from Catholicism in terms of members reaching salvation. Faith—not faith and good works (which Catholics believed)—would be *the* determinant of salvation. Bad works would not do Protestants in, according to this moral scheme of things. Faith put you in heaven, although the faithful person would probably do a lot of good works. But the emphasis on faith predisposed Americans of Franklin's era to take more moral risks—as well as political risks such as the American Revolution. Franklin was no exception to this tendency; neither was Thomas Jefferson. And like a good businessman, Franklin may well have hedged his salvation futures by participating so much in public service activities that did little to enhance his wealth or even his prestige since not one of his public offices was high-level. In his final appearance as a public servant in the Constitutional Convention just three years before his death, Franklin, plagued with numerous physical ailments, made his most eloquent plea on the necessity to do good, however, when the chips were really down. "Much of the strength and efficiency of any government, in procuring and securing happiness to the people, depends on *opinion,* on the general opinion of the goodness of that government, as well as of the wisdom and integrity of its governors. I hope, therefore, for our own sakes, as a part of the people, and for the sake of our posterity, that we shall act heartily and unanimously in recommending this constitution, wherever our influence may extend, and turn our future thoughts and endeavors to the means of having it *well administered.*"

A year later Franklin, in making out his will, bequeathed to subsequent American businessmen the legacy of compound philanthropy—even though his motivation may well have been to ease the guilt of his private sins. It was compound philanthropy because it would grow larger, like compound interest, over time. There were bequests to numerous individuals, including family members—but all that was standard legal fare. Then there were the portions of the will that were as ingenious as Franklin's business dealings: he left money that people owed him to the Pennsylvania Hospital; he gave money to the public schools of Boston; he gave the salary that he had not collected in his governorship of Pennsylvania to establish loan funds in Boston and Philadelphia, his two hometowns, for "such young married artificers, under the age of twenty-five years, as have served an apprenticeship in the said town" and who need some start-up money for the great game of life. Calculating the interest from the loans (5 percent annually), Franklin noted that within a few generations, thousands of young men could be aided and the fund would be of enormous proportions, even with some of it funneled off, as he directed, for public works projects in the two cities. Franklin's compound philanthropy would become American business's contribution to what later would become known as scientific giving. As for Franklin's humor, it too would be enmeshed in his last will and testament and not lost on subsequent generations of businessmen. ". . . considering the accidents to which all human affairs and projects are subject in such a length of time," he concluded in his will, "I have, perhaps, too much flattered myself with a vain fancy that these dispositions, if carried into execution, will be continued without interruption and have the effects proposed. I hope, however, that if the inhabitants of the two cities should not think fit to undertake the execution, they will, at least, accept the offer of these donations as a mark of my good will, a token of my gratitude, and a testimony of my earnest desire to be useful to them after my departure."

3
WILLIAM BYRD II: THE SOUTHERN EXPOSURE

The popular impression of Southerners in colonial times is one of vast plantations of tobacco manned by Black slaves and controlled by whites imitative of the English aristocracy. To a certain degree this portrait is correct: tobacco was a plantation crop that dominated the agriculture of Virginia and Maryland, whereas rice held this position in South Carolina. Black slaves would come to typify the labor force of the plantation economy, and there is much evidence to suggest that larger planters looked to England for fine imported goods and for the model of a proper social life. The only problem with this scenario is that it neglects the fact that southerners were businessmen of sorts, developing a model that was distinct from the example pursued by northerners. Profits, in the southern scheme of things, would not be as important as other objectives, nor would they be utilized in a fashion that would promote change and development of society; the labor force of Black slaves was permanent, lacked mobility, and was indefensible from a moral standpoint, yet it would still have characteristics that were positive when compared with northern society. Yankees, for example, were much more likely in colonial times to practice aversive racism toward Blacks (they avoided contact or practiced segregation), whereas southerners illustrated dominative racism: they prevailed, in other words, over Blacks but mixed with them. Black mammies suckled the planter's children, and the number of mulatto children would suggest even closer relations at times. Then there was the fact that southerners were less likely to be good businessmen. They overinvested in land and staple crops; the price of tobacco often fell as a result of overproduction; southern plantations were too often little towns within themselves, thereby preventing the development of public infrastructures and cities that would lead to a maturing business civilization. What was worse, when they ran into financial difficulties, as they often did, planters vented their spleen against northern society, which appeared to them to hum like a well-oiled, profit-making machine operating at the expense of southerners, a view that was more a scapegoat notion than reality. No matter. Southerners in their agricultural pursuits intended to make profits, which qualifies them as businessmen. That many of them, like George Washington or Thomas Jefferson, ended up with little money to show for their efforts masks the fact that they had other economic and social dividends that merit attention. The career of William Byrd II of Westover, Virginia, on the James River, illustrates these southern exposures as clearly as Benjamin Franklin models the northern entrepreneur: southerners subordinated their business activities to their home life, self-education, diary writing, social prestige, public service, quest for land, and satisfaction of basic human appetites. And their balance sheet in these areas was not unimpressive.

Byrd's father made his money as one of the first major Indian traders and planters in Virginia. Thanks to his father's fortune, Byrd was sent to England in 1671 at the age of seven to pursue his formal education, first at the Felsted Grammar School in Essex and later in Holland, which was widely believed to be the hub of European commerce and the practical school for developing businessmen. After his father died in 1704, Byrd inherited enormous wealth, which he invested in several ways: land (he owned 179,440 acres at the time of his death in 1744), tobacco, and extractive industries leading to the smelting of iron. He also served as a colonial agent in London for several years. Although Byrd's landholdings were extensive when he died, he was scarcely a good businessman. In fact, after his first wife passed away, he attempted to woo a rich London woman but was turned down by the woman's father because his income sheet was not up to snuff.

Why was Byrd a bad businessman? Because business was only a small part of his life, as illustrated by his diary entry of May 6, 1709: "In the afternoon Colonel Ludwell . . . brought us the bad news that Captain Morgan had lost his ship where I had seven hogsheads of skins and 60 hogsheads of heavy tobacco. The Lord gives and the Lord has taken away—blessed be the name of the Lord. In the evening Mr. Clayton and Mr. Robinson came and confirmed the same bad news. However I ate a good supper of mutton and asparagus. Then we went to dance away sorrow. I had good health, good thoughts, and good humor, notwithstanding my misfortune, thanks be to God Almighty." Of course, Byrd was not uninterested in bad economic matters that were caused by other than natural disasters. "In the evening," he wrote on June 14, 1709, "the boat returned and brought some letters for me from England, with an invoice of things sent for by my wife which are enough to make a man mad. It put me out of humor very much. . . ."

Unlike northern businessmen, southern gentlemen did their business usually from their homes, in a room or two reserved for such purposes and only for a portion of the day. Byrd "settled accounts" each day but that was only after he arose early in the morning and read some Greek, Hebrew, and Latin. And only after he recorded in considerable detail what he ate: food was important to Byrd and other Southerners because it was instantaneously pleasing. So too were people, visitations, and good conversation. ". . . I arriv'd at Colo. Martin's, who receiv'd me with more Gravity than I expected. But, upon inquiry, his Lady was Sick, which had lengthened his Face and gave him a very mournful Air. I found him in his Night-Cap and Banian, which is his ordinary dress in that retired part of the Country. Poorer Land I never saw than what he lives upon; but the wholesomeness of the Air, and the goodness of the Roads, make some amends. In a clear day the Mountains may be seen from hence, which is, in truth, the only Rarity of the Place. At my first Arrival, the Colo. saluted me with a Glass of good Canary, and soon filled my Belly with good Mutton and Cauliflowers. Two People were as indifferent Company as a man and his Wife, without a little Inspiration from the Bottle; and then we were forced to go as far as the Kingdom of Ireland, to help out our Conversation. There, it seems, the Colo. had an Elder Brother, a Physician, who threatens him with an Estate some time or other; Tho' possibly it might come to him sooner if the Succession depended on the death of one of his Patients. By 8 o'Clock at Night we had no more to say, and I gaped wide as a Signal for retiring, whereupon I was conducted to a clean Lodging, where I would have been glad to exchange one of the Beds for a Chimney."

Because southern businessmen like Byrd conducted their business from their homes, they were around to share the responsibilities of parenthood with their spouses. Children and good family relations were the blue-chip stocks of their lives. Byrd and his wife often walked hand in hand on their plantation, played cards and billiards together (in which he admits cheating), had numerous arguments (all attributed to his wife's being out of sorts), and sometimes cried together as a result of serious disagreements. They took afternoon naps, with Byrd boasting that he "flourished" or "rogered" his mate on occasion. As a father, Byrd was a strong disciplinarian with his children, but he was also present in their crisis times, such as when his young son died. "God gives and God takes away,"

Byrd wrote in his diary. "Blessed be the name of God. Mrs. Harrison and Mr. Anderson and his wife and some other company came to see us in our affliction. My wife was much afflicted but I submitted to His judgment better, notwithstanding I was very sensible of my loss, but God's will be done. . . . In the afternoon it rained and was fair again in the evening. My poor wife and I walked in the garden. . . ." And Byrd also spent much time in his library of 3,600 volumes, one of the largest in colonial America.

Not unlike other southern businessmen, Byrd was a Renaissance man who believed it was important to refine his pen. And indeed he did, with descriptions that are timeless for their clarity and insight. A good example is Byrd's discussion of North Carolinians:

> Surely there is no place in the world where inhabitants live with less labor than in North Carolina. It approaches nearer to the description of Lubberland than any other, by the great felicity of the climate, the easiness of raising provisions, and the slothfulness of the people. . . . The men, for their parts, just like the Indians, impose all the work upon the poor women. They make their wives rise out of their beds early in the morning, at the same time that they lie and snore till the sun has risen one-third of his course and dispersed all the unwholesome damps. Then, after stretching and yawning for half an hour, they light their pipes, and, under the protection of a cloud of smoke, venture out into the open air; though if it happens to be never so little cold they quickly return shivering to the chimney corner. When the weather is mild, they stand leaning with both their arms upon the cornfield fence and gravely consider whether they had best go and take a small heat at the hoe but generally find reasons to put it off till another time. Thus they loiter away their lives, like Solomon's sluggard, with their arms across, and at the winding up of the year scarcely have bread to eat. To speak the truth, 'tis a thorough aversion to labor that makes people file off to North Carolina, where plenty and a warm sun confirm them in their disposition to laziness for their whole lives.

Even in his short descriptions of people, Byrd gave the sort of care that if applied to his business would have made him successful. "She was a portly, handsome Dame, of the Family of Esau," he wrote on a journey in 1732, "and seem'd not to pine too much for the Death of her Husband, who was of the family of the Saracens. He left a Son by her, who has all the Strong Features of his Sire, not soften'd in the least by any of hers, so that the most malicious of her Neighbours cant bring his Legitimacy into Question, not even the Parson's Wife, whose unruly Tongue, they say, don't Spare even the Reverend Doctor, her Husband. This Widow, is a Person of a lively & cheerful Conversation, with much less Reserve than most of her Countrywomen. It becomes her very well, and sets off her other agreeable Qualities to Advantage. . . . At Nine I retir'd to my Devotions, and then Slept so Sound that Fancy itself was Stupify'd, else I shou'd have dreamed of my most obliging Landlady." And Byrd took advantage of even untoward experiences to write with verve. "The worst of it was we had unluckily outrid the baggage and for that reason were obliged to lodge very sociably in the same apartment with the family, where, reckoning women and children, we mustered in all no less than nine persons, who all pigged lovingly together."

Byrd's business activities that provided profits were a tannery business, fur trade, and coal mine. What did him in was tobacco, which was also the bane of other Virginians. For unlike rice and indigo produced in South Carolina, tobacco was constantly overproduced, thus leading to deflated prices. Because of falling prices, planters were often forced to rely on British credit to sustain them for a year and longer. The cycle of indebtedness from year to year often became vicious, leading Thomas Jefferson to remark that "debts had become hereditary from father to son for many generations, so that planters were a certain species of property annexed to certain mercantile houses in London." What was worse, the individualism of Virginia planters like Byrd was sometimes so great that ships picking up tobacco for shipment to England were forced to come to each and every plantation. Shipping charges under such conditions could amount to as much as 20 percent of the cargo's value. Then there were all sorts of fees, commissions, or charges by middlemen so that the likelihood of profit was small, provided, of course, the ship made it to its intended port in England. Mismanagement was also a problem, as illustrated by Byrd's diary entry of February 15, 1712: "I rose about 7 o'clock and said a short prayer and then gave Tom Osborne orders concerning what I would have done and then was set over the river to the Falls, where I found things in a bad way, but little tobacco, and that not well ordered, for which I reprimanded Turpin. I ate some milk for breakfast and then I rode to Kensington and found the tobacco as ill managed as at the Falls at which I was angry with the overseer and with old Robin. Then I crossed the northeast way to Falling Creek which was about seven miles and almost all on my land. I found all things very well and Mr. Mumford was there who told me all was well at Appomattox. . . . We walked about and then went in the boat about three miles up the creek to look for a stone quarry and found several and it was late before we returned."

What also helped to do in Byrd as a businessman was his insatiable thirst for land. To be sure, it was the most reliable source of wealth for colonial businessmen, but Byrd's quest resulted in enormous debts. For instance, his father left him some 26,000 acres, the best of which were located in the Richmond area. When he married Lucy Parke in 1706, he began his drive for more land, especially after Lucy's father died in 1710. Mr. Parke left his huge Virginia estate to his eldest daughter Frances. Lucy received only a sum of money. Because Parke's will stipulated that his debts should be paid from selling a portion of his land, Byrd offered, and Frances accepted, to assume the lands that needed to be sold to pay off Parke's debts. The only problem was that Parke's indebtedness, unbeknownst to Byrd, was humongous. For much of his life, Byrd was overwhelmed by debts that were in excess of the value of the land sold to repay them. And he tried to resolve the problem by buying more land: 20,000 acres in 1728, 5,200 a few years later, and in 1742 some 105,000 acres near the North Carolina border. To be sure, Byrd had a scheme in mind for all this land. He hoped to sell it to Swiss immigrants. Why Swiss? Because he believed they would be ideal immigrants, much better than the Scotch-Irish who were overwhelming the hinterland of Pennsylvania "like the Goths and Vandals of old." Byrd even wrote a *Natural History of Virginia or The Newly Discovered Eden* to encourage the settlement. The book was translated into German and supplied to prospective Swiss immigrants. In it and other writings, Byrd established a sort of first chamber of commerce for Virginia: "Besides the advantage of a pure air," he wrote to the Earl of Orrery in 1726, "we abound in all kinds of provisions without expense (I mean we who have plantations). I have a large family of my own, and my doors are open to everybody, yet I have no bills to pay, and half-a-crown will rest undisturbed in my pocket for many moons together. Like one of the patriarchs, I have my flocks and my herds, my bondmen and bondwomen, and every sort of trade amongst my own servants that I live in a kind of independence of everyone but Providence. However this sort of life is without expense, yet it is attended with a great deal of trouble. I must take care to keep all my people to their duty, to set all the springs in motion and to make every one draw his equal share to carry the machine forward. But then 'tis an amusement in this silent country and a continual exercise of our patience and economy. Another thing My Lord, that recommends this country very much: we sit securely under our vines and fig trees without any danger to our property. We have neither public robbers nor private, which your Lordship will think very strange when we have often needy governors and pilfering convicts sent amongst us. . . . Thus, my Lord, we are very happy in our Canaans if we could but forget the onions and fleshpots of Egypts. . . ."

Byrd's project for attracting ideal colonists failed. A boatload of emigrants got very close to Virginia's coast, but the ship went down before actual land was reached. A few Swiss-Germans made it, as did some of the Scots whom Byrd didn't want, but his grand scheme for a Garden of Eden failed. Byrd also put his money into other loss leaders. He tried to produce grapes in quantity as well as hemp, the latter by draining the Dismal Swamp, a task that George Washington would later contemplate. And he was absolutely convinced that ginseng was the root for all seasons—well, at least some seasons. "Its virtues are that it gives an uncommon warmth and vigor to the blood and frisks the spirits beyond any other cordial. It cheers the heart even of a man that has a bad wife and makes him look down with great composure on the crosses of the world. It promotes insensible perspiration, dissolves all phlegmatic and viscous humors, that are apt to obstruct the narrow channels of the nerves. It helps the memory and would quicken Helvetian dullness. 'Tis friendly to the lungs, much more than scolding itself. It comforts the stomach and strengthens the bowels, preventing all colics and fluxes. In one word, it will make a man live a great while, and very well while he does live. And what is more, it will even make old age amiable, by rendering it lively, cheerful, and good humored. However, 'tis of little use in the feats of love, as a great prince once found, who, hearing of its invigorating quality, sent as far as China for some of it, though his ladies could not boast of any advantage thereby." And Byrd's dreams for making money from silk culture never materialized.

Byrd's involvement in colonial matters—he was an agent for Virginia—took him away from his private business matters and led him to London for several lengthy periods of his life. He loved London, except for those early years when, on his father's wishes, he was forced to train at the counting house of Perry & Lane. Having subsequently pursued legal training in the Middle Temple and been admitted to the bar, Byrd loved the trappings of the social world of barristers. He mingled among Europe's most noted celebrities, including Sir Robert Southwell, secretary of state for Ireland and president of the Royal Society. Thanks to his association with Southwell, Byrd became a member of the society in 1696, an honor that he cherished, although his formal contributions to learning were nonexistent. Instead of a southern businessman, Byrd longed to be a wordly scholar/statesman, as illustrated by the epitaph that he wrote, which minimized his capitalistic activities in the New World:

Being born to one of the amplest fortunes in this country,
He was early sent to England for his education,
Where under the care and direction of Sir Robert Southwell,
And ever favored with his particular instructions,
He made a happy proficiency in polite and varied learning.
By the means of this same noble friend,
He was introduced to the acquaintance of many of the first persons of his age
For knowledge, wit, virtue, birth, of high station,
And particularly contracted a most intimate and bosom friendship
With the learned and illustrious Charles Boyle, Earl of Orrery.
He was called to the bar in the Middle Temple,
Studied for some time in the Low Countries,
Visited the Court of France,
And was chosen Fellow of the Royal Society.
Thus eminently fitted for the service and ornament of his country,
He was made Receiver-General of His Majesty's revenues here,
Was thrice appointed public agent to the Court and Ministry of England,
And being thirty-seven years a member,
At last became President of the Council of that Colony.
To all this were added great elegance of taste and life,
The well-bred gentleman and polite companion,
The splendid economist and prudent father of a family,
With the constant enemy of all exorbitant power,
And hearty friend to the liberties of his country.

Of course, Byrd was not alone in this quest for political and social stardom; he was simply the first of a long line of Virginia gentlemen noted more for their public service than skills as businessmen, to wit, George Washington, Thomas Jefferson, James Madison, and James Monroe. It is also one of the reasons that Byrd and his Virginia successors were constantly short of funds and even died without particular pecuniary distinction. Public servant Byrd as a colonial agent waged a spirited fight on behalf of Virginia planters who were prevented by British regulations from growing and refining cotton and flax. He was unsuccessful, in large part, because British merchants feared a loss of their export business to America if home industry were permitted. But life in London, as Byrd wanted to enjoy it, was expensive. He had therefore no qualms, after his wife Lucy died of smallpox in 1716, to pursue a rich heiress, whom he found in Mary Smith, daughter of the commissioner of excise. He made every effort to convince her father that he was financially able to meet her needs, even to the extent of attempting unsuccessfully to procure a huge loan of 10,000 pounds in order to boost his cash on hand. He also wrote nasty notes to the suitor who eventually won her hand. And as luck would have it, the whole scenario ended in a manner that left Byrd so close and yet so far. Mary married on July 8, 1718. Two days later, her father died. Mary died in 1721, twenty-three years before Byrd would pass away. Byrd tried next to marry a rich widow but failed because the taking in of his daughters by his intended wife was not attractive. After returning to America, Byrd went back to England and once more failed to marry a rich heiress, this one a granddaughter of Charles II. Finally, he wed in 1724, but wife Maria Taylor was without wealth.

Of all Byrd's failures, his inability to make a success of his tobacco business was the one that he shared with most of his Virginia counterparts. The prevalence of disease in colonial times made Byrd campaign for the employment of tobacco as medicine, and no American, before and after his time, made such a hard sell for the bad weed. "I am humbly of opinion," he wrote in *The Discourse Concerning the Plague,* "that when there is any danger of pestilence, we can't more effectually consult our preservation than by providing ourselves with a reasonable quantity of fresh, strong scented tobacco. We should wear it about our clothes and about our coaches. We should hang bundles of it round our bed, and in the apartments wherein we most converse. If we have an aversion to smoking, it would be very prudent to burn some leaves of tobacco in our dining rooms, lest we swallow infection with our meat. It will also be very useful to take snuff plentifully made of the pure leaf to secure the passages to our brain. Nor must those only be guarded but the pass to our stomachs should be also safely defended by chewing this great antipoison very frequently."

Byrd also failed in his attempt to lead a straight and narrow life. He enjoyed the pleasures of the flesh, and his sexual escapades ran the gamut from his household maids to wenches found in parks in London to women in Europe's high society. To be sure, he worried about all this gallivanting and what it might do to his immortal soul. For that reason, he constantly asked for God's forgiveness. What is more, he even took to trying to invent contraptions that would prevent his sexual misdeeds. One was a "leaden girdle" that could be worn at all times. Another emphasized clothing and as a backup a diet of "sour lemons and abundance of lettuce to cool . . . concupiscence."

As with Byrd's other business ventures, these attempts failed.

4

THE AMERICAN REVOLUTION

The American Revolution was an enormous dilemma for most businessmen. By the mid-eighteenth century economic growth in the thirteen colonies was sound, a result of incremental advances over several decades. The British mercantilist system, inaugurated in 1660, had more carrots than sticks for colonists by 1750, primarily because it was designed to effect concentration by businessmen on both sides of the Atlantic on economic efforts that they excelled in. For that reason, American merchants were assured of markets for such goods as tar, pitch, resin, indigo, rice, and lumber. British ships, which the colonists were required to use, were more expensive than Dutch counterparts, but they were the best and most dependable in the western world. Marketing fairs in the British Isles were the most sophisticated in Europe, assuring colonial merchants of the best distribution system that money could buy, even for tobacco growers with their enormous surpluses. The adverse features of the mercantilist system were that certain goods that competed with British specialties could not be exported from America, nor could colonists trade with any nation other than Great Britain with respect to certain products. Of course, America's lengthy coastline permitted smuggling, and Britain's lax enforcement helped to promote it, especially in the French West Indies. Then to maintain the regulatory system's paperwork and bureaucracy, there were modest fees placed along the trading continuum. Nevertheless, it was a good, secure, and predictable system. The dilemma was whether to risk its benefits for other laudable but elusive objectives. Businessmen would be reluctant revolutionaries by any measure, for there were scenarios much worse than a capitalistic system characterized by modest restrictions: there was, for example, the likelihood that war would evoke class conflict, violence, and destruction of property. Even worse was the specter of mob rule and anarchy. Fortunately for most businessmen, the decision for revolution was not theirs to make, nor was their participation critical.

Britain's troubles with the American colonies began in 1763. That was the year ending the Seven Years' War or French and Indian War, the last and most significant of four wars fought with France since 1689. The war, fought in the Old and New Worlds, provided the English with territorial gains. In America this meant that the French were almost totally removed, and the western terminus of English territory became the Mississippi River. In spite of these acquisitions, the war was the most burdensome one to English taxpayers, who historically had borne the total burden of support for the nation's empire. Americans, for example, paid not one cent in taxation; the fees imposed in the mercantilist system were just that and in no way analogous to the taxes that the English in Great Britain paid. Quite logically, then, the British ministry in 1763 decided that English-Americans must bear a small measure of taxation for the mother country's success in empire building.

The first revenue-raising measure in 1764 dealt with molasses imported from the French West Indies; instead of a sixpence rate per gallon that was not enforced in the old days, there was levied a threepence rate that would be enforced, specifically, by a beefing up of the British customs agency in America. There were also modest changes in import duties for certain goods, such as wines coming from various nations in Europe. Although hardly onerous, these measures came at the wrong time, at the close of a war that had given a boost to the American economy. Thus the postwar letdown combined to make the colonial reaction negative, especially among merchants in New England dependent on the molasses trade for the making of rum. Close on the heels of these enactments came the Stamp Act, designed to raise tax monies through levies placed on legal documents, newspapers, commercial papers, marriage licenses, liquor permits, and the like. The legislation not only included heavy fines for evasion but prosecution through courts that did not require trial by jury. The outcry against the Stamp Act in America grew like compound interest with each passing day, in large part because it affected those most likely to be vocal and to disseminate their views widely, namely, lawyers, merchants, and newspaper editors. The result was a boycott of English imports in various cities. And it was effective—so much so that within a year the Stamp Act, which had scarcely been enforced anyhow, was repealed. Additionally, the molasses duty was reduced from threepence to one. Sentiment throughout the colonies for Britain's actions was most favorable, with one observer commenting that "every grievance of which you complained is now absolutely and totally removed—a joyful and happy event for the late disconsolate inhabitants of America."

For most merchants, who operate more in the realm of reality and bottom line than principle, the situation by 1766 was quite tolerable. To be sure, Britain had exerted a new kind of authority over the American colonies and the next time its actual cost could be significant. But merchants worried less about renewed British legislation than the fomenting of civil disorder by elements of the population that seemed intent on regarding violence as a proper reaction to the new British measures. The stamp office in Boston, for instance, was destroyed by a mob in 1765. Thomas Hutchinson, a successful merchant and colonial administrator, had his home burned down when he acquiesced to the Stamp Act. Hutchinson identified the perpetrators as "the rabble of the town of Boston." Indeed, as many merchants recognized, there was something worse than British tyranny. It was American anarchy.

In 1767 the British Parliament imposed additional taxes on the colonies. The Townshend Acts provided for duties on lead, tea, paper, paint, and glass imported from Great Britain, with the monies going to pay British judges and civil officials in the colonies rather than relying upon American legislatures for appropriations. As with the earlier acts, the legislation sanctioned the strengthening of the customs collectors—to such an extent that they could enter any establishment to collect duties, provided they possessed a writ of assistance, which was of dubious legality. Again, merchants and their allies resorted to orderly remonstration through associations urging boycott of these particular British goods as well as others. The boycott of tea brought forth some ingenious doggerel:

Throw aside your Bohea and your Green Tyson Tea,
And all things with a new fashion duty;
Procure a good store of the choice Labradore,
For there'll soon be enough to suit ye;
These do without fear, and to all you'll appear
Fair, charming, true, lovely and clever;
Though the times remain darkish, young men may be sparkish,
And love you much stronger than ever.

Within a year the merchant pressure worked, and Parliament appeared ready to repeal all the Townshend duties except the one on tea. The only problem was that opposition to the duties became for some colonists an opportunity to demand more from the mother country than seemed prudent to merchants. Some groups, for example, wanted to boycott all English goods and demanded that citizens sign petitions to that effect. Merchants suspected of trading with the British were informally charged with treason in local newspapers, including none other than John Hancock, who was forced to write a column in his own defense. Taking a potshot at the fact that mob reaction was brewing, one merchant opposed to a total embargo of English goods declared, "I had rather be a slave under one master, for I know who he is, I may perhaps be able to please him, than a slave to an hundred or more who I don't know where to find nor what they expect of me." Outbreaks of violence occurred, the most serious the confrontation between British troops and townspeople in 1770 in what came to be called the Boston Massacre. Repeal of all Townshend Act provisions except the tax on tea permitted merchants and the general public to resume normal relations with the mother country, but merchants had again been reminded that radicalism could be the most important hallmark of any future problems with Britain.

The controversy was renewed in 1773 when Parliament passed an act designed to give the ailing East India Tea Company a monopoly of the colonial tea business. Prior to 1773 the company sold tea directly to English wholesalers who in turn passed it on to American counterparts; with the Tea Act the company could sell directly to its own agents in America, thereby bypassing traditional merchants. The price of tea, as a result, would go down, the company could get rid of its enormous surplus, and—so English ministers thought—the American tea drinker would be delighted. Of course, to merchants the Tea Act smacked of an unwarranted involvement in the colonial economic process. "The scheme appears too big," read one commentary in a New York newspaper, "with mischievous consequences and dangers to America . . . as it may create a monopoly; or, as it may introduce a monster, too powerful for us to control, or contend with, and too rapacious and destructive, to be trusted, or even seen without horror, that may be able to devour every branch of our commerce, drain us of all property and substance, and wantonly leave us to perish by thousands. . . ." In Boston where the opposition was the strongest, merchants found themselves in the dilemma of being among opponents committed to the destruction of property. When the Boston Tea Party occurred, this rift between merchants and violent opponents rivaled warfare. And in other colonies the scenario was repeated. "Whenever a factious set of People," wrote one moderate on the matter, "rise to such a Pitch of Insolence, as to Prevent the Execution of the Laws, or destroy the Property of Individuals, just as their Caprice or Humor leads them; there is an end of all Order and Government, Riot and Confusion must be the natural Consequence of such Measures. It is impossible for Trade to flourish where Property is insecure: Whether this has not been the Case at Boston for some time past, you are the best Judge. There is a strange Spirit of Licentiousness gone forth into the World, which shelters itself under the venerable and endearing Name of Liberty, but is as different from it as Folly is of Wisdom." Notable businessmen like Ben Franklin opposed the violence of the Boston Tea Party, but the problem was that their voices were becoming a minority among the adversaries of British policy.

This trend was clearly illustrated in the wake of the Boston Tea Party when Britain passed what came to be known as the Coercive Acts. The legislation closed the port of Boston until such time as the East India Company was compensated for its losses, made the upper house of the Massachusetts legislature appointive by the king (instead of elected by the lower house), and restricted the holding of town meetings. Not a small portion of the merchant community acquiesced in the parliamentary actions because the destruction of property and mob violence were worse alternatives. But there were exceptions, such as William Henry Drayton of South Carolina, who went from a conservative position to a radical one: "The same spirit of indignation," wrote Drayton, "which animated me to condemn popular measures in the year 1769, because although avowedly in defence of liberty, they absolutely violated the freedom of society, by demanding men, under pain of being stigmatized, and of sustaining detriment in property, to accede to resolutions, which, however well meant, could not . . . but be . . . very grating to a freeman, so, the *same spirit* of indignation . . . actuates me in like manner, *now to assert* my freedom *against the malignant* nature of the late five Acts of Parliament." Specifically, merchants like Drayton could agree with closing the port of Boston but could not subscribe as readily to the portion of the Coercive Acts limiting the political rights of Bostonians. In this respect, Britain's actions, however merited, could work to the advantage of radicals in America. Therefore, sympathy for Bostonians spread throughout the colonies—to the extent that resolutions supporting boycotts of British imports were passed, as well as a call for an intercolonial congress to deal with the crisis. Nowhere was the rift between moderates and radicals so evident than in Virginia, where the merchants were at odds with the debt-burdened planters who were vocal critics of the mother country. According to James Madison, merchants were among the first to contend that it was wrong for Virginians to use the Boston crisis as a pretext for reneging on their debts to British creditors. Radicals were artful, however: in an extralegal Virginia convention held in the summer of 1774, they advanced higher-sounding themes as the basis for taking issue with the British actions toward Boston. Yet within a few months of the convention, radicals in nearby Annapolis did more than destroy tea. They set fire and sunk the ship *Peggy Stewart* carrying the tea.

When the First Continental Congress convened in Philadelphia in August 1774, only eleven of the fifty-six delegates were merchants in the strict sense of the term. Half were lawyers who obviously had some appreciation of the lawful protests that the merchants were concerned about. In this sense, moderates controlled the legislation: a nonimportation agreement, modeled along the lines of earlier boycotts, was effected in late September; a nonexportation resolution, with loopholes for southern planters, was also agreed to. Afterward, however, radicals made the most of the congress's work by making enforcement of the boycott a patriotic act and violation tantamount to treason. And since many of the so-called enforcers were undistinguished men, merchants were alienated. Even worse was the fact that radical elements after 1774 rushed to control the extralegal committees and councils that implemented the congressional acts. Merchants, on the other hand, were forced to worry about their businesses and other practical matters, such as importing great quantities of goods before the actual date of implementation, which was not necessarily an unpatriotic act since colonials wanted to have their boycott as well as imported goods. When merchants in Virginia tried to enforce their debts against planters, the radicals were successful in closing the courts, ensuring that lands and other property could not be seized; at the same time, radicals offset these offensive actions by passing resolves designed to encourage industrial activities by businessmen—as, for example, in the manufacture of cloth, steel, and paper.

The fighting that broke out at Lexington and Concord in April 1775 also worked to the advantage of radicals; the only solace for merchants was that the Second Continental Congress convening the next month might be moderate. That was easier said than done, however. "We are between hawk and buzzard," summarized one congressional delegate. "We puzzle ourselves between the commercial and warlike opposition." Of the two, war seemed the more likely event, what with Lexington and Concord and two months later the Battle of Bunker Hill. George Washington was therefore appointed commander in chief of the colonial armies, with the congress passing on July 6, 1775, the "Declaration of the Causes and Necessity of Taking up Arms," written by Thomas Jefferson and John Dickinson. In short, the political and military clashes with Great Britain illustrated that what had begun as an economic fracas had moved to a human rights dispute: "They have undertaken to give and grant our money without our consent, though we have ever exercised an exclusive right to dispose of our own property; statutes have been passed for extending the jurisdiction of courts of admiralty, and vice-admiralty beyond their ancient limits; for depriving us of the accustomed and inestimable privilege of trial by jury, in cases affecting both life and property; for suspending the legislature of one of the colonies; for interdicting all commerce to the capital of another; and for altering fundamentally the form of government established by charter, and secured by acts of its own legislature solemnly confirmed by the crown; for exempting the 'murderers' of colonists from legal trial, and in effect, from punishment; for erecting in a neighbouring province, acquired by the joint arms of Great-Britain and America, a despotism dangerous to our very existence; and for quartering soldiers upon the colonists in time of profound peace. It has also been resolved in Parliament, that colonists charged with committing certain offences, shall be transported to England to be tried."

Parliament's reaction to the colonial measures fueled the fires of resistance even more—by recognizing Catholicism in Canada at the same time that the Coercive Acts were passed, by passing an act in December 1775 forbidding the colonies from trading with any portion of the world, and, shortly thereafter, approving steps to confiscate any and all American vessels along the coast of Britain. Radicals responded by attempting to appeal to all segments of the population with their grievances, including wavering merchants. In April 1776 the Continental Congress passed resolves voiding the British mercantile acts and removing all price restrictions. Radicals also wrote tracts that stressed the economic benefits of severance from the mother country. "A free and unlimited trade," was how one tract delineated the advantages, "a great accession of wealth, and a proportionate rise in the value of land; the establishment, gradual improvement, and perfection of manufactures and science; a vast influx of foreigners . . . an astonishing increase of our people from the present stock. Where encouragement is given to industry; where liberty and property are well secured; where the poor may easily find subsistence, and the middling rank comfortably support their farms by labour, there the inhabitants must increase rapidly." Indeed, it was difficult for merchants not to accept the challenge of revolution.

But in an important sense, the support of businessmen—or large numbers of other Americans—was not necessary. Most colonials, including businessmen, would watch the events of their day rather than participate in them. To be sure, a few would openly espouse commitment to Britain. They would become the infamous Tories who sometimes lost their property and were even forced to leave their home country. The American Revolution was not a referendum in which the people voted their views; rather, it was organized and directed by a small group with an uncanny ability to make the most of events. For that reason, the most momentous day in the Revolution may well have been June 7, 1776—a day that had little to do with merchants or most other Americans.

Much of the day's agenda for the Second Continental Congress was routine and unexciting: complaints about the Continental Navy, defective gunpowder, and counterfeit money. Yet the routine appearance may well have been contrived by colonial leaders Richard Henry Lee and John Adams, who openly favored enactment of a resolution of independence from Great Britain. The problem they had wrestled with at least since January, when Thomas Paine's *Common Sense* had appeared and talk of independence was broached among congressional members, was the means by which the subject could be advanced legislatively among moderates and conservatives who chafed at even the mention of independence. Moreover, some colonies had, months before, specifically instructed their delegates not to vote for severance of ties with the mother country. The strategy that had been adopted by Lee and Adams was to nudge the colonies to form special conventions establishing state constitutions and calling upon the congress to initiate independence. Not only would this take the heat off conservatives at Philadelphia, but it would counter their most effective argument: that the people were disinclined to break with the mother country.

When Massachusetts in early spring muffed a chance to be first, congresses in South Carolina, Georgia, and North Carolina led the way. They passed resolutions giving their delegates wider discretion, although not specifically in the area of the unspoken word, *independence,* save North Carolina, which permitted its delegates to concur, provided some other colony initiated the action. It was Virginia, the oldest and most prominent of the colonies, that took the great initiative. Patrick Henry was the perfect choice to lead the way in the Virginia Congress (or Assembly, as it was called). He had been influential in the initial rhetorical forays against the British, and he longed for the limelight after a frustrating tour of duty in the military. On May 15 the body passed a unanimous resolution "that the Delegates appointed to represent this Colony in the General Congress be instructed to declare the United Colonies free and independent States. . . ." Virginia's resolution reached the Continental Congress on May 27, but pressing military matters at first prevented its introduction. Finally, Friday, June 7, was selected as the date for proposing it. On the eve of introduction, Samuel Adams wrote James Warren of Massachusetts: "Tomorrow a motion will be made, and a Question I hope decided, the most important that was ever agitated in America. I have no doubt but it will be decided to your satisfaction: This being done, Things will go in the right Channel and our Country will be saved."

Lee introduced the motion in Congress and John Adams seconded it: "That these United Colonies are, and of right ought to be, free and independent States, that they are absolved from an allegiance to the British Crown, and that all political connection between them and the State of Great Britain is, and ought to be, totally dissolved. . . ." The next day, Saturday, was devoted to debate. Delegates from the middle colonies where there were no few businessmen—New York, Pennsylvania, Delaware, and New Jersey—appeared to be the most negative, and proponents had to be careful lest they provoke a walkout. Nevertheless, as debate resumed on June 10, Lee, Adams, and others continued to jab at one argument that would force what appeared to be a compromise but what was in reality a victory for independence: The *people,* they contended, were in favor of independence; therefore, let the people convene to make their will known. Accordingly, Congress voted, 7 to 5, to postpone action for three weeks, until July 1, 1776, so that delegates could "solicit the people for instructions." In the interim, a committee was appointed to draft a declaration of independence, an artful strategy in that Congress was giving the signal to the people that it was for the break with Britain. The die had been ingeniously cast by Lee and Adams, and a ground swell for independence spread through the colonies. Thus, when debate resumed on July 1, it took only until the next day for Congress to pass Lee's resolve. Twelve colonies voted positively on July 2, with New York abstaining. Only approval of the Declaration was necessary, an action that came on July 4.

The decision for independence, then, was not a challenge in which business played a leading role. But merchants would have an enormous stake in surviving the war. For it was one thing for Americans who had the least to lose to commit, as the Declaration underscored, their "lives, fortunes, and sacred honor." It was quite another thing for businessmen.

5

A GREAT MEETING

Another meeting. One after another without coming up with a proposal that would fly. This one took place in early September and, not surprisingly, only a few people showed up—twelve, to be precise. And so they talked for some days and finally came up with a plan for still another meeting, eight months hence. It was hoped that this would offer sufficient time to generate interest in the matter.

They also moved the location. It was not that the September site had been unpleasant—on the contrary, the facilities were quite good—but variety in meeting places might induce more individuals to attend. Of the seventy-four invitees, fifty-five showed up. But they didn't all come at once. They were supposed to convene on Monday, May 14, but it wasn't until Friday, May 25, that enough were present to conduct business. They decided to work diligently from that day on until they finished their proposal. They even agreed to put a lid on their deliberations.

They were a relatively young group; the average age was forty-two. The youngest was thirty and the oldest eighty-two and prone to nod during long meetings. Although some were lackluster in ability, most were able and would later move to higher executive positions. They were together for 116 days, taking off only Sundays and 12 other days. And you might have guessed it: during a very hot summer. In addition to the formal sessions of the entire group, much of the work was done in committees and after hours.

The formal sessions sometimes got out of hand. One faction had come with a proposal that was almost the reverse of an outline offered by another group. The advocates of each seemed unwilling to bend, and by the end of June tempers were flaring so much that the oldest participant suggested beginning each session with an invocation. By early June, they got wind of a way out of their impasse: adopt a portion of each plan. By compromising, they might be better able to sell their product to a broad market. Yet even this task of drawing the line between two extremes was not easy, and so some decided to go home or back to their offices. It simply was not worth the effort.

Even among those who remained there was still criticism of the final proposal. It was much too short, some argued—only 4,000 words. Four months of work and only 4,000 words! It was scarcely enough to fill a few sheets of paper. But thirty-nine of them felt it was the best they could come up with. It was good enough to sign, which they did on September 17, 1787.

And they called their proposal the Constitution of the United States.

Indeed, the drafting of the Constitution was an enormous achievement for business in that the document provided an environment in which free enterprise could work well. The new form of government gave Congress control over interstate commerce, the power to collect taxes, to defend the states, and to encourage inventiveness through a system of patents and copyrights. The Constitution protected property rights through a strong central government, so much so that critics demanded, and ultimately received, a Bill of Rights that would guarantee civil liberties. What made the Constitution especially significant to businessmen in 1787 was the form of government that had preceded it. The Articles of Confederation, the independent nation's first mode of government, put business at considerable risk in spite of the obvious new economic opportunities at home and abroad. The risks were an unstable central government incapable of controlling economic and political conditions, the diffusion of popular ideas, such as opposition to a central bank, that were contrary to sound business principles, and the lack of respect for devoted public servants—merchant Robert Morris, in particular—whose wisdom was spurned.

To be sure, the Articles of Confederation was an experiment. And like most innovations in government during a revolution, the Articles moved dramatically away from traditional moorings. Instead of a strong central government a la the British king and Parliament, the revolutionary system saw the states hold power. The federal government operating through a Congress could not tax or control interstate commerce. It shared with the states the authority to print money. Congress, based upon a one state-one vote scheme of representation, needed nine votes to pass any measure, unanimity to change the Articles. States had the power to erect tariff barriers against other states, and they did. Some states resorted to the printing of paper money with a passion that angered merchants, some of whom actually refused to accept the currency in payment of debts. Still other states provoked farmers with their paper money policies. Massachusetts is a case in point. Dominated by eastern residents, its legislature paid little heed to the inflationary demands of western farmers who saw the prices of their goods plummet as their markets in the West Indies dwindled as a result of Britain's refusal to permit continued trade. So 1,500 farmers under the leadership of one Daniel Shays, a revolutionary war veteran, organized their forces in 1786 for the purpose of overthrowing the state government. Shays's Rebellion was put down, but a dozen of its leaders were condemned to death, although all were subsequently pardoned. In another sense, the rebellion was unnerving: the state of Massachusetts appealed to the national Congress for help during the crisis, but the latter had no legal authority to act. George Washington, known for his cool disposition, said of the matter, "What gracious God, is man that there should be such inconsistency and perfidiousness in his conduct? We are fast verging to anarchy and confusion!"

Although the economic conditions under the Articles of Confederation did not illustrate anarchy, they certainly promoted hand wringing among businessmen. For one reason, war created shortages and prices skyrocketed. Some merchants took to keeping goods off the market until the price was right, a tactic that infuriated consumers, including General Washington, who suggested legislation to curb and punish profiteers. There were numerous cries for self-restraint even among businessmen. "Let us be content to receive moderate rewards for our labors," wrote one Virginian, "and recollect that the people who ultimately pay these prices are the poor soldiers and officers who are fighting for us and exposing their lives while we are trading and growing rich. . . ." But prudence was overwhelmed by the opportunities to profit from the war. Land companies, for example, rushed to get concessions from Congress regarding the western territory acquired from the British. And sometimes organizers and stockholders of the companies were members of Congress or significant officials in the government hierarchy, which led to cries of foul play from outsiders. In spite of this conflict of interest, Congress still managed to pass legislation permitting the orderly selling of the public domain as well as the creation of new states therein.

The Land Ordinance of 1785 and the Northwest Ordinance of 1787 would serve as the basis of land sales and entry of new states for more than a century. Land was sold in 640-acre parcels at $1 an acre, usually to speculators who in turn would sell it in small sections to farmers. It was still much cheaper than real estate in the east and assured rapid settlement of the western areas. Ohio, the first state to emerge from the revolutionary war legislation, entered the union in 1803 and was testimony to the wisdom of a policy that underscored settlement as a basis for economic development. What is more, because a territory could not become a state until it boasted 60,000 inhabitants, the developing areas were forced to encourage population growth by innovative means. To be sure, virgin land at relatively low prices was an inducement; better still was a political-social environment that was a cut above the situation back east. That meant that western territories offered prospective settlers more democracy: universal manhood suffrage, the abolition of property qualifications for office holding, ease of entry into business enterprises, with liberal bankruptcy laws in the event of failure. And because the western areas were playing catch-up with the east in developmental terms, they were more eager to encourage risk taking. Big risk, in short, meant big rewards—or big failures, gambles that appeared to be worth the price.

Yet there were important stabilizers in this process. The federal government sold 44 million acres of land by the 1830s, which helped to keep its budget in the black and assist western areas in economic growth. The Land Ordinance of 1785 embodied the New England system of townships, which ensured a somewhat orderly process of settlements arising. Similarly, land would be surveyed and sold by the government along this model, thereby diminishing the likelihood of squabbles over ownership by private buyers. Equally important was the concept confirmed in the 1787 ordinance that newly admitted states were equal to the original thirteen, which meant that the analogy of colonies and mother country, which Britain used to govern the Old World, was inapplicable and thus would not put a brake on western growth. In fact, the new western states would soon outshine some eastern areas in economic development, and it was difficult to maintain that the competition between the two sections was not good.

The business leaders emerging during the era of the Articles of Confederation were often controversial because of the unsettling environment. Robert Morris is a case in point. Born in England in 1734, Morris arrived in the New World as a teenager. Within ten years he was a partner in the Philadelphia trading firm of Willing, Morris & Company, which would become the largest in the nation before the first shot of the American Revolution was fired. Early on in the fracas with Britain, Morris committed himself to the radical position. He was elected to Congress in 1775 and would sign the Declaration of Independence somewhat reluctantly. Morris became a sort of unofficial secretary of the treasury during the early days of the war; he even used his own financial resources to help meet the costs of fighting the British and also solicited loans from wealthy Philadelphians. "I had long since parted with very considerable sums of hard money to Congress," he wrote George Washington in 1777, "and therefore must collect from others, and as matters now stand, it is no easy thing. I mean to borrow silver and promise payment in gold, and then will collect the gold in the best manner I can. . . . Whatever I can do shall be done for the good of the cause." To be sure, Morris's good business sense permitted him to serve his country as well as himself. For example, he bought privateer ships that preyed on British vessels, with the booty directed to the coffers of both Morris and Congress. This arrangement led to charges that he profiteered from the Revolution, but a congressional committee and a formal motion by Congress fully exonerated him. Nevertheless, the matter haunted him in his hometown of Philadelphia, and only through the intervention of leading patriots was the matter eventually downplayed.

By 1781 the financial situation of the nation worsened as a result of staggering inflation, inadequate provisions for the military, and enormous shortages of consumer goods. Congress formally called upon Morris to accept the post of Superintendent of Finance and perform economic miracles. Morris accepted, hoping "to reduce public expenditures; to obtain revenues in our own country to meet these expenses; to show foreign nations engaged in the war we must look to them for the balance." But Congress was slow to accept Morris's ideas. His plan for a Bank of North America was put on the back burner, as was his call for a mint to coin money. Small loans came from the French, but an increase in taxes was likely to cause more furor than actual warfare with the British. So Morris used his own funds and credit to sustain the military operations. He also cut whatever fat he could find in government outlays, even writing Washington to the effect that he pare his personal expenditures. Morris combined his Treasury office with the Navy office that he also headed, as a result saving a few hundred dollars in annual rents. And by the end of his first year in office, he insisted that Congress charter the Bank of North America. As one of the organizers of the Bank of Philadelphia in 1780, he believed that the economic ripple effect of such an institution was limitless: "It will facilitate the management of the finances of the United States. The several states may, when their respective necessities require and the abilities of the bank will permit, derive occasional advantage and accommodation from it. It will afford to the individuals of all the states a medium for their intercourse with each other and for the payment of taxes, more convenient than the precious metals and equally safe. It will have a tendency to increase both the internal and external commerce of North America and undoubtedly will be infinitely useful to all the traders of every state in the union, provided, as I have already said, it is conducted on the principles of equity, justice, prudence, and economy."

Congress created the bank on the last day of the year in 1781 and subscribers rushed to buy its stock. The government was the largest stockholder, owning about 600 of its 1,000 shares, the Bank of Pennsylvania was absorbed by the new institution, and the return to a peacetime economy was facilitated by the role that the BNA played. However, with war's end, the bank also became a scapegoat for the economic woes of Pennsylvania farmers, who needed the type of credit, with untimely payments, that no prudent bank could make. In 1785 the Pennsylvania legislature revoked the bank's charter on the grounds that "the accumulation of enormous wealth in the hands of a society who claim perpetual duration will necessarily produce a degree of influence and power which can not be entrusted in the hands of any set of men whatsoever without endangering the public safety." According to one of the state's leading farmers, "the government of Pennsylvania being a democracy, the bank is inconsistent with the bill of rights thereof, which says that the government is not instituted for the emolument of any man, family, or set of men." Of course, the bank had been chartered by Congress, but that meant little in an era in which the states held significant power. The new charter that the Pennsylvania legislature forced on the bank was conspicuous for its restrictions, which meant that Robert Morris's dream of a truly national institution would not come true. The government's stock was sold, and in the eyes of Pennsylvania farmers, the original Bank of North America was simply the creation and milch cow of Morris and a few other financiers.

All the while Morris bore the burden of attempting to get the states to proffer money to run the national government, in addition to fending off personal attacks of his alleged private gain from public office. He soon recognized that neither the sums received from states nor foreign loans were sufficient to make the government's ends meet. If he continued to make his personal line of credit the basis for meeting the government's obligations, he ran the risk of further accusations of conflict of interest. Therefore, in January 1783 Morris tendered his resignation as superintendent. "To increase our debts," he wrote Congress, "while the prospect of them diminishes does not consist with my ideas of integrity. I must therefore quit a situation which becomes insupportable." Ever the public servant, Morris was urged by Congress to remain longer, which he did, until November 1, 1784. And he even had printed at his own expense a *Statement of Accounts,* which set forth the government's financial statement for the years of his stewardship. Afterward Morris spent some time in politics, but most of his life was devoted to land speculation that resulted in enormous losses—so great, in fact, that he spent three years, six months, and ten days in debtor's prison in Philadelphia. The country that he had served did not come to his rescue, except perhaps indirectly through the passage of the Bankruptcy Act of 1800. Five years after his release from prison in 1801, Morris died with no public recognition, a victim of the volatile times of the era of the Articles of Confederation, which offered challenges that could not be met in public service or exceeded beyond prudence in economic speculation.

During the 1780s the new nation found itself facing some of the economic problems that confronted the United States in the early 1980s: inflation was high, taxes were low, and interest rates were unaffordable. So bad was inflation that the price of iron rose 111 percent from January to February 1779. Part of the blame was attributable to the shortages noted earlier, and exploited by certain merchants, but another culprit was government. Neither the national Congress nor the states were willing to tighten their belts. Paper money was excessively issued in many areas, and taxes were nowhere near meeting the actual costs of warfare, even though they were supplemented by foreign loans. Nor was there any disposition for wage and price controls, save in New Hampshire where its law of 1777 was largely ignored. Yet even in this bleak environment, there were some bright spots. Farmers rushed to produce more crops and found some new markets abroad. Southern tobacco planters increased their exports by more than a third by 1792 and with higher prices. Wheat farmers in the North saw an increase of 20 percent in exports, while producers of corn tripled shipments abroad—gains attributable to the fact that European nations other than Britain were interested in American products. For merchants the freedom to trade wherever they wanted seemed to confirm Adam Smith's argument in his *Wealth of Nations* of 1776: "To prohibit a great people from making all that they can of every part of their produce, or from employing their stock and industry in a way that they judge most advantageous to themselves, is a manifest violation of the most sacred rights of mankind."

Traders rushed to find new markets. The *Empress of China* set sail in 1784 with high hopes of opening up the Orient. The Chinese were very selective about their imports; nevertheless, American merchants for a while shipped ginseng—touted for increasing male virility—and, later, northwestern furs to China. To Holland merchants sent tobacco, rice, and naval stores and to France lumber, tobacco, and foodstuffs. By 1787 the tonnage moving out of Philadelphia annually was 72,000, as opposed to 45,000 before the American Revolution. Of course, Britain did much to exacerbate the American forward movement. It dumped enormous quantities of manufactured goods in 1784–85 that helped to deepen the woes of returning to a peacetime economy. At the same time, American manufacturers got some states to raise the tariff on such imports and, more important, attempted to produce items that ordinarily they had relied on Britain to provide. Thanks to the establishment of such organizations as the Pennsylvania Society for the Encouragement of Manufacturers and Useful Arts in 1787, American industrialization took root in this period. The textile industry arose, the hat industry expanded, as did the manufacture of woolens and tenpenny nails. In 1786 a newspaper reported that "the establishing of manufactories in our young country is a matter of the greatest consequence." And a Philadelphia observer of the manufacturing situation tried to delineate all the growth areas in a report in 1787:

How great—how happy is the change! The list of articles we now make ourselves, if particularly enumerated, would fatigue the ear, and waste your valuable time. Permit me, however, to mention them under their general heads: meal of all kinds, ships and boats, malt liquors, distilled spirits, potash, gun-powder, cordage, loaf-sugar, pasteboard, cards and paper of every kind, books in various languages, snuff, tobacco, starch, cannon, muskets, anchors, nails, and very many other articles of iron, bricks, tiles, potters ware, millstones, and other stone work, cabinet work, trunks and windsor chairs, carriages and harness of all kinds, corn-fans, ploughs and many other implements of husbandry, saddlery and whips, shoes and boots, leather of various kinds, hosiery, hats and gloves, wearing apparel, coarse linens and woolens, and some cotton goods, linseed and fish oil, wares of gold, silver, tin, pewter, lead, brass and copper, clocks and watches, wool and cotton cards, printing types, glass and stoneware, candles, soap, and several other valuable articles, with which memory cannot furnish us at once.

Yet, in spite of the gains of businessmen, the union was far from perfect by 1787. The biggest problem was that Congress under the Confederation had no control over interstate commerce. States took issue with other states over boundary lines and tariffs, which meant that a unified system of economic growth could not take place. Little wonder that a meeting of important leaders was called in Annapolis in late 1786 to effect what James Madison called "commercial reform." As noted, however, only twelve representatives from a few states showed up, but at least they laid the groundwork for the holding of the Constitutional Convention of 1787. To some twentieth-century analysts, the Constitution would reflect the economic self-interest of its authors, that is, the businessmen-lawyers in attendance in Philadelphia would craft a document that would preserve, protect, and increase their personal fortunes. The problem with this interpretation is that it fails to recognize the most obvious characteristics of the fifty-five attendees. According to Virginian George Mason, a Revolutionary leader and delegate to the Constitutional Convention, "America has certainly, upon this occasion, drawn forth her first characters; there are upon this Convention many gentlemen of the most respectable abilities, and so far as I can discover, of the purest intentions. The eyes of the United States are turned upon this assembly, and their expectations raised to a very anxious degree." Also, the economic self-interest view does not take into consideration the individuals who played the roles of major architects. Alexander Hamilton, who spoke perhaps more than any other individual at the convention (including a five-hour stint on a single day), was the son of a merchant but had no fortune to protect. James Madison, sometimes dubbed the Father of the Constitution, inherited much land from his Virginia family. Yet he could scarcely be called self-interested in 1787 when he was thirty-six years old since his adult life had been devoted to public service. Merchant Robert Morris represented Pennsylvania at the convention and was virtually silent throughout the entire meeting, and colleague (but no relation) Gouverneur Morris, one of the nation's richest businessmen, was vocal—but as the champion for democratic rights. He favored the idea that the president be elected by the people. Delegate James Wilson, like Robert Morris, would overspeculate in lands and flirt with perennial indebtedness, but at the convention his reputation hung on his legal expertise and advocacy of greater rights for the people. In sum, the Constitutional Convention saw no clash between economic interests so much as it did between sections: the North and the South and the large states versus the small.

To be sure, this absence of economic confrontation in the convention did not dispose the delegates to believe that such an untoward situation might not arise subsequently in America. Hamilton in his defense of the Constitution emphasized that "mutual animosities" were simply inevitable—over religion, even over political ambitions. The object of government was not to create a new order (the preamble of the Constitution read "a more perfect Union"), but one in which each of the various elements was at once the object of *freedom* and *regulation*. No more discerning view of the failures of the Articles of Confederation or of the future of pluralistic America could have been made at the time. Articulated by Hamilton, this view reflects the timeless wisdom emanating from that Philadelphia meeting in 1787:

> But the most common and durable source of factions has been the various and unequal distribution of property. Those who hold and those who are without property have ever formed distinct interests in society. Those who are the creditors, and those who are debtors, fall under a like discrimination. A landed interest, a manufacturing interest, a mercantile interest, a moneyed interest, with many lesser interests, grow up of necessity in civilized nations, and divide them into different classes, actuated by different sentiments and views. The regulation of these various and interfering interests forms the principal task of modern legislation and involves the spirit of party and faction in the necessary and ordinary operations of the government. . . .
>
> It is vain to say that the enlightened statesman will be able to adjust these clashing interests and render them all subservient to the public good. Enlightened statesmen will not always be at the helm. . . . The inference to which we are brought is that the *causes* of faction cannot be removed and that relief is only to be sought in the means of controlling its *effects*.

6

THE HAMILTONIAN SCENARIO

Of the American leaders whose portraits adorn the major denominations of paper currency, Alexander Hamilton is one of two (the other is Ben Franklin) who never served as president. To be sure, Hamilton was presidential timber, but he could never have served in the nation's highest office because his background and personality were such as to create more enemies than friends. But no early American was more supportive of business and did so much to move capitalism along a modern track. Specifically, Hamilton, by virtue of his critical role in the administration of George Washington, served as the voice and major architect of the nation's commitment to industrialism. Second, he was the initiator of the Bank of the United States, which catered to the prudent and conservative objectives of the business community. Finally, Hamilton was the chief strategist for a central government that would have economic and budgetary clout, thanks to a system of revenues that exceeded expenditures.

Hamilton's life was both mysterious and meteoric. Born in the British West Indies in 1755, Hamilton started off on the wrong foot—as an illegitimate child. His mother, Rachel Fauciette Lavien, was not married to James Hamilton, a Scotsman who hoped to make it big as a merchant in the West Indies. Nor did the senior Hamilton take much interest in Alexander or any of the children he sired. So Alexander had to fend for himself at an early age. As a clerk in a merchant's shop on the island of St. Croix, he became proficient in business matters by the time he was a teenager. In 1772 he ventured to New York City to add some academic polish to his practical business experience, attending an academy for one year and hoping because of his advancing age (he was eighteen) to accelerate through Princeton. However, the president of the New Jersey institution thought that was not possible, and Hamilton entered King's College (later Columbia) with the intention of becoming a physician. The only problem was that his extracurricular activity in the form of the American Revolution took precedence over his studies. By 1775 Hamilton joined in the war of words with the British; a year later he was a captain in the armed forces of New York in charge of an artillery company. By the spring of 1777, he was serving as George Washington's aide-de-camp with the rank of lieutenant colonel. That four-year stint with the commander in chief of the Continental Army was Hamilton's big break, and he utilized every minute to the fullest.

Washington relied on Hamilton because he needed "persons that can think for me, as well as execute orders." Indeed, Hamilton was a manager par excellence, capable of composing letters, dealing with congressmen, taking charge of the questioning of prisoners, and even directing the general's orders to subordinates in the battlefields. He also counseled Washington, who came to accept his views over the advice of any other person—during the war and as president when Hamilton served as secretary of the Treasury. Hamilton was a full-fledged critic of the Confederation Congress that, in his mind, illustrated little more than the "degeneracy of representation in the great council of America." After Yorktown, Hamilton moved to complete his education, not in medicine but in law. In July 1782 he was admitted to the bar even though his interest at the time was focused on financial matters. So he ended up accepting the position of receiver of continental revenue in New York. In this role Hamilton showed that he could switch his managerial abilities from the battlefield to the ledger sheet. No state, he contended, could be supportive of a strong business class and economy unless its government had the wherewithal to tax and pay its bills. Hamilton offered all sorts of recommendations for New York, including, first and foremost, a better plan for collecting revenues. He was insistent on devising new taxes, as, for example, on tobacco, salt, and luxury items; he even backed stamp taxes and tariffs. Although the New York legislature did not support Hamilton in all these proposals, it was sufficiently impressed with the twenty-seven-year-old public servant and elected him as one of their delegates to the Confederation Congress. Not surprisingly, Hamilton wanted to expand Congress's authority to raise monies, most specifically in the realm of import duties.

In spite of his managerial abilities and good business sense, Hamilton did not apply these talents to his own financial life. He married well, which eliminated financial worries, but he was not accumulative in his legal, business, or public life. His strong support of business as a government official, therefore, was scarcely self-interested. On the one hand, one could argue that Hamilton aspired to social prestige that he hoped to achieve by espousing conservative economic views; on the other hand, prevailing conservative doctrines would have illustrated tolerance for the status quo of farmers, merchants, and manufacturers doing their own thing, albeit with some strengthening of the federal government. Hamilton, however, wanted far more. He rejected outright Adam Smith's argument for laissez-faire because Great Britain's economic situation was totally different: the Old World was just that, overregulated, whereas the New World cried for prudent economic development and no wasted efforts. Government, in Hamilton's view, could play a critical role in effecting economic growth, and the result would be a nation quite capable of advancing the material interests of its people and quite independent of the imbroglios that typified international politics. At the heart of Hamilton's economic views was industrialization, which, surprisingly, was a turnabout from his own early life reflective of the prevailing commercial characteristic of business before the American Revolution. "The embarrassments which have obstructed the progress of our external trade, have led to serious reflections on the necessity of enlarging the sphere of our domestic commerce," Hamilton wrote in 1791. "Restrictive regulations" of foreign nations were offensive, he argued, and the Atlantic Ocean was no guarantee that the nation's restricted trade would be assured a safe voyage.

The benefits of manufacturing, however, were virtually unlimited. First, no field of economic endeavor utilized labor more productively, said Hamilton in anticipating the assembly line. "A man occupied on a single object will have it more in his power, and will be more naturally led to exert his imagination, in devising methods to facilitate and abridge labor, than if he were perplexed by a variety of independent and dissimilar operations." Machines can run day and night, need fewer employees, and combine several operations under a single roof. A classic example, according to Hamilton, was the English textile industry. What is more, factories "afford occasional and extra employment to industrious individuals and families, who are willing to devote the leisure resulting from the intermissions of their ordinary pursuits to collateral labors, as a resource for multiplying their acquisitions or their enjoyments." Women and children could be drawn into the industrial labor force, just as they were in Britain, and immigrants would be induced to come to America. Foreign manufacturers might be disposed to relocate in the New World. And even if immigrants got dissatisfied with factory work, they could always turn to agriculture. The more likely scenario, however, would be for the immigrant, and native American for that matter, to bring out their inventive side. "If there be anything in a remark often to be met with, namely, that there is, in the genius of the people of this country, a peculiar aptitude for mechanic improvements, it would operate as a forcible reason for giving opportunities to the exercise of that species of talent, by the propagation of manufacturers."

Even agriculture could benefit from manufacturing, Hamilton asserted. Farmers' basic problem, overproduction, would find an outlet in the cities that would arise to house industry. With his new markets, the farmer could buy manufactured goods "either to his wants or to his enjoyments." And even if agriculture should become less profitable as a result of continuing overproduction, it may be necessary for government to enter the scene to promote "desirable changes." That same government support should not be wanting for risk taking in business: ". . . it is essential that they should be made to see in any project which is new—and for that reason alone, if no other, precarious—the prospect of such a degree of countenance and support from government, as may be capable of overcoming the obstacles inseparable from first experiments." Hamilton went one step further. Government assistance was absolutely necessary for certain industries. Take the iron industry as an example. Certainly it had grown prodigiously in the eighteenth century, but it could expand even more with duties imposed on foreign counterparts. About 1.8 million pounds of nails and spikes had been imported in one year to America. "A duty of two cents a pound would, it is presumable, speedily put an end to so considerable an importation. And it is, in every view, proper that an end should be put to it." Firearms also necessitated duties, and for obvious reasons. On the other hand, the coal industry did not require protection from foreign imports; instead it needed bounties to stir businessmen to open new mines. And the printing business needed both protection and some loopholes: "The great number of presses disseminated throughout the Union seem to afford an assurance that there is no need of being indebted to foreign countries for the printing of books which are used in the United States. A duty of ten per cent instead of five, which is now charged upon the article, would have a tendency to aid the business internally. . . . And with regard to books which may be specially imported for the use of particular seminaries of learning and of public libraries, a total exemption from duty would be advisable. . . ."

The above views that Hamilton would enunciate in his *Report on Manufactures* to the House of Representatives in 1791 had already been formulated when he entered the Confederation Congress in 1782, but there were more pressing problems than a policy for economic development and self-sufficiency. The army was unpaid, states were slow in providing voluntary requisitions, and by June 1783 the Congress meeting in Philadelphia was, quite literally, surrounded by troops—some inebriated, others with mutiny on their minds. Congress faced the situation by moving to Princeton, New Jersey. And although the peace treaty had been effected by that time, Hamilton wrote that "much remains to be done. . . . Our prospects are not flattering. Every day proves the inefficacy of the present confederation, yet the common danger being removed, we are receding instead of advancing in a disposition to amend its defects." There was also the problem of some American businessmen becoming so disheartened by the events at hand that they were leaving the country; in fact, in 1782 alone nearly 30,000 Americans left New York City, taking lives and fortunes that Hamilton recognized could play an important role in the economy. Little wonder, then, that Hamilton hoped that a strong central government would be the result of the Constitutional Convention in which he participated as a New York delegate in 1787. Although the final product was not as strong as Hamilton had wanted, he accepted it and worked hard for its ratification. Whether he expected to play a formative role in the new government was not clear, but financier Robert Morris, whose opinion Washington solicited on the matter of a Treasury secretary, believed that Hamilton was the only person who could fill the bill.

Of course, Washington had a very favorable view of Hamilton's wartime service—so much so that his selection as the top person at the Treasury was effected without fanfare. On September 11, 1789, Hamilton was nominated and on the same day approved by the Senate. According to the September second act establishing the Treasury Department, Hamilton had his work cut out for him. For instance, he had "to digest and prepare plans for the improvement and management of the revenue, and for the support of the public credit; to prepare and submit report estimates of the public revenue, and the public expenditures; to superintend the collection of the revenue; to decide on the forms of keeping and stating accounts and making returns . . . and generally to perform all such services relative to the finances, as he shall be directed to perform." No sooner had Hamilton taken office than he found the government's coffers without funds, which meant that he had to borrow from private banks in order to pay the salaries of congressmen and the president. To be sure, earlier in July Congress had passed a tariff bill that was modest, a far cry from the protectionist stance that Hamilton would enunciate in his *Report on Manufactures* and insufficient to pay the government's bills. So Hamilton, as he had done in his post as Receiver of the Continental Revenue in New York, campaigned for a whole host of excise taxes: a tax on whiskey was the most controversial, ultimately provoking a rebellion of Pennsylvania farmers that was put down by federal troops. Taxes on snuff, carriages, sugar, legal documents, and even on houses were largely unchallenged. Hamilton also worked on the matter of coinage, proposing a mint that was approved by Congress in 1791. Although he personally favored a gold standard, his concern for the widest possible coinage system led him to urge the minting of silver dollars as well, with the ratio of pure metal in each type corresponding to their relative market values, a notion that would be quite satisfactory for a century. And he favored the minting of numerous small coins, such as pennies and halfpennies, in order to ensure that the poor could afford to buy the little things in life. In order to guarantee that states would look to the federal government for fiscal leadership, Hamilton saw to it that their debts would be assumed. The federal government's debt management would be facilitated by the creation of a sinking fund, which permitted the Treasury to meet the due dates of its obligations, often by getting new and longer loans. All this, of course, has a modern ring and quite purposefully was designed to strengthen the federal government's fiscal posture as well as to attract the support of businessmen.

Hamilton's most significant achievement as secretary of the Treasury—the creation of the Bank of the United States in 1791 —illustrated that fiscal prudence had its limits and could arouse enormous controversy even among businessmen. Hamilton looked at the new institution as a central bank along the lines of the Bank of England except for its private ownership and control. Its capitalization was $10 million, of which the government had a 20 percent stake; the rest of the stock was sold within an hour of its offering, with many shares secured by foreign investors. The bank would serve as a repository for the government's funds, lend money to the Treasury, as well as carry on normal commercial business, such as the making of short-term loans to businessmen. It would have branches throughout the eastern portion of the nation, from Boston to Savannah to New Orleans. Had the bank not been chartered, monies would flow, for the most part, into four major banks already in existence by 1791. From this perspective, the bank could be interpreted as a monopoly by its competitors, no matter that it played a stabilizing role in the expansion of credit and currency flow. Moreover, because the bank was conservatively run, it minimized the sort of risk taking that had been widespread at the time, especially among the followers of Thomas Jefferson—farmers and small businessmen alike—who began to design banking thought along the lines of "mechanics" and "farmers" banks. Symbols, in other words, helped to do in the

Bank of the United States, although it would not be eliminated until Andrew Jackson's administration when the tides of economic democracy were at their highest. A monopolistic bank under the control of foreign stockholders was simply a bad public image. Jefferson, for example, wanted to share the government's deposits with many banks, perhaps according to the political dispositions they displayed, and still other opponents attempted to charter more institutions. In fact, from 1791 to 1816 the number of banks soared, from 6 to 246, many with Jeffersonian outlooks. The biggest battlefield for political and banking confrontations was New York where Jefferson's ally, Aaron Burr, took on Hamilton on his home turf. By the end of the century, Burr had been successful in establishing the Bank of the Manhattan Company (now Chase Manhattan), which was much larger than the oldest institution in the city which had Hamiltonian ties. The Bank of the Manhattan Company grew by offering many, even aggressive services, such as selling insurance and supplying the city with water. Still other banks followed in this line by engaging in activities that were anathema to conservative Hamiltonians who worried that bankruptcy and ruin were their end results. To be sure, there were businessmen absolutely delighted with this developing scenario: business in America, they reasoned, simply could not be poured into a mold dominated by a single economic theory or party. In the words of one observer in 1804, "It is well known that previous to the incorporation of the Manhattan Company, the Branch Bank, and the New York Bank, governed by *federal* gentlemen, were employed in a great measure as *political engines*. A close system of exclusion against those who differed from them on political subjects was adopted and pursued. There were but few active and useful Republicans that could obtain from those banks discount accommodations. . . . The incorporation of the Manhattan Company corrected the evil. All parties are now accommodated."

In these early days of the nation, both Hamilton and his opponents were accommodated, in their arguments and practice. The Bank of the United States would be renewed, other banks of various political and economic persuasions were permitted to grow, and not a single institution failed until 1809. The reason for the accommodation was that Hamiltonian and Jeffersonian economics differed only in degrees, not radically. Banks generally grew under the watchful eye of state authorities; Jefferson the President did not make war against the Bank of the United States or the other fiscal programs of Hamilton. Of course, Jefferson would implement some of his own views. Excise taxes were cut, as were the pomp and ceremony of his predecessors, but no radical economic surgery was performed. Like subsequent politicians, Jefferson's rhetoric was in advance of his actual position. "He who lent his money to the public or to an individual before the institution of the United States Bank of twenty years ago," he wrote, "when wheat was well sold at a dollar the bushel and receives now his nominal sum when it sells at two dollars, is cheated of half his fortune; and by whom? By the banks, which, since that, have thrown into circulation ten dollars of their nominal money where was one at the time." Expectedly, there were occasional spurts of speculative activity, such as in the spring of 1792, but it was emotion in rhetoric that distinguished more and more the Hamiltonians and Jeffersonians. Such ultimately led to the death of Hamilton in 1804 as a result of a duel with Aaron Burr. Although this untimely end to Hamilton's brilliant career minimizes to some observers his historical significance, it is explicable for a reason other than the emotion of the era. Hamilton was a Type A personality. The economic program that he devised was successfully implemented because of the prestige of George Washington. After Washington left office in 1797, Hamilton's drive to effect his will had no moderating influence. He became head of the Federalist Party, for all intents and purposes, and immediately clashed with the personality of John Adams and with substantive matters of domestic and foreign policy. So personal and bitter were Hamilton's disagreements with Adams that Hamilton worked hard in 1800 to have Adams defeated in his reelection bid. Not only did he succeed, but he also exacerbated political animosities by supporting Jefferson over Burr, both men having received equal numbers of electoral votes in the election of 1800, necessitating action by the House of Representatives. When, four years later, Burr was unsuccessful in his campaign for the governorship of New York—all thanks to Hamilton's efforts—he provoked the former treasury secretary into a war of words that ultimately led to a duel in July 1804. Hamilton died at age forty-nine, still in the prime of his life.

However, within a few years of Hamilton's death, not only was his economic program in the form of a strong central government and national bank still intact, but his ideas on the federal government's role in supporting manufacturing would get a new lease on life. Not that the merchant capitalist had been forced immediately from center stage; in fact, the most outstanding businessman during Jefferson's presidency was merchant John Jacob Astor. At the age of twenty, Astor had set up a fur-trading business in New York State. Then in 1809 he moved westward, establishing the American Fur Company with business activities that stretched all the way to the Oregon territory. Astor traded his furs even in China and, like most merchants before him, hedged his financial bets by investing in real estate—in the ultimately lucrative area of Manhattan. When he died in 1848, his fortune was estimated at $20 million, the largest of the merchant capitalists but paltry in comparison to the sums accumulated by industrialists a few years later. The boost to Hamilton's program for support of manufacturing came not from merchants such as Astor intentionally abandoning trade as much as it came from an unintended source, namely, war. The French Revolution and the attendant Napoleonic Wars were worldwide in influence, with America's reliance on foreign trade upset by both French and British ships intercepting neutral vessels. President Jefferson, intent on avoiding war with any belligerent, imposed an embargo on trade in 1807. The effects were devastating on American merchants. Exports that had totaled $108 million in 1807 fell to one fifth that amount a year later. Imports dropped from $138 million to $57 million. Instead of investing in trade, businessmen put their monies in manufacturing. By 1808 fifteen cotton mills could be identified in the nation; a year later the figure was 102. The Du Pont Company emerged in 1802, with assets of $36,000. Whereas before 1800 there were only 8 manufacturing corporations in America, there were nearly 600 by the 1820s. States, initially hesitant to charter corporations because the concept of limited liability seemed at odds with traditional practice, began to pass incorporation bills. Even Jefferson was forced to admit that the industrial handwriting was on the wall. "We have experienced," he wrote, "what we did not then believe, that to be independent for the comforts of life we must fabricate them ourselves. We must now place the manufacturer by the side of the agriculturist." No doubt, the United States was still a long way from the nation Hamilton had envisioned in his *Report on Manufactures,* but the first steps had been taken and would accelerate. And wise merchants like John Jacob Astor also recognized that industrialization was good business. He invested heavily in the first railroad out of New York City as well as others in the East Coast area. His industrial investments increased over the years and were stopped only by his death. Like Hamilton, Astor believed wholeheartedly in the Bank of the United States and invested widely in federal government securities on the grounds that they were absolutely safe. What was more, Astor was a penniless German immigrant who was induced to come to America for the opportunities that Hamilton had prophesied in his 1791 report. Indeed, Astor's life with its evolution from merchant to industrialist confirmed Hamilton's economic scenario for America. And it was just the first chapter in the exciting book of the nation's industrial growth.

7

EXCITING
INFRASTRUCTURES

Much of the United States in the year 1800 had a rural and unfinished quality that would suggest to the foreign visitor economic underdevelopment. Even the nation's capital, occupied for the first time by Congress in November, was nothing to write home about. "I do not perceive," wrote Secretary of the Treasury Oliver Wolcott to his wife, "how the members of Congress can possibly secure lodgings, unless they consent to live like scholars in a college, or monks in a monastery, crowded ten or twenty in one house, and utterly secluded from society. . . . There are, in fact, but few houses in any one place, and most of them small, miserable huts, which present an awful contrast to the public buildings. The people are poor, and, as far as I can judge, they live like fishes, by eating each other." President John Adams was only a bit more complimentary in his view of the new city. On a visit in early June, he did not have the heart to write his beloved Abigail about the true state of the president's house, where they would reside in a few months. "You will form the best idea of it from inspection," he wrote Abigail instead. Indeed, the White House was unfinished—without staircases, fences, yard, or supply of firewood—and would remain so for some time. The audience or East Room was a shell without windows and would be used by Abigail as a room for drying clothes.

Washington was a wilderness area in 1800. Only the north wing of the Capitol building was completed, and Capitol Hill was conspicuous for its lack of amenities. There were only a few boarding houses, a tailor shop, one shoemaker store, a grocery, a stationery shop, a dry goods business, and an oyster house. Foreign diplomats who were accustomed to much more refined surroundings were appalled. "My God," exclaimed a French minister. "What have I done, to be condemned to reside in such a city!" Between the Capitol and the president's house not one house intervened—"or can intervene without devoting its wretched tenant to perpetual fevers" as a result of the wet, spongy terrain. Even the area from the president's residence to Georgetown was uninviting, according to John Cotton Smith, a representative from Connecticut. There was "a block of houses [that] had been erected, which bore the name of the Six Buildings. There were also two other blocks, consisting of two or three dwelling-houses, in different directions, and now and then an isolated wooden habitation; the intervening spaces, and, indeed, the surface of the city generally, being covered with scrub-oak bushes on the higher grounds, and on the marshy soil either trees or some sort of shrubbery."

Abigail Adams's experience in finding the route to Washington illustrated that the nation's capital was scarcely a place on the map. "I arrived here on Sunday last," she wrote her daughter at the end of November 1800, "and without meeting any accident worth noticing, except losing ourselves when we left Baltimore, and going eight or nine miles on the Frederick road, by which means we were obliged to go the other eight through the woods, where we wandered for two hours, without finding a guide or the path. . . . In the city there are buildings enough, if they are compact and finished, to accommodate Congress and those attached to it, but as they are, and scattered as they are, I see no great comfort in them." To be sure, Washingtonians didn't view their city in such dire terms. In fact, they were absolutely convinced that the town on the Potomac would soon be a capital city: "There appears to be a confident expectation," observed Secretary Wolcott, "that this place will soon exceed any in the world. . . . One of the Commissioners, spoke of a population of 160,000 as a matter of course in a few years. No stranger can be here a day and converse with the proprietors, without conceiving himself in the company of crazy people. Their ignorance of the rest of the world, and their delusions with respect to their own prospects are without parallel." Indeed, Washington's view of the future was not unlike that of other towns in America at the turn of the century. And if a foreign visitor stayed long enough in the nation, as did Alexis de Tocqueville, he too would recognize the optimistic feeling. "America is a land of wonder," Tocqueville observed, "in which everything is in constant motion and every change seems an improvement. The idea of novelty is there indissolubly connected with the idea of amelioration. No natural boundary seems to be set to the efforts of man; and in his eyes what is not yet done is only what he has not attempted to do." No better illustration of American business optimism was evident than in transportation facilities within a few decades of the century. First, there was the building of a largely private system of toll roads, along with wagons and coaches, that would be critical to the movement of goods, people, and mail. Then came the canal craze, in which even the absence of water proved to be no impediment to American ingenuity. Finally, the railroad dwarfed all other transportation innovations, affecting lifestyles from speed of movement to the time that Americans in various sections of the nation would keep.

During George Washington's two terms as president, Americans talked about the wretched state of roads but few did anything about them. By Thomas Jefferson's administration, things began to change, thanks to the efforts of business. The model for change had been set in 1792 when Philadelphia businessmen received a charter from the state legislature to build a highway or turnpike, as it was dubbed at the time, from Philadelphia to Lancaster, a sixty-two mile stretch. The road was to be a toll facility operated by its promoters, and stock in the enterprise was immediately sold to investors who were convinced of its eventual profitability. Users of the turnpike could enter through one of nine gates, and the toll depended on distance and the item being hauled. Stagecoaches moved passengers along the route; heavy Conestoga wagons (originating in the Conestoga valley of the state), pulled by as many as eight horses, would carry barrels of flour; and then there were farmers who drove their cattle, sheep, or horses along the road on the grounds that time and money could be saved. Traffic on the turnpike was always brisk, and the promoters took in as much as $20,000 annually, with almost half that going to repairs and investors receiving a modest 2 percent return in the early years. The Pennsylvania experience was soon duplicated in other northeastern states. Private road building saved states the sometimes enormous costs of construction—as much as $7,000 per mile—as well as annual maintenance costs. At the same time, the state charter to the company would impose certain restrictions, which ensured that certain classes of citizens (persons on their way to a funeral or soldiers called into service) were exempted from tolls. Sometimes states bought a portion of the stock of the construction companies, and a few actually built public toll roads, which had a greater tendency to suffer from poor construction and inadequate maintenance.

New York, Connecticut, Massachusetts, and Rhode Island had excellent systems of private toll roads in the early 1800s, most of which strove for the straight route as opposed to one with curves in order to reduce distances. Between New York and Boston the road mileage was reduced from 254 miles to 210 as a result of private construction improvements, and New York State alone chartered sixty-seven companies by the year 1807, with some 900 miles of toll roads in operation by that date. Connecticut in the same year had 600 miles of private turnpikes built by thirty firms. One of the most expensive facilities to build was in Pennsylvania between Germantown and Perkiomen, twenty-five miles apart, which cost $11,000 per mile for a surface that was modern in its hardness. It also brought a greater return to investors. Unfortunately, there were users of the roads who were dubbed shunpikers, that is, those who took shortcuts on and off without paying tolls; this dishonesty cut into the profits of private firms and defied a practical solution. Reluctantly, the federal government got into the road-building act with the National Road originating in Cumberland, Maryland. By 1818 the road reached Wheeling, West Virginia, but because of congressional squabbling over the use of federal funds for what could be viewed as state responsibilities, it took a long time to move further, reaching only Indiana by the 1850s. Of course, the post office took advantage of the burgeoning road system to move the mails. What is more, in the enterprising spirit of the times, it turned to private individuals to assist in its efforts to reach the West Coast customer. From Fort Smith, Arkansas, through Missouri, El Paso, Los Angeles, and San Francisco—a 2,800-mile circle—the post office relied upon businessman John Butterfield, who set up the Overland Mail Company. Butterfield established over 200 stations along his travel route and employed a thousand employees in his quest to meet the postal requirement that the mail from Missouri to San Francisco take no more than twenty-five days to arrive. No problem. Butterfield's company consistently ran the route in twenty-two, even when the wagons carried passengers. Eventually, Overland Mail was acquired by Wells, Fargo and Company, which became one of the best-known firms for moving mail and money in the west.

If private toll roads helped to move goods faster and less expensively across America, the same might be said for the Concord coach in moving passengers. Unlike the Conestoga wagon, inordinately heavy, wide-wheeled, and slow moving, the Concord coach originating in the New Hampshire town of its namesake may well have been the first compact car of sorts.

To be sure, it looked funny, resembling the hull of a small boat turned upside down and placed high on a four-wheel frame. Holding as many as twelve passengers in rows or benches of three, all without adequate legroom, the coach was literally supported in place by leather straps, whose give-and-take kept passengers in a constant state of motion that could occasion seasickness for the novice. On the other hand, because of its suspension feature, the coach was less likely to break down, and its cushioned, often plush interiors may well have compensated for the motion problems.

Private roads would decline in number and quality as alternative and more attractive forms of transportation arose by the third and fourth decades of the century. A trip from Boston to New York City looked good in 1825 when it took forty-one hours by turnpike, an improvement of over thirty-three hours from the travel time in 1800. But when the railroad made much greater advances in time, then the primacy that had been placed on road building and maintenance collapsed. Nevertheless, the technology of the road-building days of private developers would not be lost, as illustrated by W. M. Gillespie's *A Manual of the Principles and Practice of Road-Making* (Third Edition, 1850), which took issue with the sloppy efforts of public construction by midcentury: "A good pavement should offer little resistance to wheels, but give a firm foothold to horses; it should be so durable as to seldom require taking up; it should be as free as possible from noise and dust; and when it is laid in the streets of a city, it should be susceptible of easy removal and replacement to give access to gas and water pipes. A common but very inferior pavement, which disgraces the streets of nearly all our cities, is constructed of rounded water-worn pebbles or 'cobblestones'. . . . The glaring faults of this pavement are that the stones, being supported only by the friction of the very narrow space at which they are in contact, are easily pressed down by heavy loads into the loose bottom, thus forming holes and depressions. . . ."

*   *   *

Canals were not invented in America, but they were mass-produced there in the early 1800s. The movement to build water trenches that would provide a better means to move goods and people started off slowly, however. In 1792, for example, two short canals were constructed by private investors in Massachusetts. A year later a more ambitious undertaking was begun, a twenty-seven-mile Middlesex canal designed to bring together the Merrimack and Charles rivers. Again the brainchild of private promoters, the canal had every sort of backing except scientific. The engineering problems were mind-boggling, but virtually all were conquered by 1803 through numerous bridges, aqueducts, sluiceways, and similar patch-work contraptions. Although the cost of the canal was enormous (over a million dollars), providing little return to investors, the water route played a significant role in moving textiles and timber between Massachusetts and New Hampshire.

And it moved passengers, including Henry David Thoreau, who was more excited about the state of nature he observed along the way than with burgeoning American technology. To be sure, passenger travel on canals left much to be desired. With the boats pulled by horses or mules on each side of the waterway, the average speed was only about four miles per hour. The sleeping accommodations below the deck, one for each sex, were conspicuous for their sardinelike qualities, with beds arranged like bookshelves against a wall. But the fares were cheap in comparison to land travel—only about four to five cents per mile—and included fare, food, and bed. And there was a sort of exhilaration in the experience: ". . . such incomparable light-ness and grace as no yacht could rival," was the way one passenger described a canal trip. "The water curled away on either side of her sharp prow," he went on, "and the team came swinging down the towpath at a gallant trot, the driver sitting the hindmost horse of three, and cracking his long-lashed whip with loud explosions . . . suddenly the captain pressed his foot on the spring and released the tow-rope. The driver kept on to the stable with unslackened speed, and the line followed him, swishing and skating over the water, while the steersman put his helm hardport, and the packet rounded to, and swam slowly and softly up to her moorings." The Middlesex canal stimulated more building: a Blackstone canal (Providence and Worcester, forty-five miles), completed in 1828, as well as canals in both Connecticut and Maine. And it even set in motion grandiose schemes that were never completed, such as a canal connecting Boston via the Connecticut River with the Hudson, which would have necessitated eliminating some four miles of solid rock topography.

Without doubt, the most impressive undertaking was the Erie, a 363-mile project connecting Albany and Buffalo. Begun on July 4, 1817, about halfway between the two cities, the Erie broke with the tradition of earlier projects in that it was publicly financed. But American business ingenuity was apparent throughout its lengthy eight-year period of construction, even though there were no expert engineers in the nation at the time. There were a lot of commonsense tinkerers, however, who also relied on observers sent to England to get some insight into the nature of underwater cement that readily hardened. Some 400,-000 bushels of the product were used in the Erie. About forty feet wide at the surface, four feet deep, and twenty-eight feet wide at the bottom, the Erie was literally dug by hand, although at times some technology such as stump removers were employed. What was so significant about the planning for the Erie was the hope its promoters had for the development of the port of New York, connected to the system via the Hudson. New York State promoters recognized that the Hudson had a far greater proportion of salt in its waters, unlike the rivers surrounding Philadelphia and Baltimore, which were much more likely to freeze in the winter. Not that the area from Albany to Buffalo was a tropical paradise in winter, but surprisingly during the quarter century of its heyday, the Erie was open on the average of about 232 days a year. Until the railroad upstaged it, the Erie was a profitable venture for the Empire State. Completed in 1825, it took in $700,000 in tolls in 1826, increasing to $1.6 million by 1838. In that same year, some $65 million worth of freight was hauled, ranging from timber, manufactured goods, and farm produce to sightseeing passengers. Some 23,000 vessels traveled along the canal in 1834. To be sure, the Erie was expensive to build ($22,000 per mile), but it represented the highest state of technology for its day, replete with eighty-three locks maneuvering the various ascents and descents of the vessels. Freight rates were reduced over land transportation, New York State paid for the project without assistance from the federal government, and canal fever spread to other areas, each of which tried to add a new wrinkle to the story.

For instance, Philadelphia businessmen rushed to meet the competition of the Erie by urging a similar east-west project in their own state. The Philadelphia Main Line, as it was dubbed, was therefore built as the Erie was being dug, but with obstacles that made the New York project appear much more feasible. For between Pittsburgh and Philadelphia the Appalachian mountains intervened, thereby requiring a combination water and cable system. The Main Line had more than twice the number of locks than the Erie, and although it never drew enough tolls to pay for its annual maintenance, it drew praise from Charles Dickens, who viewed the water and cable car show during a visit. "There are ten inclined planes," wrote Dickens, "five ascending and five descending; the carriages are dragged up the former, and let slowly down the latter, by means of stationary engines; the comparatively level spaces between being traversed, sometimes by horse, and sometimes by engine power, as the case demands. Occasionally the rails are laid upon the extreme verge of a giddy precipice; and looking from the carriage window, the traveler gazes sheer down, without a stone or scrap of fence between, into the mountain depth below. . . . It was very pretty travelling thus, at a rapid pace along the heights of a mountain in a keen wind, to look down into a valley full of light and softness; catching glimpses, through the treetops, of scattered cabins . . . and we riding onward, high above them, like a whirlwind." Pennsylvania would eventually build more canal miles than New York (nearly 1,000 compared to 800 for the Empire State). Next came Ohio, a close third. In fact, every state, save a half dozen, east of the Mississippi River by 1850 boasted a canal, with the total canal mileage in that year reaching 3,700. Not surprisingly, the most successful nineteenth-century canals outside the Erie were the short lines, modeled along the earlier Middlesex model, that were promoted and run by private entrepreneurs. The Lehigh canal, forty-eight miles, was successful; so, too, was the Delaware and Hudson, which essentially moved coal out of the anthracite region. Numerous other anthracite canals made money for promoters, but virtually all the water tracks—short and long—would decline as railroads illustrated their faster speed, greater accessibility, and lower fares.

Not even the wide utilization of the steamboat after Robert Fulton proved its commercial success in 1807 could save the canal from extinction. For the steamboat, like so much American technology, was not premised on a narrow canal but the wide, navigable rivers existing mostly in the East. Its mindset was bulk and showiness. It could be as large as 210 feet, 30 feet in width, and with paddle wheels nearly as wide. It could haul and accommodate 200 passengers, with ample leg- and dining room for all. Because it never used space with an eye toward efficiency, it would ultimately be dubbed a "showboat." The steamboat illustrates that era's little concern for such practical matters as cost. Steamboats could leave Pittsburgh with freight and passengers, travel via the Ohio and Mississippi into the Gulf of Mexico, then ultimately head northward via the Atlantic to throw final anchor into Philadelphia's waters. Indeed, the canal and steamboat were the first illustrations in America of what would be called today, because of their lack of fitness, "incompatibility."

*   *   *

A lot of Americans in the 1820s thought that railroads were a giant technological step backward. They had reason to be pessimistic. Rails of that era often began where the canal ended, with horses drawing the freight or traffic along at a snail's pace. The Baltimore & Ohio line, for example, employed the animal engines at first, as did canal companies. Even with the advent of the steam locomotive in the 1830s, railroads did not mushroom nearly as quickly as turnpikes or canals. Yet American railroads still set some records. A railroad engineer boasted and actually proved in the 1830s that his train could reach eighty miles per hour, and the longest line in the world in 1834 was 165 miles running from Charleston, South Carolina, where record numbers of passengers were jamming the cars within five years. The more typical outlook about the railroad was cautious, even after the steam-propelled model came into existence. For one reason, the craft of laying rails so that trains would stay on them and maneuver with heavy loads took time to work out. There were accidents from train boilers that exploded; a good rain could wipe out the train's fire and stop it dead in its tracks; and at times the rails were rented out to individual movers whose scheduling too often coincided with the passage of the main trains. Then there was what was dubbed the snakehead, which was a spike driven loose and propelled through the floorboard, injuring passengers and damaging cargo. Most railroads in the early years were unplanned, with little thought of consolidation with other lines, necessitating movement of goods first on turnpikes and canals to rail lines and erasing savings that a planned system might effect. Little wonder, then, that by 1841 only about 3,500 miles of track had been laid; by 1848 the figure was less than 6,000, with New England and the Middle Atlantic states monopolizing the system.

Another big hurdle was government. In the first years, states like Pennsylvania, Indiana, Georgia, Ohio, and North Carolina erected lines on the theory that rails were similar to turnpikes and canals. Leasing out these state-constructed lines to individual haulers resulted in a mess. By the 1840s, however, states, and soon the federal government, gave private rail promoters large grants of land to induce development. By that time, too, technology made the rails more attractive to haulers and passengers alike: the telegraph was the single most important invention, permitting timetables to be known in advance; the iron T rail provided greater permanency and comfort than the earlier models; and the cowcatcher eased the criticism of farmers who found dead cattle in the wake of the first train movements across their grazing lands. Many lines began to rely on imported iron rails on the theory they were better and would induce Americans to use the trains because of their safety. Most of all, four integrated systems were intact by the 1850s, all employing modern management techniques: the B & O, Erie, New York Central, and Pennsylvania. Passengers, however, were the last to benefit because the railroads always looked to freight as their big money-makers. Early on, railroad owners shunned the European passenger coach with its compartmentalized and private features, accepting instead the wide-open car with its sixty seats that were reversible according to direction. With windows open, passengers had to contend with engine sparks that could light up their clothes and lives, as well as with the odors of the animal grease that lubricated the wheels. In winter with the windows closed, passengers froze, except for those nearest the stove that occupied center position in the car. Tobacco smoking was permitted everywhere; what was worse was the tobacco chewing that stained seats and floor. At restroom and eating stops there were hawkers who roamed the center aisle selling merchandise that often did not last the duration of the trip, and until George Pullman's Palace Cars made their imprint in the late 1800s there was little class to the American passenger system. Yet, trains were still an improvement over alternative modes of travel. For the first time in the nation's history, a transportation system could whisk passengers to their destinations in a matter of hours. This meant that distant visiting could be accomplished without working harm to the passenger's overall finances and available time, and often train depots were centered right smack in the center of towns and cities, ensuring that a hotel or business area was only a short distance away.

Railroads made the cost of transporting goods inexpensive. They induced farmers in the Midwest to grow more wheat and other staples, and for several decades the prices of farm produce rose, as illustrated by a Census Bureau report of 1860:

> The great bulk of the gain caused by the cheapness of transportation has gone to the producer. This depends on a general principle, which must continue to operate for many years. The older a country is, the more civic and less rural it becomes; that is, the greater will be the demand for food, the less the production. The competition of the consumer for food is greater than that of the producer for price. . . . Hence it is that New England and New York, continually filling up with manufacturers, artisans, and cities, must be supplied with increasing quantities of food from the interior west; and hence, while this is the case, prices cannot fall in the great markets. . . . But there is another respect in which the influence of railroads is almost as favorable to agriculture as that of cheapening the transportation of produce. It is that of cheapening the transportation, and therefore reducing the prices of foreign articles and eastern manufactures consumed by the farmers of the interior. . . . On the whole, the prices of articles carried from the east to the west were diminished, while those from the west to the east were increased.

Perhaps more than anything, the growth of the railroad had a ripple effect on the American economy. Even with imports of rails, the American iron industry grew significantly. Half of all iron produced by the industry by 1860 was consumed by railroads, whose total mileage reached 30,600. The size of firms in the iron industry increased, and its mass production methods boosted the anthracite coal business, minimizing reliance on wood and charcoal as fuels. The railroads needed large amounts of glass, rubber, felt, and copper tools, as well as mineral and animal oils. By decreasing transportation costs, they lowered the costs of the production of manufactured goods, which helped to increase their demand. And railroads made possible the development of new markets in the west, including major cities such as Chicago, which grew from wilderness to a million people within a few decades.

To be sure, the rails were not perfect. The visible hand of government planning of routes was not present; it did not take long before some areas were overserved by rails, others underserved, a characteristic that would not be lost on the federal government in the twentieth century when another transportation breakthrough, the airplane, threatened unfriendly skies. No burgeoning town thought it could achieve importance unless it had a railroad or two, no matter the deservedness of its economic obscurity. Hundreds of railroad companies dotting the East and Midwest before the Civil War ensured that there would be little cooperation, even to the extent of adopting a standard rail gauge. Railroads required enormous financial backing; if they relied upon foreign investors who possessed the necessary capital, they ran the risk of receiving the hostile public reaction that was generated for the foreign-supported Bank of the United States. If they gave rise to a sophisticated system of American finance capitalism—typified by large banking houses—they ran the equally great risk of contributing to the strengthening of an elitist banking system that would find tough sledding in an age of democracy.

As the nation's first big business, the railroads were forced to adopt modern management techniques, including accounting measures that the consuming public, especially farmers, had a hard time understanding. For example, railroads were among the first businesses to consider costs, variable and fixed, in the devising of rates. As a result, a rate from point A to point B, a distance of 100 miles, might be 10¢ per pound, whereas one from point A to point C, a distance of 200 miles, might be 15¢, the former representing the greater impact of fixed costs on the short haul. To the average farmer, such rate making was an outright rip-off, especially during hard times, and it induced the farmer to send goods to more distant markets where more, not less, competition might exist, thereby contributing to falling prices. What is more, the railroad looked big, sleek, and rich; its whistle could be heard for miles; its smoke blocked out the sun and invaded the nostrils with offensive fumes; and its sparks could set afire thousands of acres of dry woodlands. In a democratic nation, people can get excited in a positive and negative fashion about such imposing business, one that was seen or heard every single day of the year. The negative emotions required little stimulation—from seeming high rates to late schedules to burned forests to run-down downtown areas from which other businesses fled because of the adverse environmental conditions bequeathed by rails. When the railroads attempted to merge in order to effect economies of scale, a sensible notion given the numerous independent lines, they conjured up the negative idea that big was bad. No such mental image could be drawn of the telegraph industry, however. Although Samuel F. B. Morse hoped that his invention would become part of the postal system—an idea far in advance of his day—telegraph companies multiplied, and an outright search and merger story unfolded. Western Union whipped all its rivals, becoming a monopoly that no American minded because the mental image of the industry was a thin metal wire strung along poles that scarcely reached out and touched people's lives in an emotional way. This same characteristic permitted the monopolization of the telephone industry, also without a public squabble, less than a century later.

Yet, on balance, the railroad, invented in England, became America's initiator of industrialism that had more positive than negative tones. Unlike the European rails and locomotives that were built to last, America's were built for speed, lightweight and destined to be replaced by still speedier models. Because American passengers sometimes took a bit longer than expected to eat during the rest stops (before diners were introduced), the race to catch up on lost time meant that rails had a good share of high-speed accidents that dedicated train riders came to expect as standard operating practice. And rails and their speed became so much a part of American life in the nineteenth century that even the system of keeping time was changed in their behalf. Prior to the iron horses, each town set the time according to the location of the sun. What was worse, differences between the fifty-six "sun" areas were complex, recorded in minutes and even seconds. New York City was ten minutes and two seconds ahead of Baltimore; Sacramento and San Francisco were nearly four minutes apart. With the arrival of the railroad, time became a daymare and nightmare for travelers, who had to change their watches several times during a short trip. So railroad officials, overcome by train lag, called a time convention. The result: railway standard time, which divided the nation into five time zones. Communities were urged to adopt the idea, which officially began on November 18, 1883. But like the railroad, it remained controversial. As one cynic suggested, "The planets must, in the future, make their circuits by such timetables as railroad magnates arrange." It took decades for some citizens to swallow the new time capsule, and Congress did not approve the arrangement until 1918. By that time, the railroad sun was beginning to set on the American horizon.

8
INVENTIVE
GENIUS

The people of the United States are ingenious in the invention, and prompt, and accurate in the execution of mechanism and workmanship for purposes in science arts, manufactures, navigation, and agriculture. Rittenhouse's planetarium, Franklin's electrical conductor, Godfrey's quadrant improved by Hadley, Rumsey's and Fitch's steam engines, Leslie's rod pendulum and other horological inventions, . . . the construction of flour-mills, the wirecutter and bender for card makers, Folsom's and Brigg's machinery for cutting nails out of rolled iron, the Philadelphia dray with an inclined plane, Mason's engine for extinguishing fire, the Connecticut steeple clock, which is wound up by the wind, the Franklin fire-place, the Rittenhouse stove, Anderson's threshing machine, Rittenhouse's instrument for taking levels, Donnaldson's hippopotamos and balance lock, and Wynkoop's underlators, are a few of the numerous examples.

TENCH COXE, *A View of the
United States of America* (1794)

The U.S. Patent Office was established in 1790, but American ingenuity was apparent long before that date. Necessity mothered invention in the New World, much of which was never patented. There was no need for patents for a long time. But once the system was established, American tinkerers rushed to the patent office in a parade that was sometimes red, white, and blue in excitement, complexity, and disappointment for its participants. Some names would be well known for subsequent generations, such as Cyrus McCormick, Eli Whitney, and Isaac Singer. Most would be richly but scarcely deservedly obscure: Obed Hussey, Samuel Thomson, William Colgate, James Ritty, and William Underwood. And their inventions? Well, they ranged from still-popular soaps and foods to now-antique clocks and hairpins. There was even a patented Christmas stocking that threatened to remove the traditional evergreen symbol from the land—and it might have had not another product, electricity, cut the stocking off at the product pass.

The first inventors were handymen who devised a better way for doing farm chores or they were peddlers who would roam from town to town with gadgets they had made. And some of the time they were families, such as the Job Snelling family of Massachusetts, described by a contemporary as geniuses:

> His father was the inventor of wooden nutmegs, by which Job said he might have made a fortune, if he had taken out a patent and kept the business in his own hand; his mother Patience manufactured the first white oak pumpkin seeds of the mammoth kind, and turned a pretty penny the first season; and his aunt Prudence was the first to discover that corn husks steeped in tobacco water would make as handsome Spanish wrappers as ever came from Havana, and that oak leaves would answer all the purposes of filling, for no one could discover the difference except the man who smoked them, and then it would be too late to make a stir about it. Job himself bragged of having made some useful discoveries, the most profitable of which was the art of conveying mahogany dust into cayenne pepper, which he said was a profitable and safe business; for the people have been so long accustomed to having dust thrown in their eyes, that there wasn't much danger of being found out.

When the federal government's patent office opened, the first patentee, Samuel Hopkins of Vermont, was very much like the thousands who would follow in his footsteps in the next several decades: very average and largely obscure. His invention for making "pot and pearl ashes" (potash) made a big hit where it counted—with the patent board, composed of Secretary of State Thomas Jefferson, the secretary of war, and the attorney general. The process of securing a patent was rigorous, but it was also democratic—first come, first served—and absolutely essential to the nation's rapid industrial development. The procedure was uniform among the states, thanks to a constitutional provision empowering Congress "to promote the progress of science and the useful arts by securing for limited times to authors and inventors, the exclusive rights to their respective writings and discoveries." The process was also cheap, $3.70, plus a few cents per page for the specifications. In 1793, it was made even more democratic, making it easy—much too easy— to register a patent. In place of scrutiny by a board of examiners, a system was introduced whereby each inventor swore to the utility and novelty of the claim and simply paid a fee. Then the real fight took place in the courts. That's what happened to Eli Whitney, who could not prevent unauthorized copying of his cotton gin, in spite of long and expensive suits. But at least history would record that Whitney was the inventor of the device that would revolutionize the cotton industry. The same could not be said for Obed Hussey of Baltimore, who invented the reaper but never got credit for it.

Born in Maine in 1792, Hussey spent his early life as a sailor. His ability to invent machines soon led him from the sea to terra firma, where he became identified with a corn-grinding mechanism and a sugarcane crusher. The idea of a reaper was suggested by a friend to Hussey, who was startled with the revelation that such a machine was not already in existence. To be sure, there had been reapers of sorts in early America—as there had been even in ancient times—but none worked well. Hussey secluded himself in Baltimore in 1831, thanks to the patronage of Richard B. Chenoweth, who owned an agricultural implement factory in the city. Working on models in the loft of the firm, Hussey emerged with his invention in 1833, successfully demonstrating it before an Ohio agricultural society in July. In December Hussey received a patent. Unbeknownst to him, one Cyrus McCormick of Virginia had exhibited a reaper in 1831 but did not receive a patent until six months after Hussey's was awarded. Surprisingly, both reapers were pretty much the same, utilizing sawtooth blades attached to the side of a horse-drawn carriage, with a platform in the rear to catch the grain. They were also noisy and unsightly, often scaring the horses that pulled them.

Of course, the two men soon realized they were in competition. Hussey set up his factory in Baltimore and from 1834 to 1838 introduced the reaper in the state as well as in Pennsylvania, New York, and Illinois. But McCormick was a hustler, writing his brother: "Meet Hussey in Baltimore and put him down." The two men competed before judges, revving up their machines on open fields near the James River in Virginia in June 1843. The judges were divided, with McCormick's getting just a slight nod. McCormick's machine was bigger and stronger, but Hussey's was small and simple, working best as a mower. In subsequent years Hussey and McCormick vied for a competitive edge. They displayed their machines at the London Exhibition in 1851, battled for an extension of their patents, and did a whole lot of arguing. Hussey was the better debater, but McCormick was the salesman: he incorporated improvements, sent agents across the Midwest, advertised, and even extended credit. And he was downright bold in his warranty, saying in 1852: "I warrant them [my machines] superior to Hussey's and to all others. I have a reputation to maintain. Let a farmer take both and keep the one which he likes best." Hussey's demise was swift. Producing about 500 reapers in 1855, his Baltimore plant put out only 10 in 1859. However, Hussey was not without some rewards in his losing battle. In 1859 a court awarded him $80,000 on the grounds that McCormick had violated his patent, and the latter was ordered to pay Hussey a license fee on every machine sold. Unfortunately, Hussey had little opportunity to savor this small victory. He was killed by a train on a visit to New England the following year, bringing an end to a truly grim reaper story.

Elias Howe, who invented the sewing machine in 1841, was another American who lost his initial accomplishment to another tinkerer. For Howe, part of the problem was laziness. Working as a young boy in a Boston shop that made precision instruments, Howe was easygoing with customers and his work. When he married, he was forced to look for a better job than one earning $9 a week. But he soon quit looking. He let his father support him while he dabbled with a sewing machine. He took his model to England after getting patents, but was forced to pawn it in order to work his way back to America. By midcentury, Howe had made only about a dozen machines and was richly obscure. Enter Isaac Merrit Singer, who was equally obscure as an actor in these years, traveling with various companies across the land. Whenever the plays bombed and lost money, Singer would devise some machine, such as a rock driller in 1839, that would make his troupe enough bucks to keep it on the road again. In Fredericksburg, Ohio, the company went belly up for the umpteenth time, but Singer got a job in a local sawmill and within a short time devised a wood and metal carving machine that he immediately patented. Next Singer hoped to sell his invention to a large eastern firm and off to New York City he raced. However, the company that was interested in developing the machine was destroyed by a boiler explosion, leaving Singer down and out. But not for long. He took his type-carving machine to Boston where he hoped book publishers would be impressed. They were—but not enough to commit their funds. So Singer, still hoping to make it big with his machine, took a job in the meantime in a Boston repair shop. It didn't take him long to realize that the few sewing machines that Howe had made seemed to end up in his shop because they were notoriously undependable. The snafu was that Howe's machine mimicked his wife's arm motion as she sewed, meaning a curved needle moving in a circular, horizontal fashion. In Singer's mind, the gizmo should have moved straight up and down through a perpendicular needle, thereby assuring easy, trouble-free stitching. Within eleven days, Singer perfected his model, thanks to a little help from his friends who lent him $40. The first patent was issued in 1851, and Singer moved quickly to fight off infringement suits from Howe. Although Howe was the winner of the court battles, his victory was shortsighted, as was the case with Hussey's legal position with the reaper. For Singer went ahead and developed a production and marketing strategy, setting up fourteen branch offices, each employing a salesman, demonstrator, mechanic, and manager. Relying at first on commission agents, Singer eventually resorted to employing his own people on the grounds that they would be more committed to the full range of company services. In 1874 Singer built the largest sewing machine plant in the world in Elizabethport, New Jersey. Howe's name was then history, but Singer's would be known to every future generation of Americans.

Samuel Slater's name would not be known to most Americans studying the early history of inventiveness in their country. For one reason, Slater was not an American; for another, he was not an inventor. He stole, however, a major English invention and brought it to the United States. Not that he was a traitor in his home country. In fact, from his birth in 1768 in Belper, Derbyshire, Slater exhibited more outstanding character traits than either Elias Howe or Isaac Singer. Derbyshire was spinning country in Slater's early years, and like other youths, he sought employment in the textile mills. As a teenager he was apprenticed to Jedidiah Strutt, a partner of Sir Richard Arkwright, the inventor of the textile machinery that revolutionized the industry. Slater worked hard as an apprentice, but the industry fell on hard times as the American Revolution cut exports to the New World. No matter. Slater showed so much talent that after the war he was given responsibility for supervising a new mill in the area. By the end of the 1780s as Slater approached his twenty-first birthday, he read about the bounties that were offered by various states in America for inventions in the textile industry. So in 1789 Slater set sail for America, after having been thoroughly searched by British officials so as to make certain that he took no Arkwright plans with him, an action that was illegal under British law. Arriving in New York, Slater landed a position in a primitive American textile firm in order to get the lay of the industry. Then he wrote Moses Brown, a Rhode Island spinner, that he had a better idea about textile machinery. "I flatter myself," wrote Slater, "that I can give the greatest satisfaction, in making machinery. . . ." Brown, a Quaker, was beside himself with joy. "We hardly know what to say to thee," he responded, "but if thou thought thou couldst perfect and conduct them to profit, if thou wilt come and do it, thou shalt have all the profits made of them over and above the interest of the money they cost, and the wear and tear of them."

Never was there a better marriage of an Englishman to America than Samuel Slater to Pawtucket, Rhode Island. From memory, he reconstructed the entire Arkwright machinery, including carding, drawing, and roving machines and spindles. He trained youngsters to operate the machinery in a school-like setting, in which he himself taught religious lessons. He married one of the daughters of the family with whom he roomed in Pawtucket and even sent for his brother because he was convinced America would be good to him also. Moses Brown's mills multiplied, so did Slater's happiness, and by the time this English defector died in 1835, the American textile industry was firmly established. In fact, a report on manufactures in 1860 recognized that "the manufacture of cotton, which is now the predominant industry of this country as well as Great Britain, properly dates from the introduction of Arkwright machinery in 1790."

No inventors were more important to the industrialization of America than clockmakers. The reason was that clocks necessitated the making of precision tools. These machines had to be adjusted to a fraction of a fraction of an inch; once the technology was perfected, it could be transferred to other industries that cried for the intermeshing of gears and wheels without hitches. Of course, clockmakers relied upon the work of Eli Whitney in the area of interchangeable parts. Whitney's experience in manufacturing muskets for the United States government in 1798 was far more significant than his invention of the cotton gin, the technology of which was confined to a single product. In order to fulfill his government contract, Whitney purchased a mill outside New Haven, Connecticut, and immediately began to tackle the problems of manpower and lack of tools. He was convinced that the key to manufacturing muskets was the "uniformity system," that is, "to make the same parts of different guns—as the locks, for example, as much like each other as the successive impressions of a copper-plate engraving." He was scheduled to deliver 10,000 muskets in two years, the lion's share of 30,000 contracted by the government from twenty-seven firms. At the end of the first year, Whitney produced only 500 muskets, but he continued to make partial shipments until the full quota was met in January 1809. All the while he bore the opprobrium of skeptics who came and went with each presidential administration, and he was forced to travel to Philadelphia and Washington for periodic inquisitions. But the achievement of January 1809, combined with Whitney's continuing sophistication of the making of interchangeable parts, did not escape notice. In time, additional contracts for muskets came from Washington, as well as various states. And the word spread to Connecticut clockmakers like Eli Terry. At first, Terry produced clocks by the hundred, peddling them around the country by horseback. Consumers were wary of mass-produced clocks, but Terry persevered in both his sales technique and technology. A thirty-hour shelf clock was patented in 1816 and over the years dropped in price from $15 to $5; production, on the other hand, reached 10,000 by 1850. Another Connecticut clockmaker, Chauncey Jerome, pioneered in a small brass clock that could be readily carried in a wooden box. His goal was to cut the cost of making clocks in mass by reducing labor charges. By the 1840s, his clocks were selling for 75¢—inexpensive enough for the average American who, in an increasingly urban setting, needed to keep track of time. Not surprisingly, Jerome's clocks were even exported abroad.

New Englanders with their Yankee ingenuity were no less inventive with medicines. The first medical patent was awarded to Samuel Lee, Jr., of Windham, Connecticut, who produced "bilious pills" designed to cure not only irritability but also jaundice, worms, dysentery, and female complaints. Even though Lee would soon find numerous competitors, Americans rushed to buy pills, and Lee did well in his sales. So did makers of pills with a sugar coat: "CLICKENER's PURGATIVE PILLS, being completely enveloped with a COATING OF PURE WHITE SUGAR (Which is as distinct from the internal ingredients as a nut shell from a kernel) HAVE NO TASTE OF MEDICINE." In actuality, the first patent medicines improved upon the cures that were prevalent at the time, such as bleeding, which in colonial times took more lives than saved them. Samuel Thomson of New Hampshire agreed with physicians who bled patients that all disease was essentially caused by one factor, an imbalance in body temperature. The cure was to restore that balance through internal medicine. Thomson, a farmer, put it this way: "All the art required to do this is, to know what *medicine* will do it, and how to administer it, as a person knows how to clear a stove and pipe when clogged with soot, that the fire may burn free, and the whole room be warmed as before." Thomson's favorite medicine, which he patented in 1813, was an herb, *Lobelia inflata,* which induced vomiting. Sometimes it was mixed with red pepper to ensure the intended result, and the patient was urged to take a nice hot and then cold bath preparatory to the regurgitation. To be sure, Thomson's medication was controversial, eventually leading to a trumped-up charge that he had killed a patient. However, Thomson was acquitted, and he continued to argue that his cure was superior to bloodletting or the ingestion of harmful medicines that stayed in the body. And his medicine was absolutely democratic, requiring no doctor to administer. For about $20 a family could purchase the rights to use Thomson's medicine; by 1839 some 10,000 purchases, according to Thomson, had been made, presumably making him a rich man. Unfortunately, in 1843 Thomson died after using his medicine in excess. Nevertheless, he helped to put physicians on notice that the health field was not their monopoly and that strong remedies had to be abandoned.

If Thomson was absolutely certain of the soundness of his product, no less could be said for Charles Goodyear, who took all the kinks out of rubber products in the first half of the nineteenth century. Rubber products went back a long way, to the time when Columbus visited Haiti and found natives bouncing a rubber ball around. Between Columbus's time and 1800, a whole lot of inventors tried to make rubber into something other than a child's plaything. Cold weather turned untreated rubber into a substance harder than a rock, and hot weather made it melt. Rubber garments, for example, appeared to be a big hit when sold in the fall, but by winter they were bulletproof in weight and by August had achieved meltdown. Charles Goodyear was an unlikely candidate to correct this situation. Born in New Haven, Connecticut, in 1800, Goodyear was the son of an inventor of a light steel hayfork that made field work much easier. But Charles was a serious lad who appeared to be a good candidate for the ministry. When he shunned that vocation, he ventured to Philadelphia to enter the hardware business, but his firm went under in 1834 and Goodyear landed in debtor's prison in the City of Brotherly Love. During his prison stay, Goodyear believed that religion would not only sustain him but lead to new heights of accomplishment. In Goodyear's case, that meant tinkering with rubber since products made from the substance were so bad. As a result of his demeanor, prison officials permitted him to carry on experiments, but nothing happened. After his release, Goodyear rented a shut-down rubber factory on Staten Island and for three years literally starved his wife and children trying to effect progress. It was said of him in these years: "You will know him when you see him; he has on an India rubber cap, stock, coat, vest, and shoes, and an India rubber purse *without a cent in it!*"

Then one day in 1839 Goodyear accidentally dropped a rubber gumball onto the top of his wife's hot stove. It vulcanized, losing all the offensive qualities of its natural state. The only problem of Goodyear's discovery was that the public simply refused to believe that rubber was anything other than an undependable product. "That such indifference to this discovery," Goodyear lamented, "and many incidents attending it, could have existed in an intelligent and benevolent community can only be accounted for by existing circumstances in that community." Almost penniless, Goodyear traveled around the northeast until he began to make believers out of people. By 1844, he had his first patent, and over sixty more would follow before his death in 1860. But he never made any money from his work, which soon transformed American products. Perhaps worst of all, he had to fight others who claimed vulcanization as their idea, hiring none other than the prestigious Daniel Webster as his lawyer. "They [the defendants]," argued Webster, "attempt to prove that he [Goodyear] was not the inventor by little shreds and patches of testimony. Here a little bit of sulphur, and there a little parcel of lead; here a little degree of heat, a little hotter than would warm a man's hands, and in which a man could live for ten minutes or a quarter of an hour; and yet they never seem to come to the point. I think it is because their materials did not allow them to come to the manly assertion that somebody else did make this invention. . . ." That somebody else was Goodyear, whose fame would far exceed his fortune.

Another religious-oriented inventor, William Colgate, shunned trips to the patent office, preferring the marketplace instead. Colgate's father escaped religious persecution in England by taking his family to Maryland. In Baltimore the Colgate family dabbled in soap and candle making, with young William eventually learning the trades. But Baltimore was scarcely the center of the soap universe and William took off for New York City in 1803 when he was twenty years old. Three years later, he prospered by doing things his competitors never dreamed of: first, he added aromatic scents to his soap; next, he packaged it in bars of equal size; finally, he delivered the soap to customer homes. He also advertised extensively, gave generously to the Baptist Education Society of New York, and sent his soaps abroad. By 1837 other soap companies, such as the one started by William Procter and James Gamble in Cincinnati, cashed in on the American concern for feeling real clean all over. Not surprisingly, P & G went from door to door with their soaps, a strategy that American businessmen would extend to other toiletries and products in the nineteenth century.

Some ethically minded inventors did not achieve even as much success as Goodyear. Such was the case of James Ritty, a shopkeeper who worked in Dayton, Ohio, in its frontier days. The stumbling block for Ritty the businessman was his hired help, whose job was to sell merchandise to customers and put the money in a cash drawer. Too often employees took money from the drawer when the boss was not looking. And like contemporary shoplifting, this practice meant passing on costs to customers who, in turn, might venture to stores with lower prices and honest clerks. Ritty was determined to shortchange the crooked employee. In collaboration with his brother, he came up with the first cash register, receiving a patent in late 1879. Ritty was ecstatic over his "incorruptible cashier," as he dubbed the device. Unlike modern models, it had the primary purpose of attracting everyone's attention when it was operated. Each time a clerk opened the machine a loud bell or gong sounded to herald the event. In addition, the register had features that would assist in the recording of sales, but its hallmark was to keep all eyes front and center when the bell went off, much in the fashion of a burglar alarm.

Although Ritty's invention solved the matter of crime in his own shop, it did not spread like wildfire to other stores with pilfering problems. For one reason, clerks in Dayton put up a fuss that one of their perquisites would disappear. Second, the cash register was expensive. A company set up by Ritty to manufacture the product had to charge $50 per unit to make a profit. The sum of $50 gave rise to sticker shock, and Ritty's National Manufacturing Company looked on hard times by 1884: with thirteen employees in a superstitious age, the plant was also located in a run-down section of the city. What was worse, Ritty's great venture was the object of ridicule. So much so that when John Henry Patterson from a nearby community bought Ritty's firm in 1884 the guffaws from townspeople led him to try to get Ritty to renege on the deal, with a $2,000 sweetener for his trouble. Ritty refused. And so Patterson chose to put his act together and make his new company a going concern. He also gave it a new name, the National Cash Register Company, which soon became a household word.

That American inventions were ingenious is illustrated by the reception they received overseas, especially at world's fairs. Then, too, British agents were sent to the United States to study the state of American technology. One British report in 1854 referred to the "extraordinary ingenuity" of American machines and took pains to detail those that mass-produced little things, such as hairpins and buttons:

For another curious illustration of this automatic action we have the manufacture of ladies' hair-pins at Waterbury. A quantity of wire is coiled upon a drum or cylinder, and turns round upon its axis, as suspended from the ceiling of the workshop. The point of the wire being inserted into the machine, and the power applied, the wire is cut off to the requisite length, carried forward and bent to the proper angle, and then pointed with the necessary blunt points, and finally dropped into a receiver, quite finished, all but the lacquering or japanning. These pins are made at the rate of 180 per minute.

The reader is referred also to the automation machine for shanking buttons. The blanks being cut in this brass, are put into a curved feeding-pipe, in which they descend to the level of the machine, by which a hole is stamped in the centre of each. Then the shank is formed by another portion of the machine, from a continuous wire carried along horizontally, the wire being shaped into the shank, and pushed up into its proper place. These operations are completed at the rate of 200 per minute, the only attendance required being that of one person to feed this automation with the blanks and the wires, which he is so well able to work up to the satisfaction of his masters.

These little inventions in the nineteenth century radically changed American life for the better. Friction matches, for example, quite literally lit up lives thanks to the work of Alonzo D. Phillips of Massachusetts and others in the 1830s. Called at first "loco foco" or self-igniting matches, the new products received fame in October 1835 in New York City during a Democratic Party convention. A group of radicals seized control of the meeting, and their opponents hoped to thwart their maneuvers by cutting off the gas used for illumination. But the radicals used self-igniting matches to light up candles, went on to adopt a platform and select candidates, and entered the political arena with the appropriate name of Loco Focos. After the Civil War, a match-making machine was invented by McClintock Young of Washington, D.C., that was modern in its manner of cutting splints from a wood block and dipping them in composition. Another tiny invention was a machine for the making of pins, which were expensive in the eighteenth century, selling at times for more than 25¢ each. Inventors John Howe of New York and Samuel Slocum of Rhode Island made pins cheap, with Slocum even devising a machine for sticking them on paper in order that they might be sold and kept in an orderly fashion.

Then there was the modest work of William Underwood in the food industry. An employee of the famous Crosse & Blackwell Company in London, Underwood came to America in 1817 to establish the canning business that he had learned in his home country. Arriving in New Orleans, Underwood walked most of the way north to Boston where he opened his cannery in 1822. Using glass jars filled with various fruits and berries, Underwood found enormous consumer resistance. European brands such as Crosse & Blackwell were so well known that Americans distrusted the quality of domestic efforts. However, Underwood took his products to South America, the West Indies, and even the Far East, broadening at the same time his line to include pickles, mustard, milks, and pie fruits. In 1839 he resorted to the tin can, which caused controversy because the product could not be seen by the consumer until opened. By midcentury, though, the benefits of canned goods became obvious to housewives, and William Underwood & Company began to thrive. It limited its product line to meats and fish that could be deviled and appealed to a high-class audience that wanted more than food in the raw. Of course, by the twentieth century, the deviled ham preparations of Underwood would find a democratic market stretching from party-goers to lunch-box carriers.

Sometimes technology was so exciting that it threatened to undo American tradition. Even the Christmas tree was under siege. The problem was that the evergreen symbol was not a perfect one for the holiday—for one reason, many Americans got their trees by stealing them from parks or the estates of wealthy residents. On a single December evening in New York City in 1883, for example, 200 trees had been cut from one estate, with only a few perpetrators caught by police. Then there was the fact that in the pre-electricity days candles on Christmas trees caused extensive fires in major cities throughout the land. No wonder that *The New York Times* had a bah, humbug view of the situation. "The Christmas tree," editorialized the paper, "dropping melted wax upon the carpet, filling all nervous people with a dread of fire . . . diffusing the poison of rationalism thinly disguised as the perfume of hemlock, should have no place in our beloved land." What is more, the tree was nothing more than a "rootless and lifeless corpse."

Fortunately, in the interest of peace and goodwill in the Big Apple, the *Times* found a backup symbol to take the place of the Christmas tree. Long in disuse, the Christmas stocking was gaining a toehold. In the old days, the problems with the stocking were tradition and lack of technology. The New England stocking was too small, much too skimpy for recipients of any age; the Chicago stocking was much too big, which meant that only high rollers could fill it to the top. So exasperated parents took to the Christmas tree as a means of spreading out gifts to children. Then in 1883 came one of the most significant inventions of the nineteenth century. The Smith Christmas Stocking made its debut. It was a better idea in that it was elastic. "The economical parent," according to the *Times,* "can fill it at little more than double the cost of filling a New England stocking, while the wealthy and generous parent can crowd into it more than could be forced into the largest Chicago stocking." The Smith stocking, reflecting more than one laudable feature, was equipped with a watertight metallic toe compartment which could receive and hold molasses candy without fear of sticky meltdown or crushing. And it could be used year after year. All this simply overwhelmed consumers, and the *Times* could not say enough good things about the product: "Let us welcome back the stocking of our father—that is to say, of our female ancestors. . . . [The Christmas tree] has had its day, and the glorious reaction in favor of the sacred stocking will sweep it away forever."

And in stores throughout America, business was booming, with big holes in the stocking display.

9

THE SOUTHERN DILEMMA

Against the background of a moving, bustling West, of an East committed to the ideal of industrialism and urban growth, stands the South as a seemingly unchanging section of America in the first half of the nineteenth century. Such a still-life portrait of the states below the Mason-Dixon line is not altogether accurate. Southerners participated in the westward movement, being especially interested in the vast, fertile lands of the Southwest, which became the great cotton-producing region of the nation. They also migrated in lesser numbers to the Northwest, such as Ohio, Illinois, and Indiana. In the latter state their numbers were so impressive and their speech so different that they were dubbed Hoosiers, a name still descriptive of Indiana residents. Antebellum southerners also dabbled in industrial enterprises. Cotton textile mills were established in several states of the seaboard South, although their numbers and production quotas paled in comparison to those of New England mills. The tobacco industry, the center of which moved from William Byrd's Virginia to the western areas of Kentucky and Tennessee, was also important to the South: snuff, cigar, and chewing products totaled several millions of dollars in annual sales. Steel mills were evident in the South long before Birmingham became the second Pittsburgh in the 1870s. Richmond's Belle Isle Iron Works and the Tredegar Company were major producers of steel, their significance proven to the Confederacy during the Civil War. The manufacture of cotton gins, cotton-seed oil, and flour was further evidence of the South's participation in the industrial movement, and the growth of Baltimore, Richmond, New Orleans, and Mobile—to name but a few—was testimony to the fact that urban growth was not a monopoly of the North.

Yet for all these characteristics, the South's other economic traits made it the most contrary of the various sections of the country. In the South there were planters with slaves, as well as small farmers whose political, economic, and social importance was never proportional to their numbers; there were few immigrants, with the area remaining the most homogeneous in the nation; there was reliance on a single agricultural crop, cotton; there were factors or agents who, as in the colonial period, handled the marketing of cotton, often exploiting planters and keeping them perenially indebted in the process. There was even dueling in the pre–Civil War South, a custom that had died in the North along with Alexander Hamilton in his infamous duel with Aaron Burr in 1804. Moreover, dueling appeared as a greater indictment of the older and settled South than it did of the rawer West, where the revolver of necessity displaced the distant county court or itinerant judge as a speedy adjudicator of pressing grievances relating to land claims. On the other hand, southerners resorted to dueling to avenge their good name. Foreign visitors criticized the South for still other reasons. "The North presents me, externally at least," observed de Tocqueville in 1831, "of a strong, regular, durable government, perfectly suited to the physical and moral state of things. In the South there is in the way things are run something feverish, disordered, revolutionary and passionate, which does not give the same sense of strength and durability." Other visitors faulted southerners because they dressed, spoke, and acted differently. Slow-moving farmers in shabby dress and unrefined vocabulary and accent suggested comprehensive poverty. And whether or not they visited each other's section, northerners and southerners still conjured up an unflattering mental picture of each other: the South as a feudal, slow-paced society of Blacks and hospitable whites who had a fondness for mint juleps, the North as a reservoir of smoke, noise, and dirty immigrants. Northern writers disgusted with the section's rising industrialism also popularized these images, as did southern authors defensive about the growing criticism of slavery. What is clear is that southerners were in a dilemma: they were businessmen who produced an exported crop, cotton, that paid for the industrial goods that northern Americans imported and used. Their section, however, was becoming a political minority vis-à-vis the bustling North and West. If they resisted the economic pressures to become more like the rest of the nation, civil war was inevitable. And if the civil war were won by the North, then the South was destined to become a part of an economic transformation that was decidedly mixed in terms of its positive effects on the various classes of southerners. It was a no-win situation, which was evident even from an examination of the average southerner.

At first glance, most of the South's common folk merit little attention in terms of their difference from counterparts in the rest of the nation. They were farmers, producing by 1859 about 52 percent of the nation's corn, 80 percent of its peas—including the black-eyed variety—and beans, and even 29 percent of its wheat, which is one of the reasons that Virginian Cyrus McCormick devised a mechanical reaper. Small farmers owned sufficient land and personality to make their wills compare favorably in size and value to those of the North's middle class. To be sure, there was a poor white trash component in Dixie, many of whose members forsook the agrarian ideal of owning land and farming and took to the woods as carefree trappers, hunters, and fishermen. Because they had no roots and capitalistic principles, southerners despised them. Because they often met up with the hookworm in the backcountry, along with an unbalanced diet, they became anemic, contracted pellagra, and their resultant pallor and lack of initiative were sufficient evidence to observers that rootlessness and poverty were related. Had these same people ventured northwestward, they would have become rosy-cheeked frontiersmen and pathfinders. As it were, they became the palefaces of southern society.

The main business of the South centered around cotton, a crop that was as controversial as it was critical to the nation's burgeoning industrialism. Cotton was extremely valuable because it coincided with the English industrial revolution that centered around textiles; it had a low-bulk/high-value ratio, was virtually imperishable, and because of its short height and inedible qualities furnished its harvesters neither with a hiding place nor food on the sly. It ripened at different times, meaning that laborers were required to pick some of the crop each day from August to January. Cotton gave a new lease on life to slavery, which was becoming unnecessary in the declining tobacco culture of the upper South, and in a curious way it led to the rise of the abolitionist movement: without cotton New England merchant families would have had social and economic predominance; little wonder, then, that the leading figures in the abolitionist movement were the educated sons and daughters of merchant families who could figure out the economic twists and moral links of this emotive chain. Yet no one profited more from the cotton industry than northerners. In 1853 the secretary of the Treasury reported to Congress "that but for the exports of raw cotton, . . . more than forty-eight millions of bullion and specie would have been required annually, since 1821, to have been exported (in addition to all that was exported) to meet the balances of trade against us that would have existed but for those exportations of raw cotton. It is true that Treasury accounts of exports are not safe criteria as to values, they being in the United States, as in other countries, generally undervalued; but without the exportations of cotton from the United States, the balance-sheet would be a sorry exhibit of our condition as a commercial people, and of general prosperity. Our other exports, and especially of other agricultural products, are, when separately estimated, really insignificant in comparison with cotton." The secretary pointed out other important benefits of the cotton industry: that it was the only product—agricultural or mechanical—that increased in proportion to the nation's increase in population, even though only one in 600 immigrants came to the South; and that "the increase of importations [of all merchandise] is mainly for the use and consumption of those portions of the country that do not produce cotton." The South, in sum, was efficient in a labor system that was economically and morally offensive but permitted the importation by northerners of manufactured goods that southerners did not typically use, although their exports of cotton paid for them.

The South paid the proverbial Piper, but it did not call the economic tune. "If I mistake not," said Senator R. B. Rhett of South Carolina in the early 1850s, "from the very foundation of this Government to this day, the operation of it in its financial and pecuniary relations has had but one uniform tendency; and that has been, to aggrandize the North at the expense of the South." By 1840 New Orleans was the fourth busiest port in the world—behind London, Liverpool, and New York—but twenty years later, although still mighty, the city saw its trade with the West fall from 58 percent of its total receipts to 23 percent, in spite of the enormous growth of the new territory. Much of this loss was due to the West and North forging an economic and transportation bond—first with the Erie canal and then with the railroads—as well as a mutual political mindset. Southern leaders contended: (a) that the "general welfare" was being interpreted more in terms of one segment of the economy (businessmen) and toward other regions (the North and West) than to the South and (b) that teeming industrialism might challenge the ordered, preindustrial southern system that its residents had no wish to change. When abolitionism was added to the traits that North and West shared—although there were few Blacks in their areas—southerners by the 1850s resorted to the counterattack of "insulation." They attempted to keep their section shielded from outside disruptive forces. For that reason, they passed laws making it difficult for corporations to establish factories in the South. Steam power, for instance, was forbidden in several cities. Also, southerners saw to it that newfangled ideas or products were unwelcome, which meant that even farm plows in the antebellum days were as crude as those in colonial times. Abolitionism drew such negative fire as to move southern congressmen to seek "gag rules" in Washington and to encourage local postmasters to ban antislavery tracts from the mails.

The South reasoned that its contribution to the nation's rising economic posture in the world was not commensurate with what it was receiving in turn. It saw unproved Yankee businessmen receiving a higher tariff every few years until by 1828 it reached an "abominations" level. It contended, on the other hand, that its cotton was being sold in an unprotected market while it was forced to buy industrial goods in a protected home market. It saw the raw West receiving government-sponsored internal improvements while it received no such programs. The South's solution to this imbalance was illustrated in the Missouri Compromise of 1820, which stressed that for every two states that entered the Union at least one should have a southern mental exposure, that is, permit slavery. It also sought political balance by advocating territorial expansion (Texas, the Mexican territories of the Far West, and Cuba) in the hope that migrants to these areas would carry with them a Dixie mindset. Finally, it sought the formulation of a political theory that would ensure political balance within the nation. From such intellectual pursuits came the nullification theory, which upheld the right of states to refuse to enforce a congressional act; the refinement of the doctrine of states rights, which put limits on federal powers; and the concurrent majority thesis of

John C. Calhoun that authorized the people of each state to exercise a veto over federal legislation.

To a certain degree, the Civil War would solve some of the South's problems by making it a part of the nation's business system. First, however, the war would catapult business in the North and West to unprecedented heights. With the South out of the Union, Congress passed legislation assisting the growth of big business. The Tariff Act of 1861 was the first in a series of protectionist acts that would last, with few exceptions, to the 1930s. Congress gave ample land (45 million acres) and money ($60 million) to the building of a transcontinental railroad system by the Union Pacific, Central Pacific, Kansas Pacific, Santa Fe, and Southern Pacific railroads. Land legislation was passed making it easier for still other federal acres, with timber and mineral resources, to flow to private developers. The National Banking Act of 1864 created a system of federally chartered banks that would ultimately give rise to a national paper currency and outlaw the use of state-chartered banking notes, some 7,000 of which floated through the land, creating a currency nightmare. The Morrill Act of 1862 provided over 13 million acres of federal land to endow "at least one college where the leading object shall be, without excluding other scientific and classical studies, including military tactics, to teach such branches of learning as are related to agriculture and mechanic arts, in such manner as the legislatures of the State may respectively prescribe, in order to promote the liberal and practical education of the industrial classes in the several pursuits and professions in life." The Immigration Act of 1864 permitted the importation of contract workers whose economic bargaining power was little, tantamount to the indentured servitude of colonial days. And, of course, the federal government needed war supplies—from uniforms, which gave a needed boost to the mass-produced clothing industry, to military weaponry. Although the war was accompanied by a recession in 1861, inflation, black markets, as well as by a shortage of supplies that slowed some industries, northern industry burst forward after 1865: railroad construction doubled in the succeeding decade from the prewar rate. The same held true for the production of pig iron. Cleveland had no iron mills in 1860, but by 1866 had twenty-one. Most important, as industry got large and Americans, notably farmers, began to vent their spleen by urging punitive regulation of the large corporation, the Fourteenth Amendment to the Constitution became a legal safeguard for business. Designed primarily to uphold the rights of Blacks against southern state governments, the amendment would be interpreted by the courts as protecting the property rights of corporations from ill-founded state regulation. "No state," read the critical phrase in the amendment, "shall make or enforce any law which shall abridge the privileges and immunities of citizens of the United States; nor shall any State deprive any person of life, liberty, or property, without due process of law; nor to deny to any person within its jurisdiction the equal protection of the laws." In practical terms, that meant that state legislatures bent on regulating large business without concern for the corporation's right to a fair return on its investment would find tough sledding in the courts.

The South was brought into business civilization in America in an unintentional but direct way. Because it was the main battlefield and smaller of the adversaries in terms of men and resources, its citizens felt the bite—northerners only the pinch —of economic problems. Southern women often had the total responsibility of small farms, all landowners faced heavy tax burdens, and plantation owners were hard hit by the shaky, if sometimes nonexistent, lines of transportation. As southern military fortunes waned, these problems deepened. Small farmers could lose their lands, and planters were forced to sell parcels of their vast holdings in order to make ends meet. The new purchasers were likely to be northerners who preferred to be absentee owners. Planters and small farmers usually continued to reside on the property but in a new capacity of landlord (planter) or tenant (small farmer). Although free, Blacks were not provided with the economic wherewithal by the federal government to become independent farmers or to leave the South, so they remained on plantation lands as sharecroppers, the lowest form of tenancy because Blacks, unlike whites, had no personalty (mules and plows, for example) to bring to their economic situation. Planters had more alternatives to pursue in this scenario: they could use the income from their land sales to invest in business ventures, including the country store that supplied the area; at the same time, they could hold one foot in the soil as supervisor of tenants and sharecroppers; or they could decide to sell all their holdings and begin a business life in town. In the role of owner of the country store, the planter was unabashedly business-oriented, hoping to make as much money as possible by selling supplies to tenants and sharecroppers as well as independent farmers. To be sure, the role of storeowner existed in the antebellum period but on a more benevolent basis since customers were then essentially free men living in a peacetime economy. The Civil War undid that economic equilibrium: money was in short supply, as were banks, and the South was forced to revert to a barter society. The transportation system might be in shambles or geared to military ends. In any event, the planter-storekeeper attempted to replace as many of the dissolved institutions as possible. He accepted cotton in exchange for purchases of store supplies; he marketed the cotton of tenants and sharecroppers in return for a commission; he lent supplies to both until their crops were harvested. And because the risk to the storekeeper in these instances was perceived to be great, he charged commensurately higher prices and interest rates.

In his new capacity, the southern planter abandoned the paternalism that had typified the pre-Civil War era. Under postwar conditions, Blacks were free men who could leave the plantation without notice. White tenants could do likewise with great harm to the planter's economic situation, especially at planting and harvesting times. Because a wage system was no guarantee that renters would remain on the land when needed, an arrangement arose whereby rent would constitute a certain percentage of harvested crops, with the remainder viewed as profits. However, with the emphasis on cotton as the money crop, renters were forced to spend more than they made. They needed foodstuffs from the country store as well as fertilizers, since planting the same crop year after year exhausted the natural nutrients in the soil. A vicious cycle emerged: the more cotton grown, the lower the price, the bigger the bills at the country store, the higher the proportion of cotton to pay the rent. Both tenants and croppers were soon transformed into economic slaves, with decreasing likelihood of breaking the cycle and moving up the economic ladder.

The situation was aggravated by the era of Reconstruction. As southern states were defeated, Republican governments were imposed, often modeled along liberal views illustrated in such northern states as Massachusetts. These Republican governments, unfavorably viewed for the most part by southern whites, incorporated Blacks as voters and even officeholders. More important, they spent large sums of monies for schools, hospitals, highways, and similar programs. These debts were bequeathed by the 1870s to the southern Democrats, typifying the new planter-businessman, who recognized that the burden was antithetical to the area's economic development. Consequently, funds for the Republican-sponsored social programs were cut—even for prisons, bringing forth the convict lease system—and tax dollars went to pay the state's debts. Tenants and sharecroppers would be most affected by this turn of events, but the planter-businessman employed racial themes to keep the two groups from joining political forces against him. Although the two ultimately came together in the Populist movement of the 1890s, the planter's economic strength prevailed in the political arena, leading tenant farmers and white farmers in general to vent their frustration against Blacks. Enter the phase of disfranchisement and segregation of Blacks as well as poll taxes and the clandestine terrorism of the Ku Klux Klan.

In reality, the southern Democratic planter-businessman had no quarrel with the evolving business system that he had become a part of. He favored sound money and banks, as did his Republican counterpart in the North; because some of his investments might go to building factories or starting extractive industries, he abandoned his opposition to the high tariff. A Georgia editor spoke for southern leaders when he announced in 1865 that "with the emancipation of the slaves, agriculture ceases to be an all absorbing pursuit. Manufacturers must take their proper position, and, this fact once thoroughly comprehended, let the grand Anvil Chorus of a thousand sturdy hammers awaken the highway and the by-way with resounding clamor." Instead of the prewar policy of insulation, the South after 1865 attracted northern industries by tax exemptions and regulatory freedom. In the ten years from 1880 to 1890 railroad mileage in Dixie jumped from 16,000 to 40,000 miles, with three significant consolidations occurring by century's end (Atlantic Coast Line, Southern, and Seaboard Air Line), financed by northern banker J. P. Morgan. Cotton textile mills mushroomed: from 165 and approximately 300,000 spindles in 1860 to 239 and 1,500,000 spindles in 1890. The steel industry blossomed after the Civil War, with Birmingham becoming the second Pittsburgh by the turn of the twentieth century. Again, J. P. Morgan's money played a critical role in the industry, which primarily manufactured raw iron that was shipped northward for finishing. Even had Birmingham wanted to finish iron products, railroad rates controlled by northern owners ensured that its prices would be substantially higher and thus unable to compete outside the South. Lumber and lumber products became a southern growth industry, with some 18 million board feet cut from forests by the early 1900s. And no industry thrived like tobacco, which soon infiltrated every nook and cranny of post–Civil War America. John Ruffin Green established the famous Durham bull trademark that made his product a household word within a few years of his death in 1869. Then in 1884 James Buchanan Duke introduced machines that spewed out cigarettes by the thousands. Unlike other southern businessmen who were constrained by the directives of Yankee investors, Duke created a unique enterprise conspicuous for its innovation: first, he relied exclusively on the Bonsack machine that manufactured 120,000 cigarettes per day, then he built a factory and administrative offices in New York City, and finally, he began one of the most extensive advertising campaigns in history. And to ensure that he would not be subject to the uncertain costs of tobacco at any one time, Duke built his own purchasing, storing, and curing facilities. Of course, advertising was overwhelming, with Duke spending $800,000 by 1889, which was double his profits for the year. A year later, Duke and four competitors merged to form the American Tobacco Company, which soon dominated all manufacturing of tobacco products except for cigars.

Unfortunately, most southern business experiences, in spite of their impressive growth statistics, were not analogous to Duke's. Even the rise of the oil industry in Louisiana, Texas, and Oklahoma by 1914 did not significantly change the situation. Low wages typified most industries, with the per capita wealth of the South by 1900 still only half that of northerners. In that same year the South had only about 16 percent of the nation's manufacturing establishments, most of the colonial type, that is, cheap-labor, extractive ones dependent on northern industries for refinement and distribution. The planter-businessmen orchestrating the fine points of this economic drama benefited the most; these same individuals provided the hype that fastened on the southern population the view that the "New South" had arrived. Expositions in such cities as Atlanta, Dallas, and New Orleans were supposed to be testimony to the arrival of better economic times for all. But without significant educational facilities, southerners lived more on illusion—economic and racial—than on reality.

Instead of a hallelujah chorus of praise for the state of the southern business scene, a speech delivered in 1851, when planters ranted about the North, may have been more to the point in explaining the real situation by 1900:

> At present, the North fattens and grows rich upon the South. We depend upon it for our entire supplies. We purchase all our luxuries and necessaries from the North. . . . The Northerners abuse and denounce slavery and slaveholders, yet our slaves are clothed with Northern manufactured goods, have Northern hats and shoes, work with Northern hoes, ploughs, and other implements, are chastised with a Northern-made instrument, are working more for Northern than Southern profit. The slaveholder dresses in Northern goods, rides a Northern saddle, . . . sports his Northern carriage, patronizes Northern liquors, reads Northern books. . . . In Northern vessels his products are carried to market, his cotton is ginned with Northern gins, his sugar is crushed and preserved by Northern machinery; his rivers are navigated by Northern steamboats, his mails are carried in Northern stages. . . .

Yet all one needed was one example of southern industrial growth to substantiate that the area was on an economic roll. Take the southern town that was founded in 1871 where two railroads came together in a cotton field. Nine years later, it had 3,000 residents, in 1900 some 38,000, and by 1910 had grown to a thriving city of 132,000. "That," an Alabama state official might proudly announce to northern visitors, "was the story of Birmingham. And that was just one verse in the chapter of the New South."

10

THE BUSINESS VALUES OF SOCIETY

American business so penetrated society in the early nineteenth century that no institution was immune from its influence. The youngster was schooled in respectable business positions, and the reader of popular prose and verse was inundated with both aphorisms and longer pieces that extolled businesslike virtues. Even blue-collar workers, sometimes tempted by examples of their European counterparts, found business principles far more satisfactory than the alternatives they experimented with. Intellectuals and artists were awed in one way or another with America's business scene, and women who aspired to a better life often found a model on Main Street, as illustrated by the lives of Amelia Bloomer and Sarah Josepha Hale. To be sure, there was an underside to accepting and adhering to business values, but it paled in comparison to the benefits. Little wonder that at this early age, America could be dubbed a business civilization.

When Edward Hazen in 1842 set forth eighty-seven occupations that young boys might enter, virtually all were business-oriented. Moreover, all were described in terms of hard work and devotion to duty. Designed for schoolchildren, Hazen's list accorded approbation to the proverbial butcher, candlestick maker—and baker:

> There is, perhaps, no business more laborious than that of the baker of loaf bread, who has a regular set of customers to be supplied every morning. The twenty-four hours of the day are systematically appropriated to the performance of certain labours, and to rest. After breakfast, the yeast is prepared, and the ovenwood provided: at two or three o'clock, the *sponge is set:* the hours from three to eight or nine o'clock are appropriated to rest. The baking commences at nine or ten o'clock at night; and, in large bakeries, continues until five o'clock in the morning. From that time until the breakfast hour, the hands are engaged in distributing the bread to customers. For seven months in the year, and, in some cases during the whole of it, part of the hands are employed, from eleven to one o'clock, in baking pies, puddings, and different kinds of meats, sent to them from neighboring families.

Of course, the baker might be an employee, but that was still a "business" for Hazen, a choice of words that gives insight into the nature of the employee-employer relation of his day.

Most Americans would not rise to the level of shopkeeper or great entrepreneur, but every workingman was expected to view his condition as an employee as temporary. Newspaper editor Horace Greeley summed it up best with the admonition, "Don't strike; don't drink; save your money and start in business for yourself." Unionism was an admission that labor in America was a permanent condition, antithetical to the widespread notion of upward mobility. "Hitch your wagon to a star," said Ralph Waldo Emerson. Yet labor's success, in Emerson's view, could be measured in terms other than reaching the highest pinnacle. "Each man has an aptitude born with him," wrote Emerson. "Do your work. I have to say this often, but nature says it oftener. 'Tis clownish to insist on doing all with one's own hands, as if every man should build his own clumsy house, forge his hammer, and bake his dough; but he is to dare

to do what he can do best; not help others as they would direct
him, but as he knows his helpful power to be." Doing your
work, Emerson recognized, might get monotonous in a factory
setting. Therefore, it was imperative that the worker learn that
"self-trust is the first secret of success, the belief that if you are
here the authorities of the universe put you here, and for cause,
or with some task strictly appointed you in your constitution,
and so long as you work at that you are well and successful. It
by no means consists in rushing prematurely to a showy feat
that shall catch the eye and satisfy spectators. It is enough that
you work in the right direction." Robert Francis Astrop embodied Emerson's individualistic "right direction" in a poem
entitled "The Honest Mechanic":

> I envy no king, lord, or great emperor;
> No general, nor doctor, nor man of the law.
> No coxcomb his pleasure, nor miser his wealth
> (I live not by cunning or yet lower stealth).
> I envy no mortal that ever was made
> While I'm a mechanic who lives by my trade.

No doubt, there were American workers who found their
situations unacceptable as a result of increasing industrialization. They could accept their lot, which most did, putting all
family members to work and oversaving and underconsuming,
thereby achieving a piece of the good life in the purchase of a
home. Or if they were skilled, they could attempt to unionize
along craft lines. All carpenters in a city, for example, would
join forces. The successful unions drew upon labor's elite, those
workers that had the least competition from the factory system
(carpenters, for instance), and within that subset, those who
kept their goals realistic and limited (higher wages as opposed
to a return to the preindustrial world). Yet even the best-laid
goals and methods could be upset by strikes, depressions, and
hard-nosed employer actions upheld by court decisions. In their

frustration after losing ground, the skilled unions were often lured into thinking that a comprehensive program and enlarged membership could better effect the wage goals that they sought. This thought was influenced by the enormous increase in the number of factory workers after the 1830s, by the communitarian experiments in the West, as well as by the free-wheeling spirit of the age of Romanticism: an era of emotion, intuition, individualism, and the dignity and divinity of all men. But the experiments pursued by workers could not effectively counteract the centrifugal force of a nation dominated by business values. For that reason, workingmen's political parties—one of the first experiments—could not establish a foothold in America. Locally rather than nationally focused, the parties moved into the political arena with a platform designed to achieve both reasonable and radical objectives. The former included a reduction in the working day and universal education, the latter a renunciation of property holding—a plank almost certain to alienate the public. "Let a new State Convention be assembled," wrote Thomas Skidmore of the New York Workingmen's Party in 1829. "Let it prepare a new constitution, and let that constitution, after having been adopted by the people, decree an abolition of all debts, both at home and abroad, between citizen and citizen, and between citizen and foreigner. Let it renounce all property belonging to our citizens, without the•State. Let it claim all property within the State, . . . Let it order an equal division of all this property among the citizens, of and over the age of maturity, in manner yet to be directed."

Still another experiment of workers was to follow the example of utopians and take to the woods, establishing phalanxes that were designed to make participants happy and prolific in their work, as well as equals among each other. Workers were encouraged to bring forth their creative impulses, for talent or skill was believed to be a healthy counterpart to the new industrial order that minimized the individual. Pecuniary interest was minimized, the life of the mind maximized, as illustrated by a contemporary account of Brook Farm:

> All labor, whether bodily or intellectual, is to be paid at the same rate of wages; on the principle that as the labor becomes merely bodily, it is a greater sacrifice to the individual laborer to give his time to it; because time is desirable for the cultivation of the intellectual, in exact proportion to ignorance. Besides, intellectual labor involves in itself higher pleasures, and is more its own reward, than bodily labor. . . .

As a practical alternative to industrialism, utopianism left much to be desired. Few American workers could divorce money or advancement from their thinking; fewer still could sleep well at night with the knowledge that their creative impulses were prized by a mere thirty members of their phalanx. The same problem befell the land reformers, who looked backward into America's history for a solution to labor's economic stature and woes. Specifically, they believed that every man should be entitled to a sizable chunk of federal land. Implicit in this scheme was the confiscation of lands of plutocrats once the available public supply was gone. English-born George Henry Evans, the leading spokesman for land reform, had a difficult time spelling out the relationship between free land and labor skills, a deficiency that surely confused workers born in cities that had no veneration for the quarter-section farm. In a memorial to Congress in 1844, Evans presented a rationale for his federal giveaway program that was conspicuous for its incredibility:

> City populations would diminish gradually till every inhabitant could be the owners of a comfortable habitation; and the country population would be more compactly settled, making less roads and bridges necessary, and giving greater facilities of education. There need be no Standing Army, for there would be a chain of Townships along the frontiers, settled by independent freemen,

willing and able to protect the country. . . . It would, in a great measure, do away the now necessary evil of laws and lawyers, as there could be no disputes about rents, mortgages, or land titles, and morality would be promoted by the encouragement and protection of industry.

About the only labor experiment that made sense in the early nineteenth century combined the role of businessman and worker. "The direction and profits of industry," began a contemporary tract, "must be kept in the hands of the producers. Laborers must own their own shops and factories, work their own stock, sell their own merchandise, and enjoy the fruits of their own toil. Our Lowells must be owned by the artisans who build them and the operatives who run the machinery and do all the work. And the dividend, instead of being given to the idle parasites of a distant city, should be shared among those who perform the labor. . . ." Essentially, under this system, laborers pooled their funds and energies to establish their own businesses. Called producers' cooperatives, these experiments sometimes expanded in time into large enterprises; a few established consumers' cooperatives in addition, that is, stores that ensured that workers would get the most bang out of their consumer buck. However, most workers had neither funds nor patience to invest in cooperative businesses, for it might take several years before profits arose. Laborers were fiddle-footed, not anxious to spend their lives in one community unless economic advantages were as apparent as weekly wages. Then there was the fact that cooperatives were plagued with management problems because most laborers possessed no managerial skills. In sum, about the only arm of organized labor to survive by the time of the Civil War was the one that had initiated the experimental process, namely, the craftsmen organized into skilled unions whose major problem was to keep their blinders on. The phalanx idea, workingmen's parties, land reform, and cooperatives were tempting sideshows that diluted the efforts of skilled workers to effect reasonable objectives. The most reasonable goal of organized labor in a society dominated by business values was better wages and hours. To try to turn back the clock to an earlier era or to oppose industrialism was without redeeming social purpose. The benefits of the developing capitalistic system, in other words, outweighed disadvantages to the prudent observer. What is more, abstract economic and social ideas had little attraction for a nation of individuals who counted success in dollars and common sense. For that reason, even labor's defenders could not conjure up an economic "devil" that had the likelihood of striking a public chord. A case in point was Reverend Theodore Parker's "Sermon on Merchants," delivered in November 1846. "But this devil of the nineteenth century is still extant," said Parker. "He has gone into trade, and advertises in the papers; his name is 'good' in the street. He 'makes money'; the world is poorer by his wealth. He spends it as he made it, like a devil, on himself, his family alone, or worse yet, for show. He can build a church out of his gains, to have his morality, his Christianity preached in it, and call that the gospel, as Aaron called a calf—God. . . . It is easy to make a bargain with him, hard to settle. In politics he wants a Government that will insure his dividends; so asks what is good for him, but ill for the rest. He knows no right, only power; no man but self; no God but his calf of gold. . . . To the church he is the Anti-Christ. Yes the very Devil, and frightens the poor minister into shameful silence, or more shameless yet, an apology for crime; makes him pardon the theory of crime! Let us look on that monster—look and pass by, not without prayer."

The identification of the American businessman as bad—really bad as a devil—was not substantiated by other leading citizens. Francis Bowen in *The Principles of Political Economy* (1856) presented the widespread intellectual view that "the principal causes of the rapid growth of national opulence are moral rather than physical. . . . Neither theoretically nor practically, in this country, is there any obstacle to any individual's becoming rich, if he will, and almost to any amount that he will. . . . How is it possible, indeed, that the poor should be arrayed in hostility against the rich, when . . . the son of an Irish coachman becomes the governor of a State, and the grandson of a *millionaire* dies a pauper? The consequent of the whole is an unceasing energy and activity in the pursuit of wealth, which accomplish greater wonders than all the modern inventions of science, . . . The hope of rising in the world is the chief motive for the accumulation of capital." Educator Horace Mann acknowledged that in his own industrial state of Massachusetts there was great wealth and poverty. Yet in his view, "nothing but universal education can counterwork this tendency to the domination of capital and the servility of labor. . . . For the creation of wealth, then—for the existence of a wealthy people and a wealthy nation—intelligence is the grand condition." Mann's heavenly economy was to "change a consumer into a producer; and the next greatest is to increase the producing power—and this to be directly obtained by increasing his intelligence."

Schoolbooks in the nineteenth century reflected a favorable view of business. Authors frequently told the story of the great American inventors, from Benjamin Franklin (lightning rod) to Thomas Godfrey (quadrant) to Eli Whitney, Robert Fulton, and Cyrus McCormick. "Every man who invents a labor-saving device," according to one reader, "does a great deal of good, for he enables working-people to give more time to study and the cultivation of their minds." Still other books prophesied that American ingenuity would lead to people "floating through the air, talking to each other without regard to distance." Depictions of factory workers in schoolbooks showed healthy and happy individuals situated in clean surroundings; even child labor was portrayed as infinitely better than European conditions. Labor unions, on the other hand, got a bad shake, with strikes viewed as synonymous with riots. Laziness was one of the worst economic sins in the texts; so too was dishonesty on

the part of anyone in the business chain. Franklin's adage—
"Early to bed and early to rise will make one healthy, wealthy,
and wise"—became by 1814: "He who rises early and is industrious and temperate will acquire health and riches." To be
sure, sometimes offensive qualities were described in somewhat
morbid terms, as evidenced by "The Idle Boy" (1857), illustrated by "The Youth's Casket":

Thomas was an idle lad,
And lounged about all day;
And though he many a lesson had,
He minded nought but play.

He only cared for top or ball,
Or marbles, hoops, or kite;
But as for learning, that was all
Neglected by him quite.

In vain his mother's kind advice,
In vain his master's care,
He followed every idle vice,
And learned to curse and swear.

Think ye when he became a man,
He prospered in his ways?
No; wicked courses never can
Bring good and happy days.

Without a shilling in his purse,
Or cot to call his own,
Poor Thomas went from bad to worse,
And hardened as a stone.

And oh! it grieves me much to write
His melancholy end;
Then let us leave the dreadful sight,
And thoughts of pity lend.

But may we this important truth
Observe and ever hold;
"That all who're idle in their youth
Will suffer when they're old.

American artists, many fascinated by landscapes in the pre–Civil War era, did not neglect the rising world of business. In fact, just as landscapes were portrayed on mammoth canvases (Romanticism's Nature was big), the same was true of early industrial scenes, conspicuous for an awe and reverence of business. W. T. Russell Smith depicted a *View of Pittsburgh from the Salt Works of Saw Mill Run* (1838). There is smoke emanating from the salt works, as well as from three other establishments on the horizon, but what is impressive about the canvas is the bright blend of colors that make the city busy, active, even on fire in a dazzling way. John Ferguson Weir in *The Gun Foundry* (1866) did the same thing, concentrating on gigantic machinery and busy men but in a darkened setting lit only by a massive furnace. Weir described his view of the foundry in a religious context, perhaps as an economic baptism of industry in America:

A huge and dusky canvas—dark and sombre, spreads its surface opposite my table—opposite my table, near the wall. Charred and blackened seems its surface—impenetrable soot—but by gradual development unfolds its story to the eye—to the eye makes clear its subject—shows a forge, with grim men forging—forging shafts for floating engines—huge and ponderous—glowing hot—seething beneath the ponderous hammer hammered till its form is got—swung in chains from huge cranes—fancy makes them groan and squeak—smiths do swing these great huge masses, glowing hot with flaming gas's—from the furnace to the anvil—to the anvil 'neath the hammers—Then in anger it sputters—as its [*sic*] hammered into shape—like a thing of life it mutters—groans and sputters, sputters flaming drops of sweat.

Artist Bass Otis in 1815 depicted *Interior of a Smithy* in terms of an ordered, balanced technology: a large gear holding center stage on a twenty-eight-square-foot canvas, a wheel visible on the left, and discernible but subdued workers on the right, appearing to let the machinery do all the labor. Even Charles Willson Peale, best known for portraits, took fascination in *Exhuming the First American Mastodon* (1806)—so much so that he was the actual engineer of the real-life project, buying the rights to excavation and designing a large wheel that dominated the painting in which some seventy individuals are depicted.

Women's rights leaders viewed business as one of the most practical professions for women to enter. In the famous convention of leaders in Seneca Falls, New York, in 1848, the resolutions made no reference to women's discriminatory treatment on the farms of America; rather, they focused on business and other urban tasks. "He [man] has monopolized nearly all the profitable employments," read one plank, "and from those she is permitted to follow, she receives but a scanty remuneration. He closes against her all the avenues to wealth and distinction which he considers most honorable to himself." Some women, such as Matilda Joslyn Gage (1826–98), pointed to the fact that females had long been inventors and good business people in other countries. In *Woman as Inventor* (1870), Gage noted that the real inventor of the cotton gin was Catherine Littlefield Greene, in whose home Eli Whitney lived. "It was after a conversation . . . which had been held by some guests in her house, that Mrs. Greene proposed to Whitney the making of such a machine, and upon her idea he commenced. The work was done in her house, and under her immediate supervision. The wooden teeth first tried did not do the work well, and Whitney, despairing, was about to throw the work aside, when Mrs. Greene, whose confidence in ultimate success never wavered, proposed the substitution of wire." According to Gage, Mrs. Greene got neither recognition nor compensation for her work. Perhaps even worse in America, Gage concluded, was that women "have not dared to exercise their faculties except in certain directions, unless in a covert manner. A knowledge of mechanics has been deemed unwomanly, and yet I have known women whose natural tastes led them to be interested in everything pertaining to this science. I once had a lady friend, who, to use her own words, 'had a perfect passion for engineering,' and who if she 'had been a man, would have been an engineer.'" Some of the most successful women in the nineteenth century entered the field of business. Amelia Bloomer is a good example. Marrying a Quaker newspaper owner in 1840, Bloomer founded her own sheet, *The Lily,* nine years later. By 1853 *The Lily* claimed 4,000 subscriptions, an investment sufficient to permit Bloomer to take to the lecture circuit where she campaigned only incidentally for the dress fashion that historians would associate with her name. Sarah Josepha Hale made money as a novelist and magazine editor, utilizing like Bloomer her columns to campaign for better education of females. *Godey's Lady's Book* was an enormously successful business enterprise, thanks to Hale, with a circulation of 150,000. Then there was Catherine Beecher, sister of novelist Harriet Beecher Stowe, who pursued her feminist goals through a female seminary she owned in Hartford, Connecticut, beginning in 1823. As a businesswoman, Beecher recognized that the major problem for women was that they "had no career, except that of marriage, and for this they . . . (must) wait to be sought." First and foremost to Beecher was the "importance of educating every young girl with some practical aim, by which, in case of poverty, she might support herself."

Perhaps one of the strongest inducements for Americans to be supportive of business was the spatial mobility that it afforded. Unlike an agricultural society, an industrial one provided individuals with the inducement to move—from business or work in one place to another. The concepts of speculation and bankruptcy also aided movement. For one reason, speculation meant being in the right place at the right time, and big risk meant big reward—both for the individual and the nation. "I never saw a busier place than Chicago was at the time of our arrival," wrote Harriet Martineau, an English visitor who toured America from 1834 to 1836. "The streets were crowded with land speculators, hurrying from one sale to another. A negro, dressed up in scarlet, bearing a scarlet flag, and riding a white horse with housings of scarlet, announced the times of sale. At every street-corner where he stopped, the crowd flocked round him; and it seemed as if some prevalent mania infected the whole people. The rage of speculation might fairly be so regarded." Bankruptcy, according to the Constitution, should have been defined in a uniform manner by Congress, thereby discouraging speculation and spatial movement. But three efforts to pass enduring federal laws—in 1800, 1841, and 1867—proved futile, with each repealed within a few years after enactment. Thus, state laws determined the course of bankruptcy and usually in a lenient way. Take the case of Florida, entering the union in 1845 and years behind the rest of the eastern seaboard states in economic development. So the Sunshine State passed a liberal bankruptcy law, providing enormous exemptions (a homestead of $16,000 and personalty of $1,000) in the event a businessman would go under. Such a strategy promoted the risk taking that made for significant development, and some setbacks, for Florida. To be sure, even if business people were unsuccessful, as they often were, the inducement to get on the road again was a significant escape valve for American industrial society. Had individuals been forced to stay in one place, as the debtor's prison concept of colonial times illustrated, there would have been social ostracism, pent-up frustration over failure, and the likelihood for social disorder. In the states that had a difficult time abandoning the rigorous spirit of the colonial era as far as debts were concerned, the scene was set for some hard clashes between creditors and debtors. Connecticut is an example, passing a bankruptcy law in 1853 that was conspicuous for its pro-creditor position. Voluntary petitions were not permitted, putting insolvents at the mercy of creditors. Full discharges were authorized but only in cases of individuals capable of paying off a vast share of their debts. There were ten amendments to the act from 1855 to 1888, but the basic thrust was not altered, and economic tension typified the state.

Walt Whitman spoke for many Americans when he argued that "the extreme business energy, and this almost maniacal appetite for wealth prevalent in the United States, are parts of amelioration and progress, indispensably needed to prepare the very results I demand. My theory includes riches, and the getting of riches, and the amplest products, power, activity, inventions, movements, etc." That was somewhat the theme of novelist T. S. Arthur in *The Way to Prosper and Other Tales* (1851), which contended that even with business failures (illustrated thrice by his hero), there was an intellectual way out. "He could go up into higher regions of his mind," wrote Arthur in "Don't Be Discouraged," "and see there in existence principles whose pure delights flowed not from the mere gratification of selfish and sensual pleasures. He was made deeply conscious, that even with all the wealth, and all the external things which wealth could give, and for the gratification of the senses, and for the pampering of selfishness and pride, he could not be happy. That happiness must flow from an internal state, and not from any combination of external circumstances." Somewhat more pessimistic of America's love affair with business energy, failure, and spatial mobility was de Tocqueville. The search for wealth, in his eyes, foresaw the ecstasy and agony that twentieth-century observers would identify with a business civilization:

In the United States, a man builds a house in which to spend his old age, and he sells it before the roof is on; he plants a garden and lets it just as the trees are coming into bearing; he brings a field into tillage and leaves other men to gather the crops; he embraces a profession and gives it up; he settles in a place, which he soon afterwards leaves to carry his changeable longings elsewhere. If his private affairs leave him any leisure, he instantly plunges into the vortex of politics; and if at the end of a year of unremitting labor he finds he has a few days vacation, his eager curiosity whirls him over the vast extent of the United States, and he will travel fifteen hundred miles in a few days to shake off his happiness. Death at length overtakes him, but it is before he is weary of his bootless chase of that complete felicity which forever escapes him.

11

UNSETTLING TIMES, 1865–1900

The usually quiet and relaxed summers for members of the American Historical Association were interrupted in 1966, when its executive secretary issued a call for $50,000. The requested money had nothing to do with the financial problems of the association; rather, the solicitation was related to legal costs that the AHA anticipated would be necessary to defend historian Sylvester K. Stevens, who had been charged with libeling a business baron who lived from 1849 to 1919. Specifically, the suit was brought by Helen Clay Frick, daughter of steel and coal magnate Henry Clay Frick, and alleged that several passages in a book written by Dr. Stevens *(Pennsylvania: Birthplace of a Nation)* were libelous and defamatory of the family name. The objectionable passages read:

In the bituminous fields of western Pennsylvania Henry Clay Frick had built a similar monopoly of coal and coke production and was equally successful in beating down efforts at unionization. Frick also made extensive use of immigrant labor and cut wages to an average of about $1.60 a day while extracting the longest hours of work physically possible. Most mines of the time were without anything resembling modern safety appliances or practices, and serious accidents were common.

Still another abuse was the company town with its company store. The coal companies owned the houses, shoddy wooden shacks without any sanitary facilities, which they rented at a high rate to workers.

The power of the union was broken in the bloody and disastrous Homestead strike in 1892 by stern, brusque, autocratic Henry Clay Frick.

Instead of seeking the usual money damages in a libel suit, Ms. Frick urged the court to enjoin Random House from distributing the book, a demand that electrified the AHA hierarchy from summer hibernation. The two parties eventually settled out of court, with Dr. Stevens agreeing to make two changes in future editions of the book. Although the association was motivated at the time by what it believed to be the "constitutional right to probe history and present the results of that scholarly research without fear of legal repercussions," the Stevens case, in retrospect, is significant as an illustration of the hostility of historians toward businessmen of the late nineteenth and early twentieth centuries.

Historians, in sum, have tended to accept the complaints of various groups of the era: farmers, scattered and isolated, found inordinate frustration in dealing with problems of overproduction and falling prices, with the bleakness of life on a sodhouse frontier, or with the rapacity of the crop-lien maze in the reconstructed South. Laborers found difficulty coping with an impersonal corporation and with layoffs and pay cuts in hard times. City dwellers, many having migrated from farms, found urban life unnerving with its problems of growth, sanitation, crime, and immigration. Then there were academics of the period from the Civil War to World War I who allied themselves with the above groups in political movements against business. Because successful entrepreneurs through their philanthropy became boosters of higher education, they often attempted to reform the academic life that, in their view, ill prepared graduates for the real world. Not surprisingly, they rankled no few professors who reacted by devising rights of academic freedom and tenure and rewriting history and economics. The logic of economies of scale notwithstanding, some economists began to view giant corporations as predators that should be dissolved and punished according to the punitive standard of treble damages that the Sherman Antitrust Act of 1890 reflected. Academics would also give emphasis to critics of capitalism in the late nineteenth century, even though the reformers played modest roles in the contemporary political scene and embodied utopian schemes.

For that reason, Henry George and Edward Bellamy would become prominent in American history. George, a journalist, wrote *Progress and Poverty: An Inquiry into the Cause of Industrial Depressions and of Increase of Want with Increase of Wealth . . . The Remedy* (1879). George did not like large landowners who successfully speculated. In his economic world, there were three groups: labor, capital, and landowners. Labor and capital were all right because they made their money the old-fashioned way, by earning it. On the other hand, landowners could make a bundle by rentals and sales—and, what was worse, by doing absolutely nothing. "Like another Rip Van Winkle," wrote George, "[the landowner] may have lain down and slept; still he is rich—not from anything he has done, but from the increase of population. There are lots from which for every foot of frontage the owner may draw more than an average mechanic can earn; there are lots that will sell for more than would suffice to pave them with gold coin." George's remedy was to tax away the annual rise in the value of land that occurred as a result of population increases and not improvements. That "single tax" would be sufficient to pay the bills of all governments and require no other levies. It would also eliminate poverty, "tame the ruthless passions of greed, dry up the springs of vice and misery; light in dark places the lamp of knowledge; give new vigor to invention and a fresh impulse to discovery; substitute political strength for political weakness; and make tyranny and anarchy impossible." George carried his views to the people by running for mayor of New York City, but he died along with his reform in the midst of a campaign in 1886.

Edward Bellamy revealed his solution to an industrialized nation in *Looking Backward* (1888), which sold over a million copies. The novel dealt with a wealthy Bostonian who had died in a fire in 1887 but had been revived in the year 2000. America in the twenty-first century was a vast public business. Every person had an equal share in society; each would be assured a college education, as well as a job through the retirement age of forty-five, whereupon a carefree life of recreation, scholarly pursuit, travel, or whatever would be assured. The jobs performed in the vast state business would be geared to each individual's education and personal interest: a prestigious job, for instance, would involve more hours of work than one of menial tasks. What is more, wages were banned in Bellamy's America. Like George's scheme, Bellamy's attracted attention in large cities and among intellectuals.

To be sure, this critical treatment of big business abated somewhat by the early twentieth century as the Progressive reform movement applied some prudent rules of reason to regulation. But there were still muckraking journalists who would contribute books that academics would choose for their classes nearly a century later (Ida Tarbell's 1904 indictment of Standard Oil is still in print, no matter that the author's disposition was colored by a family member's business succumbing to Rockefeller's merger activity). Then came the economic excesses of the 1920s and the resultant depression that bred vitriolic volumes about the late nineteenth century, such as Matthew Josephson's *The Robber Barons* (1934), which still provides economic fodder for critical lectures in history classes. In reality, the economic environment of the fifty years from

1840 to 1890 cries for a delineation that is rarely stressed in the academic critiques of business. That delineation stresses the degree to which the economic temper of the times differed markedly from contemporary America—in terms of overcompetition, technology, overproduction, and falling prices. A few businessmen could deal effectively with these four factors, but most did not. And the successful would have a difficult time defending their modus operandi.

The problems in the late nineteenth century economy can best be understood by examining the previous era. From 1843, when the depression of 1837 came to an end, to 1865, the United States business environment was basically stable. Merchants and other businessmen that were among the nation's oldest had achieved specialization, evolving, in other words, from one natural state to another. Second, the railroad was still in its youthful stages, confined to areas of economic importance and population—by 1852, for instance, the nation boasted a railroad to Chicago, by 1854 to the Mississippi. One of the most successful businessmen of the time, Cornelius Vanderbilt, made his fame by refining and rationalizing the eastern corridor where railroading was still a profitable industry. Third, the period before the Civil War saw only the beginnings of the industrial revolution, as reflected by the telegraph, modest in cost and made efficient by Western Union's elimination of all rivals. Inventions were numerous but not runaway, that is, they could be absorbed into the economy without untoward effects. Business increased in numbers rather than size, which meant that the corporation—still a controversial business form—was not typical, even in urban areas. Fourth, prices rose during the antebellum years and in ways that were good for the economy. The gold rush to California in the 1840s provided new and abundant sources of ore that were put into the nation's money supply as well as sent abroad to redress unfavorable trade balances. Farm prices rose as a result of the Crimean War and crop failures in Europe. Lengthy periods of prosperity were conspicuous in the era, and recession/depression years short-lived. In March 1849 *Hunt's Merchant Magazine* pointed to a solid economic foundation:

> American produce is again selling freely at higher prices, and every element of prosperity is in action. The result is, that in all directions the desire to extend bank credit is manifest. In Illinois, Michigan, and Ohio, paper schemes are being projected. In Pennsylvania, a change in government favors the renewal of those money charters that expire in a short time; and in New York the multiplication of banks under the new law is very rapid. All of these are symptoms of growing speculation; but as yet the ground is firm, the national wealth great, and the floating capital of the country never greater than now.

In contrast, the period after the Civil War until turn of the century saw enormous business difficulties. In part, the problem was an increase of productivity occasioned by mushrooming inventions, from 36,000 patents in the era from 1790 to 1860 to 640,000 from 1860 to 1900. The result was severe price deflation, with the total index falling from 100 in 1873 to 71 by 1896, the same level that the nation reached in 1860. Farm products in 1866 had a price index that fell from 140 to 60 by 1897; food in the same period went from 173 to 71; textiles, 245 to 76; leather products, 166 to 71; fuel and lighting, 160 to 64; metals, 278 to 76; building materials, 128 to 68; and chemicals and drugs, 283 to 87. A vicious cycle that became widespread at the time included the following components: *(a)* rising technology induced individuals to enter business; *(b)* the ease of business entry led to overcompetition, at times ruinous competition; and *(c)* the result was overproduction and falling prices. Railroads built into the West where there was no demand, such as in the Great Plains area, with overexpansion of track mileage the counterpart to the overproduction of goods plaguing other businesses. Then there was the fact that technology could create products that ran counter to traditional public notions and would be difficult to sell: a case in point is packaged cookies that consumers could not see or feel as in the old days and that had a tendency to settle into a half-filled portion of the box. Consumers called that shorting and overcharging.

The strategies that businessmen pursued in this unsettling economic environment were not assisted by government at any level. One alternative that the enterprising individual could not employ was to fail to maintain his technology or to update it. That cost was fixed and necessary to remain competitive. On the other hand, investment in labor was a variable cost. Wage cuts were frequent in the period, as were strikes. In 1886 nearly 1,500 work stoppages could be identified. Yet wage cuts were not the worst case scenario for workers given the overall price deflation and labor surplus attributable to immigration from abroad and migration from American farms to cities. And wages did not fall as fast as prices. Labor, in short, was in a buyer's market, according to Charles Eliot Perkins, president of the Chicago, Burlington, & Quincy Railroad. "To say that a man is entitled to wages sufficient to maintain his family respectability is meaningless," said Perkins in 1885. "What is the measure? . . . Is it what a man wants? Suppose two men apply for work. One says, 'I am careful, frugal, have an economical wife, can get along respectably on a dollar and a half a day, and am ready to go to work at that,' the other says, 'I am more frugal than number one. I can get along respectably on a dollar a day and am ready to go to work at that.' Both being equally capable of doing the job, which shall be taken?" Another strategy that businessmen pursued as a means of extrication from the overcompetition/overproduction cycle was to attempt to sell more goods than their competitors. Of course, that was easier said than done. If they sold more goods because the price and quality were lower, they inevitably flirted with long-term disaster. On the other hand, if they reduced prices as a result of research and development—or if they expanded their product line, finding new uses for raw materials, thanks to R & D —they were likely to come out on top, provided they were able to undertake the risk in the first place and cover costs. Then there was the strategy of cutting costs through scientific management—standardization of parts, mechanical speed-up, task-on-task orientation—but this area was still in a primitive stage. Frederick W. Taylor did not undertake his significant studies until 1882 and not until the next century would scientific management take root.

Vertical combination made enormous sense to the entrepreneur whose other strategies permitted him to rise to the top. In order to guarantee adequate supplies, he might buy out raw material suppliers; to effect dependable transportation of his goods, he might purchase railroads or build pipelines; or to protect himself against producers refusing to ship goods at critical times, he might effect takeovers. Informal agreements such as pools or trusts could also be employed to bring about stability in the industry, but the likelihood of gaining agreement from all manufacturers was little. So outright mergers took place by the 1880s. Yet even with all these safeguards, a business was in a volatile position, especially if it produced goods that were not unique or likely to undergo rapid technological change. There was also the public perception of business to contend with. The farmers' movement against railroads, at first known as the Grangers and later as Populists; the uncertainty among businessmen as to the course of Congress in government financial and monetary matters; and the likelihood that rumors could cause the stock and bond markets to experience wide fluctuations—all these could bring even the healthiest firms to wiping brows and wringing hands. And hard times actually prevailed in the thirty years after the Civil War, as reflected by the following table published by the National Bureau of Economic Research in 1926, no matter the popular perception that big business was perennially rosy-cheeked:

Depression	Revival	Prosperity	Recession
1866–67	1868	1869	1870
1870	1871	1871–73	1873
1874–78	1878–79	1879–82	1882–83
1884–85	1885–86	1887	1888
		1889–90	1890
1891	1891	1892	1893
1893–95	1895		1896
1896–97			

If the public perception of business health was erroneous, the defenses of big business in the era were deficient, helping to affirm the critical popular view that in turn would be accepted by subsequent generations of academics. Englishman Herbert Spencer, whose rationale became widespread in the United States, emphasized a survival-of-the-fittest scenario resembling Charles Darwin's view of the animal kingdom. And Baptist minister Russell H. Conwell's widely delivered lecture, "Acres of Diamonds," made a religion out of the pursuit of wealth. "Money is power," said Conwell, "and you ought to be reasonably ambitious to have it. You ought because you can do more good with it than you could without it. Money printed your Bible, money builds your churches, money sends your missionaries, and money pays your preachers, and you would not have any of them, either, if you did not pay them. I am always willing that my church should raise my salary, because the church that pays the largest salary can do the most good with the power that is furnished to him. Of course he can if his spirit be right to use it for what is given to him. I say, then, that you ought to have money. If you can honestly attain unto riches in Philadelphia, it is your Christian and godly duty to do so. It is an awful mistake of these pious people to think you must be awfully poor in order to be pious." Although Andrew Carnegie took a different tack, his advice to young men on getting ahead in the world appeared incompatible with the enormous riches he had accumulated. "To summarize what I have said," concluded Carnegie's address to students of the Curry Commercial College in June 1885, "aim for the highest; never enter a barroom; do not touch liquor, or if at all only at meals; never speculate; never indorse beyond your surplus cash fund; make the firm's interest yours; break orders always to save owners; concentrate; put all your eggs in one basket, and watch that basket; expenditure always within revenue; lastly, be not impatient, for, as Emerson says, 'no one can cheat you out of ultimate success but yourselves.' "

The reality of the late nineteenth-century business environment was that profitable businesses were few in number. Those enterprises that made it drew the wrath of those that did not. What is more, a firm could have its money in the bank one day and find that the bank was insolvent the next afternoon. From 1866 to 1881 national bank failures averaged nine per year, which was considerably less than the number for state-chartered institutions; from 1882 to 1897 the average was eighteen. Railroad receiverships were rife, with nearly 20 percent of total mileage in such a state by 1894. As for the government rudder on the economic ship of state, it was nonexistent. Large and successful businessmen assumed that role. But even for them nothing was ever safe and sound as described so well by Herbert Croly in 1909 in *The Promise of American Life:*

> The early American industrial conditions differed from those of Europe in that they were fluid, and as a result of this instability, extremely precarious. Rapid changes in markets, business methods, and industrial machinery made it very difficult to build up a safe business. A manufacturer or a merchant could not secure his business salvation, as in Europe, merely by the adoption of sound conservative methods. . . . No doubt this situation was due as much to the temper of the American business man as to his economic environment. American energy had been consecrated to economic development. The business man in seeking to realize his ambitions and purposes was checked neither by government control nor so-

cial custom. He had nothing to do and nothing to consider except his own business advancement and success. He was eager, strenuous, and impatient. He liked the excitement and risk of large operations. The capital at his command was generally too small for the safe and conservative conduct of his business; and he was consequently obliged to be adventurous, or else be left behind in the race. He might well be earning enormous profits one year and skirting bankruptcy the next. Under such a stress conservatism and caution were suicidal. It was the instinct of self-preservation, as well as the spirit of business adventure, which kept him constantly seeking for larger markets, improved methods, or for some peculiar means of getting ahead of his competitors. He had no fortress behind which he could hide and enjoy his conquests. Surrounded as he was by aggressive enemies and undefended frontiers, his best means of security lay in a policy of constant innovation and expansion. . . .

12

ROCKY
AND ANDY

Both John D. Rockefeller and Andrew Carnegie are well-known names in American business history. Too often Americans tend to evaluate both men in terms of the amounts of money each made. "Too much" might well be the popular reaction. Yet the lives of Rockefeller and Carnegie involve much more than the making of money—they illustrate enormous work, artful business strategies, and the absence of a tax system that permitted them to hold on to their monies. Yet, both men chose to give the bulk of their fortunes back to American society.

The life of John D. Rockefeller and the stories of Horatio Alger have much in common. For one thing, Alger's heroes started out at the bottom of the economic heap—or close to it. John D. was one of five children of William Rockefeller, who made a living as a traveling salesman of patent medicines. His mother was a quiet and stern woman whose major possession was a worn Bible. Alger's heroes learned to oversave at an early age. So it was with Rockefeller who at the age of ten had squirreled away $50 doing odd jobs and lent it out to a neighbor at 7 percent interest. Alger's heroes were reasonably ambitious and knew that hard work was the only means to upward mobility. Rockefeller set his sights on making big money; in fact, in high school he indicated to a classmate that he would one day be worth $100,000. His first job required his presence at 6:30 each morning, a responsibility he met with determination—and for the modest weekly wage of $3.50. Alger's heroes were religious and charitable, the same for Rockefeller who tithed at an early age and regularly attended the Baptist Church. Alger's heroes never forgot from whence they came, nor did they denigrate their past, traits reflected by Rockefeller even when he became one of the nation's wealthiest men. His father, he would recall, "trained me in practical ways. He was engaged in different enterprises; he used to tell me about these things . . . and he taught me the principles and methods of business . . . I knew what a cord of good solid beech and maple wood was. My father told me to select only solid woods . . . and not to put any limbs in it or any punky wood. That was good training for me." Even when his father lent him money and then called in the loan when Rockefeller most needed it, the son was the epitome of propriety—the kind that suave politicians master—in criticizing the practice. "I confess," he noted much later, "that this little discipline should have done me good, and perhaps did, but while I concealed it from him, the truth is I was not particularly pleased with his application of tests to discover if my financial ability was equal to such shocks." Most of all, Alger's heroes exhibited massive doses of luck—being in the right place at the right time. And so it was with John D. Rockefeller.

Contrary to popular belief, Rockefeller did not initiate the oil industry in the United States. In 1859 when the first oil well was effected in Pennsylvania, Rockefeller was a partner in a commission merchant firm in Cleveland. The news of the discovery created chaos, with hundreds of firms rising immediately to get in on petroleum, the product that appeared to be an inexpensive means of providing illumination. Speculation was widespread, and a well owner could literally take all the oil from his well, thereby diminishing the sources of adjacent owners. Rockefeller lay back, believing that the whole business was a craze that would pass as quickly as it had come. But then oil became more attractive to Rockefeller when, by 1863, rail lines connected Cleveland to the Pennsylvania oil fields, and refineries sprang up in the city. Rockefeller made a modest $4,000 investment in one such firm; in the meantime, he concentrated his energies on his merchant firm. Within months, however, it became apparent to Rockefeller that refining oil presented the bigger challenge in terms of making money. "Naturally, all sorts of people went into it," he wrote in retrospect, "the butcher, the baker, and the candlestick-maker began to refine oil, and it was only a short time before more of the finished product was put on the market than could possibly be consumed." In such a case, Rockefeller noted, the price would fall calamitously "until the trade was threatened with ruin." The solution was to drive the price down even more by improving the refining processes "and to use as by-products all the materials which in the less efficient plants were lost or thrown away." In Rockefeller's first oil partnership, he began to count on those little things that can mean a lot: he purchased his own wagons to haul the oil and even established his own cooperage to build the wooden barrels in which the product was sold. Years later when he observed his workers putting forty drops of solder on kerosene cans in order to seal them, he suggested they try thirty-eight drops. Unfortunately, the cans leaked, but thirty-nine was just perfect, thereby effecting an economy that made Rockefeller jubilant. He also developed new markets abroad, and his biggest stroke of luck was finding associates for his firm who were as cost conscious as he was.

One such individual was Henry Flagler, a fellow Baptist, who worked on reducing railroad rates. Flagler contended that rails, like any other business, were amenable to bargaining. He pointed out to the general manager of the Lake Shore Railroad, for example, that the Rockefeller firm was the largest refiner in Cleveland and destined to become even larger. A reduction in freight rates was therefore prudent. Lake Shore concurred in 1867, and the practice eventually became widespread among producers of most goods—and without stigma—as illustrated by the testimony of a Pennsylvania ironmaster, which is suggestive of the twentieth-century debate over discount pricing: "In shipping small quantities along the road," the ironmaster said, "our rates are made to conform to the public toll-sheets. In selling nails or pig iron in large quantities, we find it impossible to compete with others at toll-sheet rates, to any point at any distance from our works. There don't seem to be any system about it; I have been shipping various articles for ten or twelve years, and rates seem to be entirely arbitrary, and every man seems to make a special or private bargain with the general freight agent at Philadelphia, . . . To fix the price of any commodities at points at any distance, we must have a special rate given us by the general agent in Philadelphia; we cannot live by the sheet rates. Those rates seem to be arbitrary." After formally setting up Standard Oil Company in 1870, Rockefeller, his brother William, and Flagler managed to buy twenty-two of the twenty-five refining firms in Cleveland; then they turned to refineries in New York and Pennsylvania—a grand total of seventy-six—all of which succumbed to Standard's banner. About 95 percent of all American oil was refined by the firm within ten years of its founding. And nearly 75 percent of all oil products sold in Europe by 1914 bore the Standard imprimatur.

The benefits of Rockefeller's strategy were not minor. "We soon discovered," wrote Rockefeller, "that the primary method of transporting oil in barrels could not last. The package often cost more than the contents, and the forests of the country were not sufficient to supply cheaply the necessary material for an extended time. Hence we devoted attention to other methods of transportation, adopted the pipe-line system, and found capital for pipe-line construction equal to the necessities of the business." Of course, a pipeline system required the enormous sums of money that only a large firm such as Standard was likely to raise; research and development of new products and their distribution—Vaseline, chewing gum, lubricants—were the province of the large firm, as was the low-cost production of gasoline once the automobile became a reality. German scientist Herman Frasch, thanks to Standard Oil's support, developed a method for removing the offensive-smelling sulfur from what was originally dubbed "skunk oil." Fires, one of the worst hazards in the industry, could be dealt with by Standard. "No fire could ruin us," according to Rockefeller, "and we were able thus to establish a system of insuring ourselves. Our reserve fund which provided for this insurance could not be wiped out all at once, as might be the case with a concern having its plants together or near each other. Then we studied and perfected our organization to prevent fires, improving our appliances and plans year after year until the profit on this insurance feature became a very considerable item in the Standard earnings." The company's strength also permitted it to buy its own oil fields, freeing it from reliance on the Pennsylvania producers who could gang up and exert pressure on Rockefeller's supplies and price. To be sure, Standard's success aroused the public's ire, with profits reaching between 15 and 20 percent of net assets in the two decades before 1900. Profits were emotional issues, as were the businessmen driven out by Rockefeller. Yet, as one newspaper remarked on Rockefeller's death, "His critics complained that his methods were ruthless, forgetting perhaps that the law of mathematics never is sentimentally merciful." Even Rockefeller's philanthropy became suspect. Washington Gladden, a Congregational minister in Columbus, Ohio, indirectly attacked Rockefeller in an 1895 article, "Tainted Money," and criticism grew over the years. Utilizing the same rational, even scientific, approach that he had employed in his oil business, Rockefeller established a foundation so as to ensure getting the most bang out of his philanthropic buck. But his efforts to gain a congressional charter failed as a result of rumors that the proposal was "an indefinite scheme for perpetrating vast wealth." Or in the words of Theodore Roosevelt: "Of course no amount of charities in spending such fortunes can compensate in any way for the misconduct in acquiring them." Then there was the remark of Samuel Gompers, "The one thing that the world could gracefully accept from Mr. Rockefeller now would be the establishment of a great endowment of research and education to help other people see in time how they can keep from being like him." Nothing could dissuade Congress from turning its back on the project, not even an offer to have the foundation's trustees approved by the president, vice-president, and other high officials in Washington. Rockefeller perservered. In 1913 his foundation was chartered in New York State with a bequest of $100 million. A few years earlier, the Rockefeller Sanitary Commission, which took on the hookworm disease that plagued children and adults in the South, encountered similar resistance, but by 1927 hookworm was under control in Dixie.

Rockefeller's failure to win a solid place in the world was also due, in part, to his own personality. He went to bed at 10:00 P.M. and arose at 6:30; he ate sparingly and did not gallivant around town. He could not embrace a hearty laugh and wide smile and eventually hired a public relations counselor to assist him in effecting a better image. His low-key personality was not geared to fighting off the attacks of critics, and his businesslike means of making and dispensing his money was an anachronism for the emotional times in which he lived. Rockefeller would have been more at home in contemporary America with its bent for scientific management. In his own *Random Reminiscences* (1909):

Study for a moment the result of what has been a natural and absolutely normal increase in the value of the company's possessions. Many of the pipe-lines were constructed during a period when costs were about 50 per cent. of what they are now. Great fields of oil lands were purchased as virgin soil, which later yielded an immense output. Quantities of low-grade crude oil which had been bought by the company when it was believed to be of little value, but which the company hoped eventually to utilize, were greatly increased in value by inventions for refining it and using the residues formerly considered almost worthless. . . . Wherever we have established businesses in this and other countries we have bought largely of property. I remember a case where we paid only $1,000 or so an acre for some rough land to be used for such purposes, and, through the improvements we created, the value has gone up 40 to 50 times as much in 35 or 40 years. . . . There is nothing strange or miraculous in all this. . . .

Andrew Carnegie's success story, like Rockefeller's, was Alger-like, but it differed in one critical respect. Carnegie mastered several different industries. Also, he had an intense yearning to excel in intellectual matters, whereas Rockefeller was conspicuous for his religious and family activities. Carnegie was also an immigrant—a characteristic that differed with Alger's story line that saw native Americans as upwardly mobile heroes. But Carnegie's native Scotland was in the northern European tradition of Great Britain, which meant that the discriminatory treatment and dire poverty of southern European immigrants were not part of his heritage. In fact, within a short time after arriving in America in 1848, the Carnegie family was doing quite well financially, with teenager Andrew employed in the respectable position of a telegraph messenger. Andrew would spend a dozen years in the telegraphy end of the Pennsylvania Railroad, learning not only the technical aspects of the business but also management. As a salaried employee rising to the rank of railroad superintendent, Carnegie did not make enormous sums of money. However, he invested it prudently. On borrowed money, he bought stock in an express company that skyrocketed in price, permitting him to make other good investments. He put money in a railroad sleeping-car firm as well as in an oil business, and before he left his one and only salaried position in his life, he invested in a bridge-building company that would eventually put railroad bridges across the Mississippi, Ohio, and Missouri rivers and make the

Brooklyn Bridge a household word. Of course, Carnegie was no engineer, but he found experts in the field that made his Keystone Bridge Company a big success. Carnegie also made money from commissions as a super bond salesman both in the United States and Europe. And just a few years before his interest in hawking bonds ebbed in 1872, he mused about his financial success and future:

> Thirty three [years of age] and an income of $50,000 per annum. By this time two years I can so arrange all my business as to make no effort to increase fortune, but spend the surplus each year for benevolent purposes. Cast aside business forever except for others. Settle in Oxford & get a thorough education making the acquaintance of literary men—this will take three years active work—pay especial attention to speaking in public. Settle then in London & purchase a controlling interest in some newspaper or live review & give the general management of it attention, taking a part in public matters especially those connected with education & improvement of the poorer classes.

Carnegie also philosophized over the making of money. "Man must have an idol," he wrote. "The amassing of wealth is one of the worst species of idolatry. No idol more debasing than the worship of money. Whatever I engage in I must push inordinately therefor should I be careful to choose that life which will be the most elevating in its character. To continue much longer overwhelmed by business cares and with most of my thoughts wholly upon the way to make more money in the shortest time, must degrade me beyond hope of permanent recovery."

However, by 1872, four years after his thirty-third birthday, Carnegie had not forsaken business for the life of the mind, not because he hadn't made enough money but because a new challenge, as much intellectual as economic, came his way. In his hometown of Pittsburgh, Carnegie the railroad man had long observed the iron business, in large part because rails were critical to both industries. They were also poorly made and expensive. The better steel rails, which emerged by the 1860s, were produced in England but could not be counted on, in terms of price and sufficient quantities, to improve American railroading. The English Bessemer process was another matter: it could give a needed boost to American technology, provided that an entrepreneur handle the necessary details of finance and retooling. Enter Carnegie, who was hopeful that he could establish a solid source of supply for his Keystone Bridge firm and, more important, bring integration into what was a notoriously inefficient system of production. Each manufacturing stage in the iron industry was done piecemeal, with different enterprises engaged in each one. A firm smelted the ore; still another made it into pig iron slabs; then others made sheets and plates, which then went to factories to be made into some consumer item such as hammers. Also, at each stage there were middlemen who plied their commission trade so that by the time the actual product was sold, the price was excessive. And no one really seemed to care much about the inefficiencies. "As I became acquainted with the manufacture of iron," Carnegie wrote in his autobiography, "I was greatly surprised to find that the cost of each of the various processes was unknown. Inquiries made of the leading manufacturers of Pittsburgh proved this. It was a lump business, and until stock was taken and the books balanced at the end of the year, the manufacturers were in total ignorance of the results. I heard of men who thought their business at the end of the year would show a loss and had found a profit, and *vice-versa*. I felt as if we were moles burrowing in the dark, and this to me was intolerable." Carnegie began his cost-cutting and strict accounting strategy in the Union Iron Works. Like Rockefeller, he decided it was now time to put all his eggs in one basket, abandoning the various business activities he had entered upon earlier. And he spent money, also like Rockefeller, to get expert assistance in effecting economies and integrating processes. "We found the man," he recalled, "in a learned German, Dr. Fricke, and great secrets did the doctor open to us. Iron stone from mines that had a high reputation was now found to contain ten, fifteen, and even twenty per cent less iron than it had been credited with. Mines that hitherto had a poor reputation we found to be now yielding superior ore. The good was bad and the bad was good, and everything was topsy-turvy. Nine-tenths of all uncertainties of pig-iron making were dispelled under the burning sun of chemical knowledge."

There was more, much more from Carnegie. He relied upon another German immigrant with a flair for devising an accounting sheet that was so "uniquely original" that Carnegie not only adopted it but saw the young man rise to become a partner in his firm. Because of Carnegie's emphasis on the chemistry of iron making, he was able to get the best prices for his ore. The touted mines with high prices were ignored, whereas those with lower levels of ore were sought after. One low in phosphorus but high in silicon was perfect, if properly fluxed. "It is hardly believable," explained Carnegie, "that for several years we were able to dispose of the highly phosphoric cinder from the puddling furnaces at a higher price than we had to pay for the pure cinder from the heating furnaces of our competitors—a cinder which was richer in iron than the puddled cinder and much freer from phosphorus." Additionally, the roll-scale from mills, which was usually dumped into the rivers as waste, was purchased by Carnegie for as low as 50¢ a ton because it was pure oxide of iron. Of course, in time other firms would get wise to Carnegie's strategies, but by then it was too late for them to compete. And some of Carnegie's efforts were greeted with such disbelief that competitors simply waited for an economic day of judgment that never seemed to come—except for them. An example was Carnegie's method of "hard driving," that is, producing at such a rapid rate that furnaces had to be relined more frequently than under the British system of gently coddling the process. It was still cheaper in actual dollars under Carnegie's method, but the common sense of competitors thought otherwise. Still another example was Carnegie's personnel procedures, which permitted those employees with excellent records of productivity to advance while the less efficient workers got the heave-ho. Not surprisingly, competitors saw the system as too cutthroat, likely to create worker dissension —a risk that Carnegie was determined to take.

The master salesman for iron rails and beams, which by 1875 were being produced in profusion, was Carnegie, who shunned pools and trust agreements and cut his price in half while still making profits. The master manager was Carnegie, who in 1879 scrapped his Bessemer process in favor of a new technology that made production cheaper. Carnegie integrated backward and forward, with the Carnegie Company in 1886 in command of two steel firms, a coke company, plus still other businesses separately controlled. Six years later the firm's umbrella of companies got even larger. Then tragedy struck. The disastrous Homestead strike of 1892 occurred, with its several deaths and bad publicity. Carnegie was in Scotland at the time. Although he had earlier displayed enormous ingenuity in placating workers, this time his absence was sorely felt. For his designated manager fell far short of his own proclivities. The result was a bad press for Carnegie, as well as his own insightful conviction that little things can mean a lot for laborers. " 'You were badly advised,' " he told some strikers after the Homestead incident. " 'My partners' offer should have been accepted. It was very generous. I don't know that I would have offered so much.' To this one of the rollers said to me: 'Oh, Mr. Carnegie, it wasn't a question of dollars. The boys would have let you kick 'em, but they wouldn't let that other man stroke their hair.' So much does sentiment count for in the practical affairs of life, even with the laboring classes. This is not generally believed by those who do not know them, but I am certain that disputes about wages do not count for one half the disagreements between capital and labor. There is lack of due appreciation and kind treatment of employees upon the part of employers."

Carnegie survived the deep depression of 1893 by effecting economies; two years later he strengthened his firm by leasing iron ore sources from Rockefeller and agreeing to transportation arrangements with his rail and shipping lines. The deal cost

Carnegie no money but required him to buy over a million tons of ore from Rockefeller. The savings from this arrangement, as well as from Carnegie's other cost-cutting measures, made his firm the leader in the low-price field. A ton of rails fell from $28 in 1880 to $11.50 by 1900, and profits rose from $5 million in 1895 to $40 million by the turn of the century. Carnegie was not quite finished, however; he had mastered two of three stages of his business, namely, acquiring the raw materials and processing them into steel. By 1900 he turned to the manufacture of finished goods, integrating all three stages into the United States Steel Company, the first billion-dollar industry. Stage four, Carnegie's last, would be identical to Rockefeller's—giving away his money. Although Carnegie's philanthropy began long before 1900, the entrepreneur outlined his views on the matter in a prestigious but small circulation journal, the *North American Review,* in 1889. Carnegie's essay was as well-argued as his steel business was efficient. "To-day the world," he wrote, "obtains commodities of excellent quality at prices which even the preceding generation would have deemed incredible." Carnegie went on to point out that a big price was paid for democratized goods. The impersonal relationship between employer and employee was one; so, too, was the concentration of business in a few firms. Yet there was no middle ground between the successful firm and one left by the wayside or between capitalism and socialism. Great wealth will come to the few who are truly successful, but their responsibility to society was great. "There are but three modes in which surplus wealth can be disposed of. It can be left to the families of the decedents; or it can be bequeathed for public purposes; or, finally, it can be administered by its possessors during their lives." Only the last, according to Carnegie, was the prudent choice. "Poor and restricted are our opportunities in this life, narrow our horizons, our best work most imperfect; but rich men should be thankful for one inestimable boon. They have it in their power during their lives to busy themselves organizing benefactions from which the masses of their fellows will derive lasting advantage, and thus dignify their own lives." The man of wealth, in sum, must live modestly, to bequeath moderately to family and dear friends, and then to use the rest to benefit society—"the man of wealth thus becoming the mere trustee and agent for his poorer brethren, bringing to their service his superior wisdom, experience, and ability to administer, doing for them better than they would or could do for themselves." Carnegie also stressed that most philanthropy in his day was unwisely spent: almsgiving or other giveway programs did not work; but the same could not be said for libraries, parks, museums, and recreation facilities, which would aid in the growth of the public's mind and body.

Carnegie merged theory with practice in the years after publishing his essay on wealth. Even earlier, in 1873, he had given money for a swimming pool in his hometown in Scotland and to assist what is now called the University of Pittsburgh. Less than two decades later Carnegie would donate $103,403,000 in one year alone. His benefactions included the Carnegie Foundation for the Advancement of Teaching, the Carnegie Institution of Washington, the Carnegie Endowment for International Peace, Carnegie Hall in New York City, and even a Carnegie Hero Fund Commission. The latter, organized in 1904 with a $5 million gift, was designed to reward heroic persons in the United States and Canada, especially those who were injured in their efforts to save lives. The two areas that would affect the intellectual lives of millions of Americans were Carnegie's libraries—some 1,700 built in communities throughout the land at a total cost of $64 million—and Teachers Insurance and Annuity Association, designed to ensure that college and university professors would have the economic wherewithal to retire with dignity. One of the nation's largest pension funds today, TIAA is rarely recognized as a Carnegie institution by contemporary academics disposed to criticize businessmen of a century ago. Ironically, one of the biggest brouhahas of the pension fund in recent years has been its conservative investment policies that bring forth returns that some academics have found inadequate. Carnegie would have delighted over this state of affairs among intellectuals, perhaps believing that they had finally arrived at his state of capitalistic wisdom, which emphasized that

> our duty is with what is practicable now—with the next step possible in our day and generation. It is criminal to waste our energies in endeavoring to uproot, when all we can profitably or possibly accomplish is to bend the universal tree of humanity a little in the direction most favorable to the production of good fruit under existing circumstances. We might as well urge the destruction of the highest existing type of man because he failed to reach our ideal as to favor the destruction of Individualism, Private Property, the Law of Accumulation of Wealth, and the Law of Competition; for these are the highest result of human experience, the soil in which society, so far, has produced the best fruit. Unequally or unjustly, perhaps, as these laws sometimes operate, and imperfect as they appear to the Idealist, they are, nevertheless, like the highest type of man, the best and most valuable of all that humanity has yet accomplished.

13

R. W.
AND
J. C.

It's difficult for contemporary Americans to conceive of the country store or mining town retailer in negative tones. Both establishments were mom-and-pop enterprises, with a homey atmosphere that delighted farmers and miners: there was a potbellied stove in the store's center spot, a place for warm hands and good conversation; there were goods that opened eyes and delighted the senses, including the herbs, spices, and teas that were delightful counterparts to the odors on the farm or in the mines. And there was that personal service for each customer, including a free stick of licorice for the kids. The problem with these establishments was that they were the only retail games in town. In the long run, they made the lives of farmers and miners rather unbearable in terms of poor-quality goods with no guarantees, a usurious credit system, and high prices. Enter Richard Warren Sears and James Cash Penney, businessmen who would offer farmers and miners a great deal —and a great deal more.

It was a cold December 7 in Stewartville, Minnesota, in 1863. Not that the weather mattered much to Eliza Sears, who had other things on her mind, namely, the birth of her first son, Richard Warren. Her husband was off fighting in the Civil War, Stewartville was a frontier outpost where Indians comprised the majority of the population, and family and friends were few and far between. Eliza and her child would have to rely on each other for a long time. But it was a good relationship, and young Richard would grow up confident and enterprising. In fact, by age seven he captured his first job that paid 25¢ a day. At sixteen he began a career as a railroad telegrapher, moving up quickly to station agent, a position that permitted him to learn the freight business. Not surprisingly, Sears soon learned that a lot of freight was refused by purchasers, with sellers frequently negotiating with station agents to buy the merchandise at a fraction of the cost. Sears took an interest in buying such discounted goods, especially watches, and sold them at a profit to other station agents; by 1886 he had amassed about $5,000 from this side business, enough to set himself up in his own firm. So the R. W. Sears Watch Company was born, operating out of a small office in Minneapolis, but business was so good that a year later a move was made to Chicago where better shipping and rail facilities existed. Sears sold his watches by mail, advertising in farmers' magazines and putting his good name on the line: "We guarantee," he said in one 1889 ad, "every watch we sell to be exactly as represented and if not found so, they can be returned at any time and we will refund all the money paid." Sears also hired a crack watch repairman by the name of A. C. Roebuck, but it was his low prices that attracted the attention of country folk.

Perhaps more than any other group in American society, farmers in the late nineteenth century had a tough time getting the most purchasing power out of their dollar. Widely scattered and isolated, they depended primarily on the country store for their necessities and wants during their Saturday visit. The store proprietor was a father confessor of sorts, knowing the farmer's children by name (to whom he dispensed a little candy on the side), but as a businessman he left much to be desired:

prices were rarely placed on goods, negotiated instead according to the economic strength, weakness, and/or gullibility of the farm customer. Markup was enormous no matter the transaction, and credit, which the farmer was forced to use, was often outrageous. Part of the problem could be attributed to middlemen who slapped on charges along the production and distribution processes and to the fact that many farmers were such poor risks who reneged on debts, the costs of which were passed on to other consumers. There were other buying alternatives for farmers. The first mail-order business to emerge was Montgomery Ward in 1872. Ward eliminated all middlemen and sold directly to farmers organized in a politico-social organization known as the Patrons of Husbandry, or the Grange. He sold a wide variety of goods, offered guarantees, advertised in farmers' weeklies, and sent out invitations for customers to visit his Chicago plant during the 1893 World's Fair, some 285,000 actually obliging. Other mail-order firms included R. H. Macy and Company of New York, which began its catalog in 1874, and Spiegel's, organized in 1882.

So Sears's watch firm had its work cut out for it, both in terms of competition from country stores and other mail-order companies. And mail literature had no monopoly of virtue at the time, especially in terms of exaggerated claims and statements. No wonder that Sears included a statement on references in his 1889 catalog: "To those unacquainted with our reputation for fair and honorable dealings, on application we will be pleased to furnish reference in any State in the Union; or will refer you to the managers of any Express Company doing business in this city; the Fort Dearborn National Bank, or any old reliable business house in Chicago." Sears did not lose his shirt in the watch business as a result of the obstacles at the time, but he did not make the bundle of money that he had expected either. By March 1889, he sold the business and took off for Iowa with a nice chunk of cash in his pocket to invest in some land dealings in his mother's name. Not a bad situation for a twenty-five-year-old man.

Iowa, however, was no rose garden for Sears: the long work-days and evenings in his Chicago firm had geared him to something more than the quiet life of rural America. Within six months Sears headed for Minneapolis to open another mail-order business consisting of watches and jewelry, this time under the name of the Warren Company. Again, Sears made money, but again he sold out, this time in 1891 to his former associate Roebuck. But within a week Sears persuaded Roebuck to let him back into the firm, now reorganized as A. C. Roebuck. Again, the business was conducted much in the fashion of earlier ones: heavy stress on advertising, low prices, guarantees, and customer satisfaction. Within two years, however, the product line was expanded to include items varied enough to fill a sixty-four-page catalog under still another name, Sears, Roebuck and Company. A Chicago branch was also opened. Richard Sears concentrated his energies on writing copy for the catalog, appearing at long last to have found a place for his restless genius. "If you don't find what you want in this book," he wrote in 1895, "write us. We may have the very thing in stock; if we haven't, we can no doubt get it for you at a great saving. Don't hesitate to write us at any time. We are always at your service." And even if a customer didn't have an order form, Sears also advised, a request on a plain piece of paper would be honored.

Sears worked hard on his ad copy in order to reach his farmer audience, harder still to drum up new lines of merchandise. The pace was too much for Roebuck who, concerned about his health problems, decided to sell his share of the business in 1895. No problem, for by late summer Sears, Roebuck and Company was reincorporated with a greater capitalization, thanks to the investment endeavors of Aaron E. Nusbaum and Julius Rosenwald, who were convinced that Sears had a better idea. Rosenwald, a clothing merchant who had pulled himself up from his bootstraps, would play the formative role as manager after 1896 when first brother-in-law Nusbaum left and Sears concentrated his efforts on promotion. And Sears refined his promotion techniques as Rosenwald sweated the administrative details. He advertised for the first time in religious magazines that went to farm families, filling each ad with copious details about his products so as to convince skeptical readers that they knew the truth, the whole truth, and nothing but the truth. He offered buyers a free trial period for his clothing line and dropped prices way below what anyone else could sell for —either by mail or in a shop. There was more—even a consumer's guide, chock-full of artful writing. "We have learned in several cases," read the 1897 catalog, "where a small error has cost us the loss of a valuable customer although the error was unavoidable, and we would have gladly corrected it if given opportunity. In this way we are sometimes blamed for things of which we are entirely innocent. Don't fail to report any oversight, shortage, inattention, or error on our part. Do it pleasantly if possible. If not pleasantly report it anyway, and you will find us quick to right any wrong." Sears offered a 3 percent discount for all orders accompanied by full payment; the discount was increased to 5 percent on orders over $100. "Nearly all our customers send cash in full. It's the best way. You save the cash discount, save the return charges on money to us, besides, we can, as a general rule, make prompter shipment of cash in advance order than of C.O.D. order." How could Sears provide its customers with the cheapest and best goods money could buy, the farmer might ask? Simple, explained Sears. We have the best buyers roaming the land for the best bargains; we buy our goods with cash, and "we add the smallest percentage of profit possible consistent with honest goods and honest representations, and that is our net price to one and all, the price against which no other concern can compete; prices that establish us as the cheapest supply house on earth." And then there were the testimonials that Sears printed in his catalog, some downright apologetic for getting so much for so little: "The clothes and shoes I ordered of you have been received and am well pleased with your fair and honest dealings. Have been trading with you for eighteen months and am always surprised when I receive goods from you, as they are so good for such little money. Wishing you many better customers than myself, I am Yours truly, D. J. Meade, Pollock, La."

The significance of Sears's strategy is best seen in the prevailing prices of goods before his firm made a dent in the consumer market. Men's suits cost $10 before Sears, but only $5 in his catalog. In 1897 bicycles ran anywhere from $75 to $100 in retail stores. When Sears first sold them, the price was affordable. According to an 1898 magazine, Sears sends a "bicycle Catalogue free to anyone who asks for it, and, we are told, shipping several hundred bicycles every day to every state, direct to the riders at $5 to $19.75, on free trial before paying. If Sears, Roebuck & Co. continue to wage their bicycle war throughout the season it will be a boon to all those who want bicycles, but a sad blow to bicycle dealers and manufacturers."

Of course, Sears made some mistakes in his attempt to win customers with low prices. A premium plan introduced in 1904, giving customers special prizes after they had bought so many dollars of goods, proved to be too expensive and was dropped; charging for the four-pound catalog also proved to be shortsighted and was abandoned in 1904; and the "send-no-money" inducement left hundreds of thousands of unclaimed goods at freight offices, necessitating a change to a cash system of ordering. But the firm learned from its mistakes and sometimes high costs. It set up its own printing plant in 1903 in order to cut costs, experimented with just the right size and weight of catalog paper as to insure postal savings, and bought linotype machines to accelerate the production process. Sears undercut five-and-dime stores by offering customers some small goods at 2, 4, 6, or 8 ¢, the theory being that while a minimum order for business was 50¢, a starter order in which the firm made no money would induce the first-time buyer to continue purchases. Sears made certain there were adequate supplies for its orders by buying into various plants; it worked on getting out orders in the fastest possible time, within twenty-four hours, thanks to mail-opening machines that processed 27,000 missives per hour by 1905; and balanced its modest wage policy for employees with various benefits, such as health services, a savings plan that paid 5 percent interest, an employee discount of 10 percent on purchases, and permanent employment. ". . . While it is the policy of very many institutions," read a 1907 policy manual, "to lay off a large percentage of employees on Christmas Eve, or in the early summer, Sears, Roebuck & Co. have stood for the permanency of employment and if employees are dismissed in these seasons of the year it is from the fact that after being weighed in the balance, they have been found absolutely wanting. . . . The only exception lies in certain instances where a number of people may be employed temporarily and are so advised at the time."

Sears, Roebuck took a great deal of abuse from small retailers and country stores that were hard hit by the firm's low prices. There were public burnings of Sears catalogs in some small towns. Along with stores such as A & P, Sears was depicted as a "chain" that threatened to undo the "independents." Rumors circulated about both Sears and Roebuck as to their race and legitimacy, and Rosenwald's Jewish background became a target for anti-Semitic stories. Jokes circulated throughout small-town America about "Rears and Soreback," but the most frequent claim made by critics was that Sears did not help the employment and overall economic stability of small towns where the real Americans lived. The extent to which the small-town merchant crusade against Sears bordered on lunacy was best seen when Congress debated the extension of parcel post between 1910 and 1912. Prior to this time, rural customers of Sears had to go to the railroad freight office to pick up their goods; with an extended parcel post, convenience of home delivery and less cost would have been introduced. Yet although virtually all farm groups supported the congressional proposal, small-town merchants gave it the thumbs down. Of course, the measure passed as it was simply untenable to be against bettering the nation's mail service. As for Sears, it remained rather magnanimous in the matter—even historic in its words, as reflected by one early twentieth-century catalog:

> With malice towards none and charity for all, we extend to all mankind our sincere wishes for greater prosperity and happiness. . . . Let us all believe as we do, that every successful dealer, retailer, catalogue house or otherwise, is reliable. Let us rise above the jealousies and differences that so often grow out of competition so that in the evening of the day's work your competitor will be as welcome to break bread at your table as would be your doctor or your banker. We have a high regard for every honorable and reliable dealer and even though we may at times differ in our opinions, we bear no ill will against any maker or seller in our land.

As a result of its ingenious marketing strategies and increasingly respected name, Sears, Roebuck was making money hand over fist by the early twentieth century. Its capitalization of $150,000 in 1895 mushroomed to $5 million in less than ten years. Its sales in 1906 amounted to nearly $51 million. Profits were mostly reinvested in the business, and when Sears sold his interest in 1908 for about $10 million, the firm was the undisputed leader of the mail-order houses, way ahead of Montgomery Ward. And when Richard Warren Sears passed away in 1914, he left behind an American institution that would be as well-known as ice cream, apple pie, and baseball.

James Cash Penney would also lend his name to American posterity but in a somewhat different way. Like Sears, he was a midwesterner who grew up under the influence of a strong parent, his father, a Baptist preacher intent on making an economic man out of his son at an early age. Young J. C. took to raising pigs on his family's Missouri farm, an enterprise that netted him $60 by the time he was ten. His first job as a clerk in a retail store in his hometown made a good impression on the proprietor as well as Penney's banker: within a short time the young man stashed away $300. But the Missouri climate did not agree with Penney, and medical opinion feared that consumption might well develop in his lungs. Colorado, it was suggested, was a much better place to breathe free and easy. So in 1897 at age twenty-two Penney took his first train ride, entering a brand-new world. The change, however, was mostly in scenery and climate; the dry goods store that Penney first clerked at was similar to the shop he had known in Missouri —except for the fact that unethical practices seemed to prevail. Penney was urged to have several sets of prices for various customers, depending on their degree of gullibility. He refused to clerk in this fashion, taking his $300 in savings and promptly opening his own butcher store. Butcher man Penney was not, nor businessman, and his enterprise soon went the way of a Rocky Mountain high. Penney learned from the experience, namely, that religious scruples alone were not sufficient to succeed in business. Morals needed bolstering with storewise knowledge. Back to clerking in a dry goods store Penney went, this time with a winner businessman. Not only was the firm operated honestly, but it had several branches across the state, usually managed by partners, that is, former clerks who had shown promise and been given the opportunity to invest their own money. Two years after he began working, Penney became a partner in a new store being opened in a ranching and mining town in Wyoming. It was dubbed Johnson, Callahan and Penney: The Golden Rule Store.

Penney ran a tight shop. His hired help were forbidden to smoke or drink and expected to give each customer their best shot in terms of attention. They were to "hustle," in the better sense of the term, and Penney made no bones about the fact that his store catered to the average person who needed to get the most value for his dollar. When his partners decided to sell their interest in three stores, Penney jumped at the opportunity. By 1907, he was a businessman who had come a long way from his initial childhood ventures as a producer of pigs. He had also learned that the partnership idea could be employed with advantages to prospective businessmen and himself. As a result, by 1908 Penney's Golden Rule stores had expanded to four, with gross sales of $208,000. Three years later the number was twenty-two, with $1 million as the sales total. In each store Penney emphasized to customers that his people were here to stay, that they had no intention, a la the fiddle-footed and mysterious traveling salesman of the time, to skip town in the middle of the night. Just as Sears concentrated on eliminating the deficiencies of country stores in the East, Penney focused on the mining shops that ripped off their customers. "Our stores," he recalled, "were the simple kinds of places they felt at home in, we were their kind of people. They liked our cash and carry plan. They knew that they usually paid dearly for credit, which with many of them, the miners especially, meant a coupon system that kept them in a kind of bondage by depriving them of the full and free control of the money they earned when they earned it."

Critical to Penney's success was the careful selection of men to be his partners. They not only had to have business talent and the drive to work unlimited hours, but they had to be willing to accept less money—sometimes as much as 50 percent less—than they were earning elsewhere. Penney's theory was that a sacrifice on their part illustrated their commitment to prove themselves. It was also a religious act. "Men who in their relation to their customers and to the public generally are guided by the knowledge that their sins as well as their good deeds will be visited on every other man in the organization" was the way Penney phrased it. In terms of specific strategies for determining whether an individual manager of a store was a prime candidate for a partnership, Penney mixed the quantitative and qualitative. For example, he knew the inventory of the store, the markup, and the anticipated expenses. If the manager hit the profit figure that Penney had in mind, he was halfway to a partnership. The other test was a trial by the juries of cleanliness, economy, and customer relations, determined by Penney when he visited stores frequently and without notice.

Still another challenge for Penney was incorporation so as to obtain its benefits; this came about in 1913, but the partnership idea was continued in the sense that the only stock was preferred issues held by Penney and his partners. No less challenging for Penney was effective coordination of his growing chain of stores. A Salt Lake City warehouse was established, then came a New York City office to serve as a basis for refining buying and selling techniques. Because Penney shunned the concept of "sales" on products (goods, like people, were equal; therefore all should have the same treatment), managers were under the gun to buy carefully. They visited New York twice a year, and they and they alone were responsible for making the final choices for their stores from the buyers that Penney and his staff had selected because of their quality goods. By 1917 the system was changed in that buyers went directly to individual stores, but the managers still made the final buying decisions. All this meant that it was incumbent on managers to know their communities, even to the extent of getting involved in their activities. "We told our store managers," Penney wrote, "that, unless they knew their communities and unless they were prepared to enter sympathetically into community life, they could not make a success of their stores. We pointed out to them that the men who represent our organization before the public are under much the same obligation to take the public into their confidence with respect to their public interests and the motivation and conduct of their enterprises as are men who enter public service in the more restricted political sense of that term."

If Richard Sears was the master of explaining to customers the qualities of goods they could not immediately touch or test in their catalogs, J. C. Penney excelled in urging customers to meet him halfway in keeping down costs. "You are always willing," read an early ad, "to carry your purchases home with you. That may not always be a pleasant thing for you to do, but it helps keep down the overhead expense that would be necessary if you obliged us to maintain a delivery system. The fact that we do not have to hire extra men and keep an automobile for that purpose permits us to keep the expense of doing business down to a minimum. We give you the benefit which rightly belongs to you because you carry your own purchases home with you. We have no business, nor has any other mortal man, to charge you for a service we do not give you. To keep down prices and to play the game squarely with all our customers is our policy. Then, too, another element that works in your favor is this: You pay cash for all you buy at our stores. We have no charge accounts. That fact enables us to save the expense of a bookkeeper in each store. Consequently, we have no loss on bad accounts; and most of all it enables us to pay CASH for our merchandise which means thousands of dollars saved in cash discounts."

To be sure, both Sears and Penney's in time would undergo changes from their original policies, although Penney's clung more tenaciously to a cash-only system. Sears would introduce retail stores in the decades of the 1920s when America became an urban nation, yet continue a catalog system for those who still wanted their fingers and their postman to do the walking for their purchases. Its decentralized system of management would become a model that other corporations would emulate; on the other hand, its guarantee system would function in much the same manner that the founder had employed it. Some of Sears's strategies would be more successful than others: its growth program after World War II was in marked contrast to the policy of Montgomery Ward, whose more centralized management viewed the future with visions of another Great Depression. While Sears expanded, Ward retrenched—until it was too late to catch up with the competition. On the other hand, Sears's older managers and directors—fifty-six-year-olds were the average among officers by 1979—continued to think that the typical Sears customer would always be the Norman Rockwell man and woman: the husband who worked every day and bought Sears paint and Craftsman tools on Saturday and the wife who stayed at home and bought Toughskin jeans for Timmy and Sally and Kenmore appliances for herself. The youth of the 1960s and 70s with their significant purchasing power were ignored, as was their disposition, mostly anonymous. Their desire to shun salesclerks, to make purchases with the same dispatch that they bought fast food, created a new infrastructure of retail stores that competed more successfully than Sears for their consumer dollars. Sears would eventually respond, as, for example, by devising new businesses for the future, in financial services and real estate. As for Penney's, it would remain under the tutelage of its founder much longer than Sears. Richard Sears left his firm in 1908; even though A. C. Roebuck came back to Sears in 1933, he worked first as a clerk and then as a celebrity touring company stores and greeting customers. Penney's relation to his firm was never honorific; long before the term was coined, he practiced management-by-walking-around, visiting stores to keep employees and managers on their toes. In fact, my very first job while a high school student in 1952 was at a Penney's store during the Christmas holidays. In my orientation session with the department manager, I was shown not only Penney's venerable portrait but was also cautioned about the possibility of Mr. Penney introducing himself to me during one of his unannounced visits. I was so frightened of that eventuality that I went out of my way to ooze courtesy to customers, especially those with even the faintest speck of silver in their hair. More important, I did some research on the man, including getting a copy of his autobiography, *The Man with a Thousand Partners,* which I read in a couple of sittings. Afterward I felt good about my employment —and in some mysterious way I believe I became a partner in business history through that experience.

14

AN AMERICAN INSTITUTION: HENRY FORD

Henry Ford was the classic example of the American tinkerer. And no American would be more well-known in his lifetime: Russians marveled in the 1920s over "Fordizatzia," Germans over "Fordismus," and Americans simply over the word *Ford*. Born on a farm outside Dearborn, Michigan, in the midst of the Civil War, Ford was at war with the monotony and drudgery of farm work during his formative years. His mental highs came when he could fix various appliances or wander to other nearby farms for the same purpose. But there were only so many things that needed fixing in rural areas, so in 1879 Ford decided to head for Detroit to become a machinist and repair more things in a day than he had contemplated during a long, dreary winter. For eight years Ford worked as a machinist of marine engines, both steam and gasoline. It should have been a good life in a city that was conspicuous for its rising industrial prominence, but Ford exhibited the kind of mental restlessness that was more indicative of a creative artist than a blue-collar machinist. He returned home to the farm at age twenty-four, gladly accepted a forty-acre plot from his father, got married, and appeared to settle down to the life that his parents had always wanted for him. To be sure, Ford was busy with his farm chores

—eking out an existence wasn't easy—but he also found some time to do tinkering. For two years he sweated the details of what might be called a mechanical plow, a device he was absolutely certain would revolutionize American farming. It did not work, however, and back to the big city Ford, now twenty-eight, headed, this time with a wife and a sense of both failure and relief. Landing a job with Detroit's Edison Illuminating Company, Ford stayed with the firm for eleven years, rising to the post of chief engineer and taking in all the mechanical contraptions that the metropolis illustrated in this age of inventiveness. Indeed, Ford may well have become an ex-inventor turned secure with a good blue-collar job. Then something caught Ford's fancy, something far more attractive than a mechanical plow, something that he would develop as no other American before and after him. That something was the automobile.

The motor car that made its debut in Detroit during Ford's years in the city laid little claim to American ingenuity. A European by the name of Gottlieb Daimler devised and displayed the internal combustion engine in 1886, and a French firm pioneered in putting the motor into a frame that could be sold to consumers. And the automobile was sold in France in large numbers before the turn of the century. The first American to get in on the auto act in a leading role was Ransom E. Olds, who began a mass-production scheme in Detroit in 1899. One company, the Dodge brothers, made the engine, another firm the transmission, and then Olds used his plant to assemble the final product. The Oldsmobile was more than "merry"; it was a quality product far cheaper and better than the autos that would be produced by nearly 180 competitors that eventually tried their luck in the industry. Even before Olds had begun his enterprise, Henry Ford was absolutely fascinated with the possibilities of the automobile, an excitement that was fanned by his friendship with Charles B. King, a Detroit businessman who assembled a motor car. Ford soon built his own model and for the next five years tried to get the kinks out of it, exasperating Detroit residents with his frequent breakdowns and rush back to home base for spare parts. He joined forces with several investors to form the Detroit Automobile Company in 1899, the same year that Olds led the field. But Ford's product was a bomb that had no market. His model was a high-speed racer that was mostly designed to break speed records on barren stretches of roads. By 1900 Ford left the company to put more time and energy into his race car, which he demonstrated as its "chauffeur" (note the influence of the French) for the next three years.

In sum, Ford was on his way to becoming the nation's speed demon, a somewhat unusual role for a middle-aged man, one that was almost certain to give him rich historical obscurity. Fortunately, a Detroit coal dealer interfered with Ford's plans; Alex Y. Malcomsen wanted Ford to be his chief honcho at a new automobile plant. In 1903 the two men cut a deal, with the Ford Motor Company coming into existence. As with Ford's earlier economic decisions, this one was nothing to write home about, at least initially. However, Malcomsen was smart to bring outside contractors into the picture: as the Dodge brothers brought forth excellent parts that were assembled at the Ford plant, Henry in the first year continued to race his own special models. However, he soon began to pay attention to the need to produce his cars with dispatch so as to be affordable to average Americans. His first model, priced at $850, was a two-cylinder car that sold well, priced $100 below what Olds charged. Then Malcomsen urged that a high-priced, luxury car be produced, selling from $1,000 to $2,000, depending on model. That was done by 1906, but the result was calamitous in terms of reduced sales. So Ford campaigned for producing a good, inexpensive model—a campaign that led to Malcomsen's selling out in July 1906 and the reintroduction of a

1903-type car in 1907, a depression year. The strategy paid off, and Ford Motor Company made a profit of $1,250,000 as other automakers were flush with red ink.

Henry Ford next set his sights on production. A Ford car contained about 5,000 parts and was ordinarily assembled by men in the same way that construction workers built a house. Observing the overhead trolley system that Chicago meat-packers used in dressing beef, Ford experimented with the assembly line. "It must not be imagined," he wrote in retrospect, "that all this worked out as quickly as it sounds. The speed of the moving work had to be carefully tried out; in the fly-wheel magneto we first had a speed of sixty inches per minute. That was too fast. Then we tried eighteen inches per minute. That was too slow. Finally we settled on forty-four inches per minute. The idea is that a man must not be hurried in his work—he must have every second necessary but not a single unnecessary second. We have worked out speeds for each assembly, for the success of the chassis assembly caused us gradually to overhaul our entire method of manufacturing and to put all assembling in mechanically driven lines. . . . Some men do only one or two small operations, others do more. The man who places a part does not fasten it—the part may not be fully in place until after several operations later. The man who puts in a bolt does not put on the nut; the man who puts on the nut does not tighten it. On operation thirty-four the budding motor gets its gasoline; it has previously received lubrication; on operation number forty-four the radiator is filled with water, and on operation forty-five the car drives onto John R. Street." Within a year of Ford's introducing the assembly line, the time required to put together a car was reduced from twelve hours, twenty-eight minutes to two hours, thirty-eight minutes. In another year the time was cut to one hour, thirty-three minutes.

The low-priced car that Ford introduced after Malcomsen left was called the Model N. Its secret was tough vanadium steel, that is, strong and yet light so as to permit the car to be economically run. Steel makers in America could not produce this type of steel, however. It required a temperature of 3,000 degrees when the maximum employed in United States furnaces was 2,700. Ford hired an Englishman with a knowledge of vanadium production and guaranteed a small steel company against any loss from making the product. Instead of a tensile strength of 70,000 pounds for regular steel, vanadium reached 170,000. One auto magazine described the Model N as the best of any car. "This . . . position of first importance and highest interest," it went on, "is due to the fact that the Model N supplies the very first instance of a low-cost motorcar driven by a gas engine having cylinders enough to give the shaft a turning impulse in each shaft turn which is well built and offered in large numbers."

In 1908 Ford announced that his company henceforth would build only one car, the Model T, which was a distillation of the best features of his previous models. "I cannot say that any one agreed with me," said Ford of his decision. "The selling people could not of course see the advantages that a single model would bring about in production. More than that, they did not particularly care. They thought our production was good enough as it was and there was a very decided opinion that lowering the sales price would hurt sales, that the people who wanted quality would be driven away and that there would be none to replace them." When Henry Ford was right, as he was about the early attraction of the Model T, he was absolutely right. Praise about the car came from all quarters, even the U.S. Board of Tax Appeals writing in retrospect in 1928: the Model T, it said, "was a utility car. It was a good car. It had a good reputation and a thoroughly accepted standing in 1913. It was used by all classes of people. It was the cheapest car on the market and was a greater value for its price than any other car. Because of its low price it had a much larger field of demand than any other car. It was within the purchasing power of the greatest number of people and they were rapidly availing themselves of it. There was a greater demand for it than the car of any other company." Until World War I, each year saw the number of Model Ts increase:

> 1909—12,292
> 1910—19,293
> 1911—40,402
> 1912—78,611
> 1913—182,809
> 1914—260,720
> 1915—355,276
> 1916—577,036
> 1917—802,771

And each year saw the price fall:

> 1909—$950
> 1910— 780
> 1911— 690
> 1912— 600
> 1913— 550
> 1914— 490
> 1915— 440
> 1916— 360

Ford set up assembly plants in twenty-seven areas by 1915; shipping parts from factories located in the Detroit area to the assembly plants was cost effective because they were less bulky and hence much easier to ship than a finished automobile. Another advantage of this system, according to a Federal Trade Commission *Report* on Ford,

> was that stocks of parts could be accumulated at the various assembly plants, economizing storage space at the Detroit factories and permitting production of the parts in those portions of the year in which business was slow, thus eliminating the sharp curves of production. The assembly plants also established immediate sources of supply in the regions in which they were located. Dealers were furnished with stocks of parts from these assembly plants; and in many cases were able to drive the cars from the assembly plants

to their places of business instead of having them transported by rail.

To gain name recognition the Model T was driven through all sorts of obstacle courses. It won a transcontinental race in 1909, whipped competitors in various hill climbs, and in 1912 bested the worst of the West, the Grand Canyon, via a driver who was forced to use dynamite to clear a path through the rocky terrain. Ford also had to whip inventors in the patent court, and for a time had to assure buyers protection against legal suits. By 1911, however, an appeals court settled the matter in Ford's favor. Critical also to Ford's success were the strategies of business manager James Couzens. As the firm's sales increased, Couzens negotiated the best terms from manufacturers of parts in order to keep costs down, sometimes even getting parts below cost from manufacturers who hoped to make their profits from sales to other companies. Couzens also saw to it that the freight costs priced into each auto were considerably reduced in practice, thereby assuring an additional source of profits. Most important, Couzens got 7,000 dealers to market Ford cars by 1912. He went to various towns, made a nice deposit in the local bank, and urged the institution to lend money to the newly emerging Ford dealer in his community. Then Couzens shipped an overload of cars to the dealer, ensuring that he would have to work like the dickens to sell them all. Henry Ford also admonished dealers:

A dealer or a salesman ought to have the name of every possible automobile buyer in his territory, including all those who have never given the matter a thought. He should then personally solicit by visitation if possible—by correspondence at the least—every man on that list and then making necessary memoranda, know the automobile situation as related to every resident so solicited. If your territory is too large to permit this, you have too much territory.

In 1914 Ford even introduced the first rebate to the customer, a $50 sum that amounted to a total of $15.5 million dispensed by the company in one year. Of course, the advantages of the automobile to the average American were exceeded only by those to major cities in the United States. Before cars became widespread, New York City streets were the daily repositories of 60,000 gallons of horse urine and 2.5 million pounds of manure, to say nothing of the forty dead horses whose carcasses had to be removed each day.

Ford Motor Company was not without its problems in these heady years. Labor was the most difficult to handle. The usual working day for the firm's assembly-line employees was nine hours, the maximum daily wage $2.34 in 1913—both indexes quite respectable. Not so respectable was the regimentation and speed of the assembly-line routine, which gave rise to a 10-percent daily absentee rate and an enormous turnover, nearly 400 percent in 1913 alone. Ford, in sum, had done what any prudent business at the time would have done, that is, put its money into machines, and scarcely a working day went by without the introduction of another laborsaving piece of machinery. By 1913 serious attention had to be given to Ford's working force not only because of absenteeism and turnover but also labor radicalism, best illustrated by the Industrial Workers of the World, who hoped to take advantage of the situation. Yet Henry Ford's solution was more radical than the ideology of the IWW: in January 1914 he announced a $5-a-day wage plan, based upon a profit-sharing formula and a reduction of the workday to eight hours. Although some editorial opinion was critical because of the fear that other workers would strike their employers for similar wages, the immediate reaction of Ford's employees was positive. In fact, in spite of bone-chilling cold at the Highland Park, Michigan, plant at the time of the announcement, some 10,000 men created a mob scene in hopes of gaining employment, ultimately having to be dispersed by police with fire hoses. This incident aside, worker productivity increased, absenteeism and turnover plummeted, and Ford profits skyrocketed—from $24 million in 1915 to $60 million a year later.

However, the $5-a-day scheme had its underside. Ford Motor Company expected the worker to be productive *and* accept the firm's rules; otherwise, the employee would get the boot or never come close to attaining the maximum wage. For instance, a worker would have to move through probationary status before being eligible for the $5 wage. Next he would have to satisfy Ford's Sociology Department, whose staff would visit his home, advise him on saving money, buying reasonable and nutritious foods, abstaining from liquor, and turning away male boarders on the grounds that they might violate the females of the residence. Families found deficient in the Ford rules were ineligible for the big bucks, even though those receiving the maximum wage helped to fuel inflation for the entire community in which the plant was located. But to most workers, the benefits of Ford's paternalistic program outweighed the liabilities, and most believed that the scheme devised to judge eligibility for profit sharing, described below by John R. Lee, who headed the investigative unit, was fair:

As a result of this work our employes were grouped as follows: *First Group.* Those who were firmly established in the ways of thrift and who would carry out the spirit of the plan themselves. . . . *Second Group.* Those who had never a chance but were willing to grasp the opportunity in the way every man should. . . . *Third Group.* Those who had qualified but we were in doubt about as to their strength of character to continue in the direction they had started in. . . . *Fourth Group.* And the men who did not or could not qualify were put into a fourth group.

The first group of men were never bothered except when we desired information for annual or semi-annual reports or something of that kind. The second group were looked up as often as in the judgment of the investigation department, so called, we could help them or strengthen their purpose by kindly suggestion. The third group were dealt with in much the same fashion, although some detailed plans had to be laid for them. The fourth group were very carefully and thoroughly studied in the hope we might bring them, with the others, to a realization of what we were trying to accomplish, and to modifications, changes and sometimes complete revamping of their lives and habits, in order that they might receive what the company wanted to give them. During the first six months 69 per cent of our force qualified. At the end of the first year about 87 per cent were on a profit sharing basis, and at the present time about 90 per cent are receiving the benefits under this plan.

Again in January 1919 Henry Ford showed his adaptability to changing labor conditions by announcing a $6-a-day wage. Recognizing that the glow of $5 had faded in five years, Ford reacted in order to ensure a solid work force in the postwar years, speed up the assembly line, and fill the enormous demand for Model Ts that World War I had put on hold. "The payment of five dollars a day for an eight-hour day," he wrote in his autobiography, "was one of the finest cost-cutting moves we ever made, and the six-dollar day is cheaper than the five." Ford, however, was less adaptable to changing competitive conditions in the automobile industry. After a postwar boom led to a sharp collapse in 1920–21, which Ford handled by significant cost cutting, the firm was perched at a crossroads in the early 1920s. On the one hand, there was competition, most notably from General Motors, which had about 12 percent of the market. GM hoped to increase its share by having each one of its product lines, sold through autonomous departments, appeal to a different market: Chevrolet as the low-priced car; then Buick, Olds, and Pontiac; finally, Cadillac as the most expensive. On the other hand, Ford was convinced that the way to meet competition, a la the examples of Rockefeller and Carnegie, was to drive down the cost of the Model T even more. The focal point of this strategy was the building of an enormous central production plant on the River Rouge near Detroit, capable of turning out more cars at less cost each and every day of the year. Yet by 1923 it was clear that Ford's pricing policies were not inducing buyers, nor was Ford's personal rule doing for him what GM's decentralized management was doing for its sales. GM's marketing strategy focused on the American buying cars on credit (which Ford did not permit) and on changing styles, if not cars, every year or so. In Ford's rational world of production, that was downright heretical. "We want to construct some kind of a machine that will last forever," argued Ford in 1922. "We want a man who buys one of our products never to have to buy another. We never make an improvement that renders any previous model obsolete. The parts of a specific model are not only interchangeable with all other cars of that model, but they are interchangeable with similar parts on all the cars we have turned out. You can take a car of ten years ago and, buying to-day's parts, make it with very little expense into a car of to-day. Having these objectives the costs always come down under pressure. And since we have the firm policy of steady price reduction, there is always pressure. Sometimes it is just harder!"

Executives at FMC urged Ford to modify his basic policy in order to meet the competition. But Ford refused until most of his lieutenants had left and sales plummeted. By 1927 he closed all thirty-four of his plants for six months in order to retool for his new car, the Model A, which wasn't put into full-fledged production for a full year after closing. The Model A was an excellent car, made easier to purchase because Ford gave in to buying on credit, and it stayed on top for two years. But that was it for the company: by 1936 it was number three behind GM (43 percent) and Chrysler (25 percent) in passenger car sales (in that same year the Ford Foundation was established to avoid excessive taxation and maintain family control of the firm). GM's strength after 1927 lay in its annual fanfare in introducing new styles and models, research and development that brought forth enclosed cars with better running features, and its savvy handling of the used-car business. Ford, for example, had traditionally treated used-car sales as a means of profit for its dealers, whereas GM from its beginning believed that losses could be sustained if used cars could be related to increases in new car sales. And in 1926, General Motors also employed the first reconditioning and guaranteeing of Buicks under a "gold seal" plan that was ahead of its day; in the same year it devised a forecasting system that was modern by any reasonable standard. Henry Ford, in the meantime, liked to make fun of such scientific management. Organizational charts were compared to a tree

> heavy with nice round berries, each of which bears the name of a man or of an office. Every man has a title and certain duties which are strictly limited by the circumference of his berry. If a straw boss wants to say something to the general superintendent, his message has to go through the sub-foreman, the foreman, the department head, and all the assistant superintendents. Probably by that time what he wanted to talk about is already history. It takes about six weeks for the message of a man living in a berry on the lower left-hand corner of the chart to reach the president or chairman of the board, and if it ever does reach one of these august officials, it has by that time gathered to itself about a pound of criticisms, suggestions, and comments.

Henry Ford was more than a tinkerer. He was the embodiment of the American caught between farm and city. His values were rooted in the farm, as were the values of most Americans of his day. City values with their mass-produced goods made sense to Ford so long as the products were increasingly affordable (the Model T reached a low price of $290 in 1925), unencumbered by gimmickry, and illustrative of a handshake between seller and buyer as to longevity. "A manufacturer is not through with his customer when a sale is completed," wrote Ford. "He has then only started with his customer. In the case of an automobile the sale of the machine is only something in the nature of an introduction. If the machine does not give service, then it is better for the manufacturer if he had never had

the introduction, for he will have the worst of all advertisements—a dissatisfied customer. There was something more
than a tendency in the early days of the automobile to regard
the selling of a machine as the real accomplishment and thereafter it did not matter what happened to the buyer." To give
service was also being neighborly in the good farm tradition.
Some city and farm values did not mix for Ford, however.
Bringing down the price of the car had limits that rarely applied
to the low-cost goods sold by Sears, Penney, Rockefeller, and
Carnegie. For the automobile by the 1920s became an extension
of the American's personality. With more people living in the
city than on the farm for the first time, Americans cried for the
individuality that they had known on the farm but was stifled
amongst the huddled masses yearning to breathe free on urban
streets. The sameness of the Model T ("Any customer can have
a car painted any color that he wants so long as it is black" was
the way Ford put it) was all right until consumers were exposed
to different styles and models affordably provided by General
Motors ("A car for every purse and purpose" was GM's slogan). Ford's notion of credit, like that of Sears and Penney, was
country bred. Don't go in debt, he admonished for a long time.
Sure, that worked for watches and underwear, as Sears and
Penney demonstrated, but not for cars. Like country people,
Ford detested banks and bankers; he was anti-Semitic, anti-
union, and antimilitaristic. War promoted government to the
forefront of an economy that it was ill equipped to handle,
unionism emphasized collectivism instead of the individualistic
spirit, and Jews were sharp city slickers who manipulated
money and credit. Ford's commonsense notions even extended
to good and evil in the world:

> I believe that the smallest particle of matter—call it an atom or an
> ion or what you like—is intelligent. I don't know much about
> atoms and the like, but I feel sure that they know what they are
> doing—and why. They swarm all around us. If a man is working
> his level best to do what he believes is right, these invisible elements

pitch in and help him. If he is doing what he knows is wrong, they will work just as hard against him.

Torn between farm and city, Ford let the farm end of his personality win out, which made him an enormously popular American—a folk hero of sorts—in the 1930s and 40s and a less-than-successful businessman. "I have tried to live as my mother would have wanted me to," he said to the delight of Americans caught between devotion to mother and its antithesis in the city, the license to do anything. "It is all the same to me if a man comes from Sing Sing or Harvard. We hire a man, not his history," Ford announced to Americans witnessing for the first time the complexities of a society that necessitated more than readin', 'ritin', and 'rithmetic. ". . . It is not a bad thing to be a fool for righteousness' sake. The best of it is that such fools usually live long enough to prove that they were not fools—or the work they have begun lives long enough to prove they were not foolish," argued Ford in defense of his ideas as they became less popular. And no argument was more potent to Americans caught between the rushing streams of farm and city than the either-or dichotomy that Ford enunciated. "What this generation needs is a deep faith, a profound conviction in the practicability of righteousness, justice, and humanity in industry. If we cannot have these qualities, then we were better off without industry. Indeed, if we cannot get those qualities, the days of industry are numbered. But we can get them. We are getting them." Little wonder, then, that Ford was an attractive candidate for the presidency by 1923, with more Americans in a major magazine poll naming him first choice over all other leaders.

After Ford died in 1947, his firm would regain some of the economic leadership that it had held in its early years; it did so by becoming more and more like General Motors with its decentralized staffing, wide product line, affiliated industries (Auto-Lite and Philco), and union labor force. Ironically, in recent years much of the leadership in producing cars at low cost would come from foreign nations that adopted the spirit of Henry Ford's sameness and quality and put effort on improving worker morale and motivation through quality control circles and robots as opposed to Ford's high wages and paternalism. Model changes that used to occur yearly among American manufacturers have been slowed to three-, five-, or even six-year cycles. And the most popular American in the mid-1980s is Lee Iacocca, an automobile manufacturer who has run his firm in much the same centralized fashion as Ford called the shots. Frequently mentioned as a presidential candidate, Iacocca is no farm boy perched at the crossroads of urban/suburban America, but an Italian-American nurtured on city streets with a savviness somewhat reminiscent of Ford's, even to the extent of paying off Chrysler's government loans years in advance of their actual due date—no matter the unwisdom of such a decision from an investment standpoint. All this may suggest that automobile history has come full circle, visible to old-timers who recall the good old days. Or to put it in Ford's own words, "History as is sometimes written is bunk. But history that you can see is of great value."

15

THE
PROGRESSIVE
COMPROMISE

The closest thing to an economic and social breakdown in American society occurred during the last quarter of the nineteenth century. That's not something contemporary Americans like to accept. But the scenario of labor strife and violence, of a third party committed to sometimes socialist objectives, and of a massive depression in 1893—all these actually unfolded. Fortunately, the American disposition to find a middle way to solving its political and economic problems prevailed, leaving the business environment in good shape and setting the tone for subsequent reform of private enterprise. Not surprisingly, businessmen played critical roles in achieving what came to be known as the Progressive Compromise, although their names have been lost as a result of the prominence of political leaders such as Woodrow Wilson and Theodore Roosevelt.

Just one year after the nation celebrated its centennial with a marvelous exposition in Philadelphia—in which American industrial ingenuity was the focal point—Pennsylvania became a sort of crucible of labor strife. In fact, in a matter of a few weeks, it had enough trouble to set historical records: on June

21, 1877, six Irish miners, members of the Ancient Order of Hibernians (Molly Maguires, as they were commonly known), were hanged in Pottsville; on the same day four others were executed at Mauch Chunk. Both episodes were later referenced as "Pennsylvania's Day with the Rope." Later in the same year, seven other Pennsylvania miners were put to death; however, it was not until two Molly Maguires were executed in January 1879 that the movement came to an end. Although the Mollies were viewed by some as radical revolutionaries, more likely they were miners who took part in strikes that often, for a variety of reasons, witnessed violent confrontations. Also in 1877, within a month of the double executions, the nation experienced its first major rail strike. Stirred by wage cuts and starting with workers on the Baltimore & Ohio, the strike spread to the mighty Pennsylvania Railroad and other lines, ultimately resulting in ten states putting about 60,000 militia in arms.

The strike on the Pennsy centered in the Pittsburgh area where rail workers were supported by numerous sympathizers. And to add insult to injury, Governor John F. Hartranft was on a railroad junket to Wyoming—paid for by the railroad—and the adjutant general was given authority to deal with crises in the governor's absence. So National Guard troops from Philadelphia were called to the scene on the grounds that Pittsburgh's militia might be sympathetic. At the time Philadelphia was the City of Brotherly Hate for Pittsburgh folk because the home office of the Pennsylvania line was located there. Then there was a rumor to the effect that the Philadelphia militia were hell-bent on putting their traditional cross-state rivals in place. In spite of the urgings from strike leaders to avoid a confrontation, no sooner had the Philadelphia troops arrived than the assembled crowd of greeters unleashed a torrent of invectives. The troops were ordered to fix bayonets and within minutes panic ensued. "Seventeen Citizens," read a headline in an Extra edition of a Pittsburgh newspaper, "Shot in Cold Blood by the Roughs of Philadelphia. The Lexington of the

Labor Conflict at Hand. The Slaughter of Innocents." What followed was even worse than the initial bloodshed. Rioting became widespread, railroad and other buildings were burned, and looters were silhouetted against an inflamed scene. "People were hurrying up the hill," an onlooker noted, "with all kinds of shipping cases, webs of cloth, silk, brooms, hams, bacon, umbrellas, liquor of every kind, in fact every kind of portable merchandise. . . ." Total damage from the fire and looting was estimated at $5 million, including 104 engines, 46 passenger cars, and over 1,200 freight cars. Additional gunfire from the Philadelphia troops raised the number of deaths to about forty.

In its Maryland manifestation, the strike began at the B & O terminus in Martinsburg, West Virginia, in mid-July as a result of wage reductions. There had been minor incidents earlier at Camden Junction outside Baltimore but these were contained. Martinsburg, however, was another matter. Several hours removed from the city where railway constables were present, the area was a relay station critical to the B & O system. Firemen, then brakemen began to refuse to move freight trains. Militiamen were called in, a scuffle ensued, and one striker was wounded. The strike spread to nearby areas, and the B & O urged the governor of West Virginia to request the intervention of federal troops. The governor complied, President Rutherford B. Hayes responded, and the whole matter seemed to be over as quickly as it began. But then a major incident developed in Baltimore, where there was widespread sympathy for the rail workers as well as the existence of other strikes: on July 20 crowds of people and the assembling of militiamen combined to ignite a riot. By day's end, Baltimore's streets became the scene of what was dubbed the "second Battle of Bunker Hill." Although the casualty figures were disputed at the time, it was believed that as many as eleven people were killed and another forty wounded. There was little disagreement, however, over the fact that the instigators of the incident were individuals other than railroad strikers. Although the Baltimore *Sun* emphasized this aspect of the incident, Governor John Lee Carroll was mostly alone in criticizing the strikers. "You are responsible," said Carroll, "for the violence that has been done, whether you were actually engaged in it or not. You on your part must drive away from you the evil-disposed people who have done so much harm, and discountenance in the plainest way everything tending to violence."

Both Philadelphia and Baltimore returned to normal times as the railroad strike was cooled by the presence of more and more troops, but the incident would be referenced repeatedly in the years that followed. The significance of the strike depended on one's perspective at the time. For some observers, the strike represented clear and convincing testimony to the abuse of economic power by industrialists; for others it confirmed the influence of foreign forces at work. This was the view of the *Annals of the Great Strikes in the United States,* published at year's end in 1877. "It was evident," read the book, "that there were agencies at work outside of the workingmen's strike. The people engaged in these riots were not railroad strikers. The Internationalists had evidently something to do with creating scenes of bloodshed. The threats of their leaders made at meetings held the same evening were evidently not merely idle vaporings. Women frenzied with rage, joined the mob and incited the men to stand firm in the fight. The scenes . . . in the city of Baltimore were not unlike those which characterized the events in the city of Paris during the reign of the Commune in 1870." This theme would be repeated in a bestselling book published several years later. In *Our Country* (1885), Reverend Josiah Strong contended that it was the technology, mostly of foreign nations, that was largely to blame for the unsettling times. "It must not be forgotten that, . . . [there] has been developed, in modern times, a tremendous enginery of destruction, which offers itself to every man. Since the French Revolution nitroglycerine, illuminating gas, petroleum, dynamite, the revolver, the repeating rifle, and the Gatling gun have all come into use. Science has placed in man's hands superhuman powers." Technology, argued Strong, was a double-edged sword: through the railroad and telegraph it heralded a new age of investigating and touching the world; it also illustrated some concern for human life by making work easier. At the same time, technology lessened the moral guard. "Divorce religion and education," the book argued, "and we shall fall prey either to blundering goodness or well-schooled villainy." Crime and immorality also had a tendency to increase faster than church membership. Strong's solution was to bring the nation into a moral and religious rebirth, exporting its dividends to the world in a sort of rendezvous with destiny: "We stretch our hand into the future with power to mold the destinies of unborn millions. 'We are living, we are dwelling, In a grand and awful time, In an age on ages telling—To be living is sublime.' " Such an entry into the world arena was not "a plea for America's sake, but America for the world's sake."

Neither the end of the first great rail strike nor the publication of Strong's book lessened social strife in America. Labor uprisings moved across the country like grain bowing to a strong wind, with Chicago the scene of the worst incident in 1886. A strike by a few workers mushroomed into a major crisis in Haymarket Square in the wake of May Day. A bomb exploded, killing seven policemen and wounding numerous others. Eight anarchists were summarily arrested, and police punctuated the violence with gunfire of their own, thereby adding to the casualty list. Four of the anarchists were executed, one committed suicide, and the rest were sentenced to long prison terms that were commuted in a controversial decision by Illinois governor John Peter Altgeld in 1893 on the grounds that the evidence presented at the trial was flimsy. Back in New York City, journalist Jacob Riis raised the panic level of well-heeled residents with a sensational description of slum life in *How the Other Half Lives* (1890):

A man stood at the corner of Fifth Avenue and Fourteenth Street the other day, looking gloomily at the carriages that rolled by, carrying the wealth and fashion of the avenues to and from the big stores down town. He was poor, and hungry, and ragged. This thought was in his mind: 'They behind their well-fed teams have no thought for the morrow; they know hunger only by name, and ride down to spend an hour's shopping what would keep me and my little ones from want a whole year.' There rose up before him the picture of those little ones crying for bread around the cold and cheerless hearth—then he sprang into the throng and slashed around him with a knife, blindly seeking to kill, to revenge.

Matters got worse by 1892 when the Populist Party was formally organized on July 4. To be sure, there had been third parties earlier in American history, and the Populist antecedents (the Grange, the Northwestern and Southern alliances) could already lay claim to some success—the Interstate Commerce Act of 1887 and the Sherman Antitrust Act of 1890. But 1892 was a jittery year for business. The Homestead strike at the Carnegie Steel Company lasted for more than six months and was marred by violence, including the slaying of ten strikers and three Pinkerton agents. Although a revival period in the economy was underway, it faded as quickly as it appeared. Then came the disturbing preamble of the Populist platform:

. . . we meet in the midst of a nation brought to the verge of moral, political, and material ruin. Corruption dominates the ballot-box, the Legislatures, the Congress, and touches even the ermine of the bench. The people are demoralized. . . . The newspapers are largely subsidized or muzzled, public opinion silenced, business prostrated, homes covered with mortgages, labor impoverished, and the land concentrating in the hands of capitalists. The urban workmen are denied the right to organize for self-protection, imported pauperized labor beats down their wages, a hireling standing army, unrecognized by our laws, is established to shoot them down, and they are rapidly degenerating into European conditions. The fruits of the toil of millions are boldly stolen to build up colossal fortunes for a few, unprecedented in the history of mankind; and the possessors of these, in turn, despise the Republic and endanger liberty. From the same prolific womb of governmental injustice we breed the two great classes—tramps and millionaires.

More worrisome to business was the actual Populist platform, which called for government ownership of the railroads, telegraph, and telephone. The platform also demanded that all land owned by railroads and other corporations in excess of their actual use be reclaimed by the federal government. In order to raise prices of farm goods, the Populists called for the coinage of silver dollars. And they opposed "any subsidy or national aid to any private corporation for any purpose." The Pinkerton detective agency drew the wrath of Populists as did garment manufacturers in Rochester, against whom a national boycott was urged. What was worse to businessmen, the Populists did exceedingly well in the 1892 election, with their presidential nominee garnering over a million popular votes and twenty-two electoral votes. No third party had done better, which meant that the Populists hoped to win the White House by 1896.

In the wake of the 1892 election, however, the American economy came apart in the worst depression in its history. The Panic of 1893 lasted four years, giving rising to numerous business failures, including 600 banks in the first year alone. There were other untoward events: Coxey's Army, a group of 500 unemployed men, marched on Washington in 1894, urging Congress to spend $500 million for public works; in the same year, the American Railway Union struck the Great Northern line, then moved on to Pullman, Illinois, where it got the cooperation of employees of the Pullman Palace Car Company. The strike eventually spread to twenty-seven states and territories, bringing forth the use of the injunctive powers of the Sherman Antitrust Act against the ARU, the firing of the first shots by federal troops in a labor controversy, and the jailing of ARU leader Eugene Debs. The election of 1896 exacerbated matters. The Democrats were assured of the support of most Populists by nominating Nebraskan William Jennings Bryan for the top post. But Bryan was a mountebank whose sole claim to fame was a booming voice in a premicrophone age and the ability to make extraordinarily complex issues offensively simple. In his famous "Cross of Gold" acceptance speech, Bryan intensified the emotional level of the times by making the Populist pitch for the minting of silver dollars and the Republican adherence to the gold standard as the basis for determining good and evil in America: "You come to us," he said of his political foes, "and tell us that the great cities are in favor of the gold standard; we reply that the great cities rest upon our broad and fertile prairies. Burn down your cities and leave our farms, and your cities will spring up again as if by magic; but destroy our farms and the grass will grow in the streets of every city in the country. . . . Having behind us the producing masses of this nation and the world, supported by the commercial interests, the laboring interests and the toilers everywhere, we will answer their demand for a gold standard by saying to them: You shall not press down upon the brow of labor this crown of thorns, you shall not crucify mankind upon a cross of gold." Bryan's nomination meant the repudiation of incumbent Democratic president Grover Cleveland, who, for all his shortcomings, was level-headed about political and economic realities. And although Bryan's candidacy would not prevail, the election was razor thin, with only 700,000 votes separating winner and loser out of 14 million cast.

The most salutary aspect of the events of the last quarter of the nineteenth century was that they moved business to exert efforts in behalf of prudent reform. Their ventures were joined with those of middle-class reformers who were appalled at the radical nature of Populism and its scurrilous leaders, such as "Sockless" Jerry Simpson, whose very name suggested social impropriety. By the turn of the century, business leadership was changing, from the great entrepreneurs to managers whose lives were likely to be more bureaucratic than daring. These businessmen had little choice other than to work in a disorderly status quo or to mold society into something better than the radical alternative that Populism illustrated. The payoff of the latter strategy was more stable economic growth in place of big booms and bigger busts as well as the forging of a working relationship with professionals and government bureaucrats. The formal reform movement emerging from this philosophy, Progressivism, dominated the American political scene in the years from 1900 to World War I, an era of prosperity. Progressivism was simply a fancy term for reform that fell between doing nothing and moving in the direction of socialism. It was compromising and in need of periodic tinkering, although sometimes in the case of the Mann Act (outlawing the movement of women across state lines for immoral purposes) and Prohibition, the movement was moralistic. Progressivism rarely solved problems as a result of its middle-of-the-road nature, but it provided a wide degree of consensus among Americans. And it laid the foundation for subsequent reform in the twentieth century.

One of the best examples of the business Progressive was Gerard Swope. Born in 1872 in St. Louis, Swope was one of four children of Isaac and Ida Swope, German Jews who emigrated in 1857. His schooling in the St. Louis public schools brought forth an interest and talent in mathematics. So Swope attended the Massachusetts Institute of Technology majoring in electrical engineering. As a student, he returned to Chicago in the summers, attending the World's Fair there in 1893 as well as working for the fledgling General Electric Company. Upon graduation in 1895 Swope accepted a position at Western Electric Company where he worked himself up from a lowly helper to vice-president in charge of domestic sales by 1913. According to Henry Ford, no easy judge, Swope was the best salesman in America. Long before he was selected as president of General Electric in 1922, Swope took a keen interest in Chicago's urban problems. In fact, from 1897 to 1899, he lived and assisted at

Hull House, the social settlement created by Jane Addams who, in the tradition of Progressive leaders, knew neither economic disadvantage nor discord in her life. Like Swope, she was well educated, attending Rockford Medical Seminary and the Women's Medical College in Philadelphia. Urged to refine her womanly graces rather than professionalism, Addams took two trips to Europe that left her with other convictions, especially as she took the opportunity to view the worst sections of London. "The poorest people wait until very late Saturday night," she wrote in 1883, "as meats and vegetables which cannot be kept on Sunday are sold cheaper. . . . It was simply an outside superficial survey of the misery and wretchedness, but it was enough to make one thoroughly sad and perplexed." On her return home, Addams bought an old building on Chicago's West Side and in 1899 began the nation's first settlement house, designed to provide assistance to the city's industrial masses. Hull House would evolve into an educational, welfare, and social institution with thirteen buildings ranging from classrooms, a coffeehouse, theater, music school, nursery, and a gymnasium to a boarding school for working single females. At Hull House Swope taught the essentials of electricity to immigrants and other working class families who were tempted to equate the new form of energy with electrocution rather than its enormous domestic uses. He also met another Progressive, college-trained Mary Dayton Hill, who devoted her free time to teaching and whom he would later marry. To be sure, Swope was not a typical businessman, but reform movements, like revolutions, rarely involve large numbers as much as they do concerted leadership of a few people. Under Swope's leadership, GE was transformed with corporate social programs in the form of workmen's compensation, accident insurance, and pension schemes. A small man who bristled with energy and ideas, Swope had the ability to get to the heart of organizational and substantive matters in his own business and to take a pragmatic view of change in industrial society, which would reach its height during the crises of the Great Depression.

Below Swope's enlightened capitalism were businessmen who viewed reform as an outgrowth of organization and bargaining on political matters. The rise of civic associations—Rotary in 1915, Lions in 1917—and the growth of chambers of commerce, including the formation of a national body by 1913, were testimony to the desire of businessmen to work up front for programs that required a public airing rather than employ the strategy of smoke-filled rooms and the secret greasing of the palms of city bosses. The Chamber of Commerce of the United States used referenda of local bodies to determine its position on various issues, but it stopped short of becoming a pressure or lobbying group. It also tried to ensure that no one segment of the business community dominated its leadership or membership. Then there were hundreds of other business organs, such as commercial clubs or boards of trade that dotted American towns and cities. Members worked in behalf of such reforms as licensing of businessmen as well as the implementation of the city manager–city commission form of government. Both reforms became popular because they were good compromises. Licensing, for instance, was only a modest screening of prospective businessmen; the payment of a fee was not onerous except for the fly-by-nighter who was the worst-case businessman that licensing focused on. The city manager–city commission form of government, on the other hand, mixed the expert (the manager who was the engineer) with selfless democracy (the nonpartisan commission members who relied on their own businesses or professions for their income). Business Progressives also urged the adoption of civil service for local government employees as well as municipal ownership of various utilities or, alternatively, regulation of private firms through a scientific rate-making scheme. The latter combined both democracy and sound business management: a utility commission held open hearings for citizen comment while employing quantitative data to gear rates to agreed-upon rates of return. Moreover, an appointed commission was likely to be a good compromise between elected bodies setting rates and the utilities having full freedom to do so. Of course, some Progressives in cities charted their own unique course. Such was the case of Tom Loftin Johnson (1854–1911), mayor of Cleveland, who was a successful steel manufacturer in his early days. When he became mayor in 1901, Johnson vigorously pursued improvements in the city's street-railway system and campaigned for less state control over Ohio's municipalities. At the same time, Johnson went around the city pitching a tent and inviting citizens to come talk to him as well as listen to his ideas about making the lake city the best place in the nation to live.

A good example of business pursuing prudent, middle-of-the-way reform on a state level was through workmen's compensation legislation, adopted by forty-three states and the federal government from 1900 to 1920. The problem was not only the rise of industrial accidents as a result of dangerous machinery but the common law and legal system that worked harm to the injured employee through the time delays and to the employer through liability for potentially large damages. Private insurance was costly and then provided only a small portion of the actual cost of injuries. A workmen's compensation law enacted by the state legislature appeared the best alternative. For one reason, it became compulsory for all employers and workers. They could reject the system but at the loss of their rights to use traditional legal defenses or sue in court. Second, compensation was substituted for liability, which meant an emphasis on the lesser of two burdens. Third, the system was a state-supervised insurance scheme that induced safety through the lower premiums charged the accident-free employer. As summarized by a University of Chicago law professor at the time of Illinois' passage of one of the first state laws, workmen's compensation brought forth

social solidarity. The nexus of employer and employee in a common understanding, the inevitable risk of accident and the apportionment of loss through a system of measured benefits not aiming to give full indemnity—these are the elements of solidarity which

are entirely absent from the common law principle of liability.
. . . Workmen's compensation carries no stigma or disability, and
by its conditions or terms rather seems to be in the nature of the
discharge of a debt that the community owes to its members, a
deferred payment for previously inadequately rewarded service, or
a compensation for some kind of injustice suffered.

Businessmen were involved in Progressivism on a national
level. There was substantial business support for food and drug
legislation in 1906, even from the National Association of
Manufacturers, which had a greater tendency to drag feet on
regulatory legislation. Although tariff revision divided businessmen, there was the beginning of a reciprocity movement,
mostly by midwesterners, who effected the National Reciprocity League in 1902. The Federal Reserve Act, which took a year
to negotiate and write, had a little bit for each business group:
for the large banks that wanted a private central bank there was
some concession in the form of Federal Reserve Banks that had
a public-private imprimatur; for members of the American
Bankers Association, mostly opposed to a private central bank,
there was at least some change from the status quo; and for
farmers who hated all banks there was some form of government control through the Federal Reserve Board. The Clayton
Act of 1914 was a helpful reform for businessmen in that it
delineated practices that constituted manifestations of anticom-
petitive practices, and although businessmen were not about to
recognize unionism in these years, the act's provisions exempting labor unions from the injunctive provisions of the Sherman
act, employed in the Pullman strike, seemed fair, given the fact
that labor unions were not intended to be the objects of regulation in the 1890 legislation.

The Federal Trade Commission Act of 1914 also represented
a blend of reform ideas generally acceptable to business. To be
sure, the FTC was not the first arm of government to keep track
of industry. In 1903 the Bureau of Corporations had been established to compile and publish data that would assist the attor-

ney general in determining antitrust suits authorized by the Sherman act. Although such suits became more numerous after 1903, the courts, adopting the Progressive spirit, were less inclined to render strict justice—and for good reason given the unsettling economic effects dissolution could bring. Instead, they began to adhere to a "rule of reason," which suggested that there was a reasonable restraint of trade as well as an unreasonable one. Only the latter was illegal. Some reformers reacted to the court stance by demanding passage of two laws, one that would delineate proscribed monopolistic practices, the other creating an agency that would maintain fair rules of competition among businesses engaged in interstate commerce. By the time these demands were being debated, Woodrow Wilson had entered the White House after beating the third-party attempt of Theodore Roosevelt to win another term. TR's campaign, however, was not without its contagious effects on Wilson. Adopting a reform program identified as the New Nationalism, Roosevelt stressed that big government should rationalize big business. Wilson, on the other hand, adhered to reformism, dubbed the New Freedom, that centered on small economic units as the preferable form of business organization. By 1914, however, Wilson moved in the direction of blending the New Freedom and New Nationalism. The Clayton Act would outlaw certain activities, but it had an escape hatch that the courts had already recognized: the activities had to "substantially lessen competition." The FTC would have teeth—Section 5 empowering the commission to issue cease and desist orders—as well as the likelihood of bleeding gums in that weak commissioners could be appointed to go easy with industry on the matter of fair practices. This scenario occasioned cries of alarm, some reformers worrying about a weasel-like administration of the laws, some conservatives about massive interference with business prerogatives in practices such as advertising. For most businessmen, the situation seemed to reflect as much give-and-take as one could expect, as illustrated by the reaction of the Chamber of Commerce of the United States. "The Commission's value," it said, "would have to be judged on the basis of its future course of action."

Without doubt, Progressivism was not ideal: halfway solutions tend to cure problems only halfway and even less, and economic depression would bring into sharp focus the limits of compromise. But Progressivism muted the cries of radicals, induced the beginnings of employer welfare programs that would lessen the degree and number of labor confrontations, and, most important, would bring about conclusions to strikes that were far different from the ones of the late nineteenth century. An example was the national coal strike called by the United Mine Workers in May 1902. The grievances of miners centered mostly on pay, but their leadership tended to forego the strategies of earlier quests by labor for better wages. Shunning violence, UMW president John Mitchell called for passivity among strikers as well as arbitration. If the arbitrators, said Mitchell, "decide that the average annual wages received by the anthracite miners are sufficient to enable them to live, maintain and educate their families in a manner conformable to established American standards and consistent with American citizenship, we agree to withdraw our claims for higher wages and more equitable conditions of employment, providing that the anthracite mine operators agree to comply with any recommendations the above committee may make affecting the earnings and conditions of labor of their employees." Although Mitchell sounded like a Progressive, the representative of the mine owners, George F. Baer, appeared the antithesis, hard-nosed about breaking the union. As the strike dragged on for several months, cries arose for suppression of the miners a la the earlier labor stoppages. President Theodore Roosevelt took a different tack, inviting both sides to the White House in early October. Although the UMW was eager to arbitrate, the mine owners were not. So TR let the word out that the government would take over the mines—a strategy that induced Baer to accept arbitration. The final settlement was compromise in wage and hour demands but no recognition of the union. Washington had made its mark as an impartial umpire, and Roosevelt illustrated that radical threats could bring about give-and-take solutions. As he said of Baer, "If it wasn't for the high office I hold, I would have taken him by the seat of the breeches and the nape of his neck and chucked him out of that window." Roosevelt's example would not be lost on subsequent presidents and business leaders.

16

MORE
INVENTIVE
GENIUS

A small but interesting device in the aid of business is the slot machine. Early uses appear to have been in telephone booths, on transportation vehicles, and for the sale of small articles, such as chewing gum and candy. Lately the principle has been used in restaurants, soda fountains, cigar stores, breweries, and even in homes. The slot machine is also employed in selling sandwiches, fruit, peanuts, handkerchiefs, stamps, pencils, nameplates, combs, towels and prophylactics. The principle has been applied to scales, musical instruments, mechanical shows, games, museums, shooting galleries, gaming devices, toilets, shoe shining machines and turnstiles. It facilitates speed and is a further step in the mechanization of life, saving labor and bringing a new kind of salesmanship into being. One gasps to think of the possible extensions in the future.

Report of the President's Research Committee
on Recent Social Trends (1933)

Some inventions in the early twentieth century, like the slot machine, were easily adapted by business to American society, but many more took a long time to work out before they became widespread. In fact, one could argue that the major products

204

that Americans enjoy today—from electrical appliances to shower curtains to zippers, venetian blinds, telephones, and mattresses—had to go through several stages of production and marketing before they became household words. And some inventions, like those by Oscar Hammerstein for the tobacco industry, never caught the public's admiration as much as the life-style and public activities of their originator. But that was the varied way of the American business scene—a sort of uniqueness that was at once exhilarating and agonizing for both business and the public.

For example, the tin can went back to 1811, but it took until 1903 to perfect the device, especially to eliminate the danger of solder getting into the canned food. Thomas Edison believed that his phonograph would become a sort of Dictaphone for individuals who lay on their deathbed and needed to effect a will; by the twentieth century this loss leader was transformed into a popular appliance by virtue of the music industry, even adapting to competition from the radio industry in the 1920s.

No industry had a harder time entering the front door of American homes than electricity. Like so many technological forces, electricity was applied to big machinery and the nation's infrastructure—the streetcar system—before directly affecting the home consumer. The problem with electrical usage was stereotypic. Edison, of course, lit up American living rooms with his incandescent bulb after 1879, but the power companies that grew to meet this demand transmitted electricity to homes only at night—when it was needed. The firms simply could not perceive of the home as anything other than a light receptacle; the same was true for the consumer, who for decades would refer to the monthly charge as a "light" bill. One utility worker, Earl H. Richardson of Ontario, California, was determined to bring more good electrical appliances to life, especially after talking to housewives during a monthly tour of reading meters.

Not surprisingly, he found that their primary complaint was ironing, which was then done with implements that rivaled industrial machinery in terms of weight.

So Richardson invented an electric iron in 1903 and persuaded his power company to provide current to homes during the day on Tuesday, which was the usual time for ironing after the Monday wash. The only problem was that Richardson's iron was a real scorcher. Its heat was confined to the center, which led to holey finished garments. Richardson went back to the drawing board, sweated the details, and came back with a model that provided for heat at the tips: Hotpoint, as it was dubbed, helped to stir consumer interest in the electric iron. But there were still other problems. Electricity, other than perhaps in lighting, was perceived by many Americans to be synonymous with electrocution; newspapers of the day gave no little space to the gory details concerning accident victims. Then there was competition from gas irons; in fact, by 1904 a Baltimore firm, the Bolgiano Manufacturing Company, was a leader in their production. Most of all, electric irons were in dire need of additional improvements, especially in cords that burned because of the constant heat. The development of the automatic thermostat came about in the 1920s but went unnoticed as inventors hoped to extinguish burnout by devising a cordless iron. The attraction of an electric iron that was preheated, then unplugged during the ironing period, was enormous, as reflected by the logic of one advertisement:

No annoying cord to tangle and pull and get in your way!

No cord or plug breakage!

Fire hazard reduced to a minimum.

Plenty of heat during the entire iron period!

But keeping heat for more than a few minutes was a big obstacle that cordless irons could not overcome. By the 1930s the automatic thermostat put the cordless iron on the back burner. So too did the development of the steam iron, which became a sort of practical tool for certain clothes as well as a fire extinguisher. Steam-o-Matic was a popular model: rustproof, all aluminum, 3½ pounds, and a $9.95 price tag in 1938. Before World War II manufacturers of steam irons were in hot pursuit of one another, with Steam King competing against the Challenger as well as the Steam Queen. And in subsequent decades they would take on one another in terms of devising the most holes in their steam models, reducing the weight, and assuring easier maintenance.

To be sure, no electric iron was of much use unless the ironing board kept pace with it. The original ironing board was just that: a board or plank placed between a table and another piece of furniture. By the turn of the twentieth century, some manufacturers, specializing in ladders for the most part, came up with four-legged wooden versions that could be taken apart. But that was the rub, as was the fact that they tended to wiggle. By 1914 an inventor got a leg up on the competition by constructing a three-legged ironing board that was guaranteed not to "wiggle, wobble, jiggle, slip, or slide." Within a few decades such a model became widespread, with manufacturers concentrating on refinements ranging from metal construction to height adjustments.

Electric toasters ran a course not dissimilar from that of irons. The first toasters, like the first irons, were hardly conveniences: they were forks placed over a fireplace. By the sixteenth century in England, toasted bread was being added to drinks (which would give a double meaning to the phrase "to toast"). And then toasters began to look like a flat, wrought-iron contraption, made by blacksmiths in the Old World and America. Because of the fireplace's unpredictable flame, toasted bread had a hard time finding a warm place in the home. With the spread of wood and coal stoves in the nineteenth century, however, inventors began to devise appliances that could utilize the heat from stove tops. Made mostly of tin and wire, the toasters resembled a lid with four sides, each of which held a slice of bread. In the center was a pyramid of metal designed to direct the heat. The maker of one model boasted that all four slices could be toasted in two minutes. Others fitted directly over the vented area, serving as stove-top stuffers. When electricity entered the home in the early twentieth century, the toaster began to take on a new glow, after, of course, the iron broke a little of the path of consumer resistance. The major problem of the early electric toaster was that the product's open coils could burn fingers as well as bread. General Electric's Radiant Toaster of 1912 stressed points other than safety: "On a severe life test one G-E toaster remained in perfect working order for 13,865 hours. The toaster—making 10 slices of toast for every breakfast—would have lasted one family over 225 years. It was a regular stock toaster."

By 1922 Estate Electric Toaster of Hamilton, Ohio, came out with a four-winged device capable of making as many slices. "One movement of the lever knob to right or left turns over all four racks. Turns them positively—no jamming or sticking," according to one ad. With improved safety came the problem of knowing just when to turn the knob to prevent burnout. Two inventors raced to come up with a better idea. D. A. Rogers of Minneapolis constructed a model in the 1920s that featured a dial which automatically cut the toaster off after a certain period of time. Another Minnesotan, Charles Strite, devised a pop-up toaster that was totally automatic—"perfect toast every time without watching, without turning, without burning." Intended primarily for commercial use, Strite's toaster was eventually dubbed Toastmaster, with his firm taken over by the McGraw Edison Company. Advertising was a critical part of the task of promoting Toastmaster for home use, for the mechanism looked complicated. "First, you drop a slice of bread into the oven slot," read a 1927 ad. "Second, you press down the two levers. This automatically turns on the current and sets the timing device. Third, Pop! up comes the toast automatically when it's done, and the current is automatically turned off." Other manufacturers got into the automatic toaster business, producing models that rang bells and even brewed coffee. But the biggest need was to fine-tune the toaster so as to ensure the precise color and doneness the consumer wanted. Preheating the toaster was sometimes recommended, as was keeping bread in a dry place to reduce moisture content that would foul up the toasting time. As better sensors were devised in the 1930s, manufacturers next looked to making the toaster as quiet as possible and to reducing size. The Chicago Electric Company in 1935 came up with a streamlined version guaranteed to make customers "stop, look, and loosen." Ironically, as time went on, the toaster reverted to a bigger size and sound: in 1956, for instance, GE came out with an oven-type toaster that was first introduced in 1922 by the Best Stove and Stamping Company of Detroit. GE's Toast-R-Oven would be just right for the emerging singles and small-family generation wanting to combine several cooking functions into one.

Perhaps the most controversial of all electrical gadgets was the refrigerator. In fact, the idea of a mechanical icebox that kept foods frozen or stored at cold temperatures encountered enormous consumer resistance. Although refrigeration was well developed by 1900, only a few homes boasted fridges by 1920. Industry sales totaled only 75,000 by 1925, which meant that most American homes favored the natural ice delivered by the iceman, even though it suffered from meltdown. Of course, refrigeration went back a long way—to at least March 1626 when Sir Francis Bacon left his coach in search of ice to keep a dead bird cold—an experiment of dubious value since Sir Francis caught a chill that led to his death. Nearly 250 years later, American Nelson Morris shipped frozen meats from Chicago to Boston in a regular railroad car, but then an inventor gave businessman Gustavus Swift another idea: a refrigerated railroad car. Swift gave his bright yellow and white cars great-sounding names ("Tropical Refrigeration Express," "California Fruit Transportation"), but he had a difficult time convincing consumers that refrigerated food was good. By the early twentieth century, the debate over "cold storage food" was on. An electric show in New York's Madison Square Garden in December 1905 featured an electric fridge; it was a bomb. Four years later a *New York Times Magazine* article written by a Brooklyn physician noted that frozen vegetables "look perfectly like the real thing. They taste something like the real thing. But believe me, son, the vital energy that keeps us alive is not in them." Even refrigerated fruits got a thumbs-down assessment from the doctor. "A diet of cold storage fruit would delight your palate and starve you to death."

Government officials, such as the head of the chemical bureau of the Department of Agriculture, tried to steer a middle course through the controversy. Dr. Harvey W. Wiley conceded that some items such as meat could be frozen for a limited time, but he was suspicious of cold storage plants that put away items for months on end. "I often wonder," he said in an interview, "what they do with the things they put in cold storage, and what the cold storage rooms are for anyway?" State legislatures objected to frozen food warehouses for two reasons. First, they feared that food costs would rise as plants purposely withheld produce and meat; second, they firmly believed that refrigerated items were a health menace. Even when the latter notion was disproved by scientific evidence, state and local laws still required the use of the words *cold stored* or *frozen* on all such goods. Moreover, it did not matter whether the food had been stored for an hour or six days. "It shall be a violation of the provision of this article," read a New York statute, "to sell any article or articles of food that have been kept in cold storage without representing the same to have been so kept." By the 1930s, the cold shoulder that Americans had given to the fridge was easing, but it was not until the post–World War II era that the industry was able to take off.

One other illustration of an electrical appliance that got its cord caught in the American home was the vacuum cleaner, the idea of James Murray Spangler, who came up with the idea in 1907. Spangler, who worked as a janitor in an office building in Canton, Ohio, found that carpet sweeping each night nearly did him in. The dust caused him to cough and wheeze so violently that flaking out was not hard to do. So one night Spangler put an electric fan motor on an old soap box, attached a brush and a pillowcase, and voilà, he had built a better dust trap. Although he received a patent on the device and began distribution, no one beat a path to his door. But Spangler sold them, catch-as-catch-can, to his friends and relatives, including Mrs. William H. Hoover, a cousin who also lived in Canton. Mr. Hoover was in the tannery business at the time; in fact, he employed over 200 men in the making of such items as horse collars and harnesses. He obviously had a lot of horse sense because, after examining Spangler's contraption, he thought he could lead it to customers and make them buy. Exit Spangler and enter Hoover, who hoped his new feedbag would be the Hoover Suction Cleaner. But the name was scarcely a come-on, so Hoover in 1908 changed it to the Electric Suction Sweeper Company. Still a tongue twister, the name became the Hoover Suction Sweeper Company in 1910. By 1922 Hoover was forced to sweep the wordy mess under the rug and call his firm The Hoover Company.

Hoover's cleaner cost only 3¢ of electricity each week in 1909, but the initial outlay for the machine was a lot—$70, with attachments an extra $15. No matter. Hoover's advertising was extensive and even offered a free trial. By 1919 the beater bar was being touted, as well as house-to-house selling, complete with demonstrations of the cleaner's effectiveness. As for Hoover's tannery business, well, it bit the dust. However, there were numerous competitors, including a Swedish cylinder-type model brought to America in 1924 under the hard-to-pronounce name of Aktiebolaget Electrolux. And there were American firms that first produced electric hair dryers and vibrators before going to the mat with a vacuum cleaner. Although Spangler and Hoover got much of the credit for the development of the American model, there was an inventor who entered the sweep stakes even before they did. That was Ira H. Spencer, who in 1905 devised a turbine vacuum cleaner or central cleaning system. Spencer urged that buildings and homes be installed with ducts for taking dust from each room to a central bin in the basement. Within a few years, he was making $2 million annually from office buildings that adopted his system. But the application of his theory to private homes was not widespread, although there were various companies that arose which offered portable cleaning based on the same principle. A horse-drawn, and later motor-driven, van replete with long hoses and suction units would encamp outside a house, emitting loud noises that somehow suggested that a whole lot of cleaning was going on. These dust busters would soon fade from the scene, but the duct makers would return several decades later, preventing manufacturers like Hoover and Electrolux from making a clean sweep of the market. Not surprisingly, broom manufacturers were not about to let competition from the vacuum cleaner industry do them in. A 1919 issue of *House Furnishing Review* bristled with their rationale to keep a part of the household turf:

> The medical profession, in numerous instances, advises women to take up housework, especially sweeping, to offset their ills. Sweeping is exercise of a highly beneficial nature, and therein lies a fertile field for the writer of advertising. . . . By educational copy the home maker will have the opportunity of knowing that she can 'Sweep and still be sweet.'

Sometimes the products of American business in the early twentieth century were diminished by peripheral problems. Such was the case for the shower bath. Of course, the bathtub became common early on in America, as illustrated by the 1897 Sears, Roebuck catalog, which advertised a six-foot model with tin sides and a wooden bottom, weighing fifty pounds and costing $5. By the turn of the century, bath sprays were introduced, permitting the users to sit in a tub and spray themselves with water from the faucet. One model produced by a Brooklyn firm in 1909 was a bit more advanced, complete with a faucet chain, "the only practical attachment ever made for preventing the strongest pressure of water from forcing the bulb off the faucet." The modern shower faucet attached to the top of a bathtub typified some homes by the 1920s, but the problem that would plague users for years was the shower curtain. The first curtains were made of a heavy canvas material called white duck, which was basically used for feedbags for horses. Not only was the fabric heavy and unattractive, but it also mildewed in nanoseconds and provided unpleasant odors that were unconditionally guaranteed to last. Other materials were tested, such as rubberized cotton mattress ticking, which could be spruced up in design but not in the elimination of the bad qualities that plagued white duck. What was worse, rubber cracked and peeled.

By the late 20s, a lacquer-type substance was put on curtain fabrics, but the result was heavy and did not stand up to repeated use. Then, by 1932, oiled silk became the rage. The process was developed in the electrical industry, which used oil and varnish to waterproof cables. Silk ensured that the curtain would be lightweight. An advertisement touting General Electric's oiled silk referred to a secret process that made the shower curtain "strong, durable, waterproof, transparent, light in weight. It can be dry cleaned or laundered, will not stick, crack, harden or get lumpy in any weather. This fabric contains no rubber and will not deteriorate with age." Like previous curtains, however, oiled silk could not stand the test of time, producing bad odors and a sticky quality that made a shower a real bath. Within a decade researchers recognized that the ideal shower curtain had to stand up to sunlight, hot water, soap, and the residual moisture in the bathroom. And it had to be affordable. Oiled silk met this last characteristic, as low as $2. Around 1938, the B. F. Goodrich Company came up with a better product, a vinyl film called Koroseal. It could stand alone without attachment to a fabric and could be made into various thicknesses, still retaining its light weight. The biggest problem with vinyl, however, was that nothing stuck to it, not even ink. So all kinds of research went into developing a technique to embellish the vinyl with various designs. By the early 1950s, the goal had been reached, and "fashion" shower curtains became widespread. "Let the water fall where it may," read a 1952 Lord & Taylor ad, "as long as it hits Koroseal shower curtains! Designed by Florence Isles, in a wide array of wonderful patterns and colors. $3.95 to $12.95."

Earlier B. F. Goodrich had given a name to overshoes containing hookless fasteners. "Zip 'er up," the slogan for the galoshes coined by Goodrich's president in 1923, would still not make the "zipper" a household word until the Great Depression. In fact, the zipper had struggled for a tiny hold on America from the 1890s when Whitcomb L. Judson of Chicago got fed up with using hooks and eyes and buttons to keep his clothing attached and came up with what he dubbed a slide fastener. At the 1893 World's Fair in his hometown, Judson exhibited his invention. One Lewis Walker saw the Chicago exhibit and was convinced that Judson had no fly-by-night product. A lawyer, Walker knew the business world, having sixteen companies as his clients before he was thirty-one years old. With Judson's cooperation, Walker organized the Universal Fastener Company to manufacture the zipper. The company started out in Chicago, then moved to Elyria, Ohio; Catasauqua, Pennsylvania; and Hoboken, New Jersey. After so many moves it deserved a new name and got it: the Automatic Hook and Eye Company. By this time in the early twentieth century, Judson had exited and Walker was left holding a product that was receiving a mixed public reception. Sure, the slide fastener worked but not all the time, popping loose when it should have stayed closed and vice versa. Enter one Gideon Sundback in 1906, a Swedish engineer who worked on large dynamos for Westinghouse. The small slide fastener caught his inventive eye. Joining with Walker, he spent years working on the gadget, finally devising an improved product by 1913. It was called Talon and the firm became the Hookless Fastener Company, which like its product was always on the move—this time to Meadville, Pennsylvania. Then in 1937 HFC became Talon, Inc. By this time all the kinks had been taken out of the zipper, and Americans very cautiously began to use the device. For example, a Brooklyn tailor used the fastener on some money belts, the Navy on flying suits. Most important, a dress manufacturer, to prop up sagging sales in the Great Depression, made the zipper a gimmick that soon became a mark of fashion. By 1938 Talon was on its way to becoming a household word.

The Great Depression did the same thing to venetian blinds, which had been around for over 400 years by the time Franklin D. Roosevelt became president in 1933. The Japanese beat the Venetians to the punch in terms of the original blinds, using bamboo rods, but the Venetians got the credit, especially in America where the name and usage were evident as far back as colonial times. St. Peter's Church, at Third and Pine Streets in Philadelphia, had venetian blinds installed in 1761. Nine years later the *Virginia Gazette* carried an advertisement from carpenter Joshua Kendall who claimed to make "the best and newest invented Venetian sun blinds for windows, that move to any position so as to give different lights. They screen from the scorching rays of the sun, draw up as a curtain, prevent being overlooked, give a cool refreshing air in hot weather, and are the greatest preservatives of furniture of any thing ever invented." Actually, the colonial version was strikingly similar to modern venetian blinds: it had tapes and cords that were used to adjust the wooden slats. And about the only refinement in technology came on August 21, 1841, when John Hampson of New Orleans was awarded Patent No. 2,223 for his "Manner of retaining in any desired position the slats of Venetian Blinds."

Yet venetian blinds were expensive for the average American homeowner. By the turn of the twentieth century, Kirsch Manufacturing Company of Sturgis, Michigan, turned away from blinds to concentrate on making flat, extension curtain rods. Venetian blinds would not see their heyday until the 1930s —odd, given their high prices and the hard times of the decade. In 1934, for example, Kirsch was making wooden venetian blinds; two years later, it turned out a metal version, with aluminum slats. Most models produced in the 1930s were made of basswood and cedar, and the color range was as wide as the spectrum. All models had chromium ornamental tassels; a few were made with tin. In New York City alone, $210 million worth of venetian blinds went on the market in a single year, 1936. They were used almost everywhere—over skylights and bathroom shelves, between booths in restaurants, even as wall decorations. "Most people are bored, and they like things they have to 'adjust,'" wrote Margaret Russell in *The New York Times Magazine* that year, trying to explain why blinds had grown so popular among the rich. "You can't get much fun out of a window shade. All you can do is to pull it down or pull it up. If you shoot it up and let it spin it loses its snap." Venetian blinds, on the other hand, gave people a new slant on life. "You can pull cords on it all day," Russell continued. "You can spend hours just trying to decide which way to tilt the slats. And if you let them fall suddenly they make a nice shivery sound. If you're out on the street you can play peek-a-boo with people inside. And at night if you look at a window and the light is on and the slats aren't quite closed you can see everything in the room through dots—it looks like a pointillist painting." Of course, after World War II, the venetian blind would become democratized in price and style and toned down to conservative hues.

The telephone had a much easier time catching hold of the American consumer. By 1933, the Committee on Recent Social Trends indicated that the number of phones

testify to the permeation of the nation by a new agency, and indicate its acceptance, not as a luxury or a desirable convenience, but as a necessity. The disadvantages of not having the telephone close at hand are so great that it is installed even where the total number of calls may be relatively few. The telephone directory has assumed importance as a city directory, and is useful in establishing contact. To be without a telephone or a telephone listing is to suffer a curious social isolation in a telephonic age.

As early as 1884 when American Bell Telephone, a Massachusetts chartered corporation, held its fourth annual meeting, it reported that its balance sheet cracked the $2 million barrier in terms of net earnings. "The session," according to one newspaper account, "was harmonious." To be sure, the session was harmonious for other reasons. Ma Bell was well on its way to winning every one of the more than 600 lawsuits that would be filed against it in its first decade for patent infringement, including some that had the makings of a good melodrama, such as that of Antonio Meucci. In 1857, Meucci, a candlemaker and brewer from Staten Island, effected sound through a tight wire connected to two cans, but the courts were unconvinced that he could reach out very far and touch someone. Bell was making money hand over fist because its rates were as high as satellites and did not decline significantly for a number of years. Annual charges ranged from $150 to $240 based upon 1,000 or 2,500 message units, and business was increasing at a good rate. But the service was not good. In fact, in the 1880s the electric light and trolley systems in major cities caused static on the lines as a result of the phenomenon known as electrical induction. Worse still was a good old-fashioned thunderclap, which made the sounds on the lines downright scary.

Next, Bell was getting its way with regard to planting telephone poles all over major cities, leading to veritable dark forests, thanks to the dozens of wires strung horizontally from pole to pole. New York legislators got so uptight about the matter that they passed a law in 1884 requiring underground wires in big cities. Bell claimed it did not have the technical know-how to do the job, and the law was put on hold in 1885. Three years later when the Great March Blizzard made its way up the East Coast, wires were draped all over the Big Apple, as well as New England cities. As a result, Bell's technical knowledge about underground wires was stirred up in the next few years. Lastly, Bell was doing its thing with regard to employees. When it first opened shop, it employed teenage boys as operators. The lads appeared to be perfect, for their tasks required speed and coordination as well as strength (they also served as janitors) and stick-to-itiveness (they collected fees from subscribers). However, teenage boys were not always pleasant, and their voices had a tendency to change or get hoarse. The boys were also mischievous at times. So Bell turned to teenage girls who were not only more courteous but less expensive, starting out at $10 a month, well below the rate for male employees. What is more, the prospect of female operators was even getting an intellectual defense by March 1884, as illustrated by one newspaper's commentary: "The aspect of a telephone office is curious enough to an outsider. A number of young girls sitting before a cupboard-like structure into the apertures of which they are busily chattering, holding in the meanwhile an instrument like an ear trumpet to their heads, would appear ridiculous enough were it not well known how indispensable the telephone has become to civilization." Bell did have one major setback in these years. As a Massachusetts corporation, it had to abide by the state's severe restrictions on growth, including the provision that the state legislature had to approve increases in the firm's capitalization. But Bell found a circuit breaker of sorts: a long-distance subsidiary that it had formed in the less-regulated New York State would simply take over the assets of American Bell. So on December 30, 1899, the company left Boston for New York City, assuming the name of its parent, American Telephone and Telegraph. By January 1, 1984, Bell's story would come full circuit—with its breakup from AT&T—and thus have a familiar ring.

Some business products in the early twentieth century were the objects of public hysteria in terms of health matters. A case in point was the mattress industry, which became subject to

Public Law 489 of the Sixty-ninth Congress in 1926. The major concern of the "mattress law" was contagious disease: "No person in the District of Columbia who is a renovator of mattresses shall use in whole or in part, in the renovation of any mattress, material which has formed part of any mattress theretofore used in and about any sanitarium or hospital, or used by any individual having an infectious or contagious disease." According to the act, secondhand material could not be used in mattresslike furniture unless it had been sterilized and disinfected. States also rushed to pass similar legislation, and Minnesota's law was even more detailed in its stipulations of approved sterilization procedures, which ran the gamut from dry heat to live steam to sulfur and formaldehyde processes. Even the sterilization room had to be somewhat akin to an operating room. "The moist atmosphere shall be produced by thoroughly sprinkling the floor of the room with warm water just prior to the process of disinfection. The room shall be provided with a separate air inlet and an exhaust connection, and shall be equipped with tight dampers or closure gates which can be operated from outside of the room." Both the Minnesota and federal laws provided penalties including fines and imprisonment, with the former statute more severe in its definition of a violation: "Any person who shall remove, deface, alter, or shall cause to be removed, defaced, or altered any label or tag upon the article of bedding so labeled or tagged under the provisions of this act, shall be guilty of a violation thereof." Ironically, even to this day, upholstered furniture and bedding carry a tag referencing those original laws and stipulating that "under penalty of law this tag not to be removed except by consumer."

The early twentieth century gave rise to inventions that were as outstanding as their originators were distinctive in life-styles. In 1913 the invention of a machine that utilized the tobacco stem as well as leaf in the making of cigars was a major breakthrough in the industry, leading to inexpensive cigars. The machine also provided its inventor, Oscar Hammerstein, with the opportunity to blend business success with a revolution in the arts. Hammerstein was the grandfather of the lyricist who would scintillate the musical world in the mid-twentieth century with such hits as *Show Boat, Oklahoma!,* and *South Pacific.* Like so many other American success sagas, Hammerstein's began as an immigrant, running away from his Berlin home during the American Civil War. He had $2 in his pocket, his passage financed by selling his violin for $35. Jobs in the cigar industry in New York City were plentiful at the time, thanks to rush orders from soldiers and the lack of technology. And so young Hammerstein entered the field, within months creating a name for himself by devising the first of nearly a hundred machines that would transform cigar making. Later he would edit the *United States Tobacco Journal.* To be sure, Hammerstein's inventions brought forth no little money, but they were merely conduits to his great love, music. By the time of his death in 1919, he had distinguished himself as one of the great theatrical and operatic managers in the nation. His artistic dreams were daring: to provide grand opera in English at popular prices. He opened at one time or another seven opera or music halls in New York. He also started one in Philadelphia. He wrote operas—one of which was staged in forty-eight hours as a result of a wager. And between his composing and impresario activities, he retired to a small workshop across the hall from his office on West Forty-second Street to tinker with the machinery that would incite his inventive mind and permit him to continue his musical ambitions.

Although his artistic funds were ample, the same could not be said for the public's patronage. Oversupply-side economics characterized the state of the arts, and opera houses in particular had a short life span. Hammerstein's most enterprising act of taking on the big boy, the Metropolitan Opera, in 1906 was rewarded only by a short-lived spotlight dimmed by the Met's takeover and Hammerstein's agreeing not to open another opera house in the city before 1920. Undaunted, he went abroad where he established the London Opera House, then returned to New York and built the American Opera House, the use of which was restricted by the courts. Making and losing fortunes never seemed to dampen Hammerstein's spirits. A striking figure seldom seen without a high hat and a black cigar, he once summarized the ecstasy and agony of an inventor/artist who could not revolutionize all of his worlds: "I've had the ideas but I've worked harder . . . just getting them than most men do in the course of a whole lifetime, to say nothing of putting them into execution. I have guarded my health zealously. I live a life of incredible simplicity—I never drink and I smoke only 25 cigars a day. Don't think in telling you this that I'm boasting of my qualifications for a proscenium-box seat above, for I have no immediate desire to leave my life of usefulness here to go to heaven, where there is sure to be a chorus which I have not selected, like as not with wings, too."

When Hammerstein unveiled for the public his revolutionary tobacco machine in the spring of 1913, it was at an unconventional yet symbolic location: the roof of his Victoria theater.

17

BUSINESS
AND
GOVERNMENT:
THE 1930s

The reaction of Americans in general and businessmen in particular to the Great Depression was similar by 1932. Some Americans decided to put an end to it all—New York City experienced the highest suicide rate in twenty-five years. Numerous businessmen decided to close up shop as evidenced by the 31,822 commercial and industrial failures in 1932, also a record. Most Americans pursued a policy of retrenchment; they cut out unnecessary fringes ranging from the telephone to coffee. Some items Americans regarded as indispensable, such as gasoline, canned milk, radios, electric refrigerators, and cigarettes, held steady or increased during the Depression decade. Most businessmen tried to cut back production and prices. Zenith cut the price of one of its popular radio models from $135 in 1931 to $78.75 in 1932. The Pullman Company offered a 20 percent discount on upper berths, and drug companies capitalized on the lethargy, frustration, and disillusionment of the populace to market their wares. "Don't be a victim of ASTHENIA," warned one advertisement. "Don't think just because you're *regular* that you are *immune*. Physicians will tell you that daily elimination not only must be *'regular'* . . . it must be *complete.*" Mail-order businesses focused around the selling of inexpensive products designed to "defeat" or "relieve" Depression blues also reflected the adaptability of American business. Manufacturers of men's clothing took cognizance of the declining sales of traditional styles and eliminated such nonessentials as garters, vests, and bathing suit tops. Easily assembled frocks illustrated economy in women's fashions. Of course, retrenchment was obvious in the securities business: the Dow Jones average reached its nadir in 1932 and sales were one third the 1929 volume.

The recorded business failures of 1932 were offset by the increase in the number of unrecorded businesses. Unemployed citizens and marketing agents combined to bring forth hordes of independent salesmen on city streets and country roads. The apple-selling idea, introduced by the Pacific Coast Apple Growers, caught the fancy of the unemployed in big cities. Shoe shining was especially attractive to those who felt the shine kit a more permanent investment than prone-to-rot apples. In June 1932, New York City's police department estimated the number of shoe shiners at 7,000. In one block, nineteen were counted. Vegetable hawkers did not invade Wall Street in 1932, but they moved into neighborhoods where they had been unknown. Even newsboys displayed business ingenuity. "Selling Sunday papers has become a science," read a contemporary account. "Youngsters have found that it is extremely profitable to invade apartment houses between 11 and 12 o'clock Sunday morning, knock on each apartment door, and offer the Sunday editions. Their profits are usually between $1.50 and $2.00." To be sure, the increase in the number of small entrepreneurs aggravated the spiraling business scene, especially among food retailers. It was easy for a vendor to get a shop and merchandise on credit, live therein, and then at the end of the month sell at whatever low prices were necessary in order to pay a little on his rent and inventory. To prudent businessmen, this scenario led to what was at the heart of the economic debacle and what had been a problem for years: overcompetition, overproduction, and falling prices. The cure to the dilemma was obvious to some business leaders: the cartelization of American industry, that is, the easing of antitrust laws and permitting businesses to regulate production, marketing, and pricing of their commodities either on a geographical or industrywide basis or on both. The idea was neither new nor revolutionary. During World War I businesses had been permitted to organize in this fashion under the aegis of the War Industries Board. They were encouraged to eliminate waste, standardize products, fix prices, and maintain production quotas. American industry achieved unheard-of heights of success under the WIB: shoe styles, automobile wheel sizes were reduced; efficiency was almost robotlike as salesmen were permitted only so many trunks, elevators only so many ups and downs. And enough steel was saved each month in the making of women's corsets to build many an American tank. In sum, perceptive businessmen who advanced the WIB model provided a key ingredient, the rationalization of the American economy, that would aid in the easing of the Great Depression; thus, for a while, their relationship with government was a partnership. That this accommodation would come apart by the mid-1930s is testimony to many conflicts, but it also underscores the fact that the business approach to bringing about recovery worked—especially for business.

One of the leading advocates of the WIB approach to defeat the Depression was Gerard Swope of General Electric. When the downturn of 1929 lasted longer than the one year he had predicted, Swope announced an unemployment program for the 75,000 GE employees. Under his plan workers and the company would contribute equally to an emergency fund—with management contributing its share during the hard times when it was most needed. At the same time Swope attempted to eliminate production practices that would result in an excessive number of styles or models. In one department of GE, the implementation of the unemployment plan, coupled with elimination of certain styles of light bulbs, resulted in a guarantee of fifty weeks of work in 1931 for employees with at least two years' service. In a speech before the National Electrical Manufacturers Association in September 1931, Swope outlined his proposal for national legislation resurrecting the WIB model. He called for relaxation of the antitrust laws; industries with fifty or more workers would be urged to form trade associations for the purpose of fixing prices, trade practices, and accounting procedures. Federal supervision in the form of a national economic counsel was provided for. Swope also recommended that a national workmen's compensation scheme be implemented and that the trade associations provide for a benefits package for employees similar to that which GE had adopted, with both employer and employee contributions. Within a month after Swope's speech, the Committee on Continuity of Business and Employment of the Chamber of Commerce of the United States, chaired by Henry I. Harriman, came out with a scheme similar to what was now being called the Swope Plan. Harriman was the New England Power Company's counterpart to GE's president. And like his colleague at GE, he was an articulate spokesman for a more planned business world. Writing in the *American Economic Review* a few months later, Harriman outlined the philosophy behind "The Stabilization of Business and Employment." No Malthusian, he believed that American society had reached a population level that would not expand greatly in years to come. A stabilized society could not exist under the old game rules of competition and struggle, at least not without adversity to the general welfare. By dividing the market on an equitable basis among the various units, prosperity and fair play would result. Although Harriman differed with Swope on minor details, the planned economy idea caught fire among businessmen in the early months of 1932, even though President Hoover believed the proposal to be unconstitutional. The election of Franklin D. Roosevelt, however, brought the matter to the White House again.

In fact, in an address before the annual convention of the Chamber of Commerce of the United States in May 1933, FDR

MADE IN THE U.S.A.

promised that the federal government would assist businessmen in eliminating abuses that had led to the economic crisis. A few days later the president delivered his second fireside chat in which he referred to industrial recovery in terms of a "partnership in planning, and a partnership to see that the plans are carried out." In mid-May, the National Industrial Recovery bill was sent by Roosevelt to Congress. It became law a month later and was basically in line with the Swope-Harriman plan. Although the latter included a host of benefits ranging from unemployment insurance to workmen's compensation, the NIRA focused instead on essentials: the elimination of industrial abuses through codes devised by trade associations. These codes would center on "fair competition," that is, the eradication of cutthroat competition and bad labor practices through fair-trade prices, production, and wage-hour practices. The codes would attempt to blend what industry and labor wanted. And both groups may have gotten more than they had reckoned on. Section 7(a) of the act affirmed the right of employees to organize and bargain collectively, and as far as business was concerned, the law provided almost total exemption from the antitrust laws. Moreover, although the president had to approve each code and, in the event of disagreement within a trade association, could impose a code, the bureaucratic red tape was cut a month after the bill's passage: a blanket code was created dealing with prohibition of child labor, payment of a fixed minimum wage, adherence to a maximum hours schedule, and the avoidance of price increases. The implementation of the recovery bill involved no great outlay of government funds; the National Recovery Administration operating out of a few rooms in the Commerce building would assist business units in writing codes. Except for Section 7(a), the NIRA was no radical or unexpected pill for businessmen to swallow.

Under NIRA administrator Hugh Johnson, who played a key role in the WIB experiment, the recovery program was widely publicized to businessmen and the public. Thanks to Johnson's initiative, labor leaders, notable business leaders, and actors such as Al Jolson took part in parades that led presidential advisor Raymond Moley to remark that "nothing like this, short of war, has been seen in any nation since Peter the Hermit and others incited the Crusades." It was Johnson who devised the Blue Eagle as a symbol of compliance with NIRA codes—the eagle decorated the windows of businessmen and the products they sold. So caught up were Americans with the eagle symbol that a Philadelphia professional football team that was emerging at the time took the bird's name. Businessmen appeared as enthusiastic as Johnson in the NIRA drive, as illustrated by a Wanamaker advertisement:

FORWARD! AMERICA!

Wanamaker's "Partnership" Sales Help the Quick-step. Industry is moving forward—manufacturers, distributors, workers in factories and workers in field.

There's a new note of courage, clear and loud as the call of a bugle, and we are responding to it.

Business is definitely better. Industrial production is increasing. Car loadings are up. Consumption of electricity is greater. The steel and automobile orders are ahead. Retail sales are climbing. Employment is larger.

Here, in these "Partnership" sales, is the Wanamaker contribution to "Forward America."

Businessmen were pleased with the advisory body of industrial executives (there were also consumer and labor boards) that Johnson set up. Commerce Secretary Daniel Roper also obliged businessmen by establishing a forty-one member Business Advisory Council in June 1933. Less than three months after the NIRA had been enacted, Henry I. Harriman characterized the change in America from "fear and discouragement" to "hope." In spite of the problems that businessmen were having in writing and implementing codes that they feared would result in closed shop unions, Harriman called the NIRA and the agricultural recovery bill "sincere and probably effective efforts to coordinate and rationalize American industry along democratic lines and to assure economic security and industrial liberty to employers, employees, and those who work on the farm." While Hugh Johnson in a November speech used a bit of hyperbole in his contention that only 1 percent of the American public opposed the NIRA, there was widespread business support. Even the National Association of Manufacturers, no friend of government entry into the economy, mellowed. Resolutions adopted at its December convention were conciliatory. Its NIRA resolution praised the president's "decisive leadership" and called the recovery law a great measure to restore prosperity, in spite of the "confusion and hardship that were to be anticipated in a period of rapid and decisive change." The resolution went on: "We pledge ourselves to make every rational effort to cooperate in and to test fairly experimental legislation under which industry has been placed by the Congress but we consider it a duty to offer constructive criticism as defects in policy or plans of operation appear or as administrative improvement may be suggested."

To be sure, there were some problems by the autumn of 1933. Oil company executives did not want price fixing; retailers, on the other hand, were ecstatic over the price-fixing mechanism as a means of eliminating cutthroat competition. The National Founders Association, an organization representing metal manufacturers, devoted a convention day to hearing critics of the recovery law but failed to agree on a resolution voicing its discontent. Even the Chamber by November became somewhat disenchanted with the law because of the failure of the codes to distinguish between small-town and big-city industries, the unenforceability of some codes, and the "coercive attitude" of government administrators. Nevertheless, Chamber president Harriman conceded that business was impatient, that "all present opposition . . . is a natural reaction to the unrealized hopes for a speedy and instantaneous recovery." The NIRA was still good legislation, as long as it was "wisely amended and constructively administered." Yet for every criticism of the recovery act, there were numerous businessmen in support, as illustrated by letters written to the White House. A San Francisco executive wrote that "most business men admit the greatness of the new policies, and agree with me in the belief that the administration have made few if any mistakes, which is historical when the great strides taken are considered." Two western businessmen, one a member of the St. Louis Chamber, were so thin-skinned about any criticism of the New Deal, even the few reservations advanced by the national Chamber in November, that they lodged formal protests. And one canceled his membership in the Chamber. Businessmen who traveled widely throughout their states often provided the president with regular reports of business opinion. "I have today made it my business to talk to the business men here in Palestine [Texas]," wrote one attorney. "They all report that business has been a great deal better. . . . I talked to them about President Roosevelt and his policies. Some of them object to the N. R. A. but even though they object to the N. R. A. they are for Roosevelt. Roosevelt is stronger now at the present time than he was when he first went in as President." A small businessman wrote of his distrust of "Big Business" and of his delight with the recovery legislation. "For the first time in a generation, the small and medium business man finds there is a chance that Big Business must play according to the same rules as himself." An importer from New York City was even more ecstatic about business conditions and the New Deal. "We have had more government sponsored social progress in the last six months than in the previous sixty years," he recited with obvious pleasure. Believing that the business outlook was good and commending the president for steering "a middle course between the inflation siren and the standpat fog horn," he prophesied a political transformation of America: "I wonder if you know who would reelect you if ballots were cast today? In the opinion of many you would be reelected by the aid of Republicans who never voted for a Democrat before. . . ."

A Michigan businessman wrote the president that the New

Deal was taking hold in his state in a "wonderful way." The NRA, he confided, was the major topic of conversation at political meetings, picnics, and fraternal outings. "Now my thought is why not have some phonographic records made which could be purchased by clubs, boards of commerce, political associations or others interested in securing full cooperation for the N. R. A. or other programs which you may inaugurate for the welfare of the country." The president's recorded voice would assure the success of any New Deal program, he asserted. Most of all the record and phonograph program could snowball into a really big business:

> A service bureau could be established by local business men in each community, to give or rent the service of the phonograph and the current records, so that they would be of service to the various organizations having meetings. Thousands of persons would want to purchase them for their own home. And any royalty resulting from the sale could be turned over to some form of national welfare.

The idea was not so farfetched. An investment in confidence was a good risk; its dollar value imprecise, it was the most obvious glamour stock of the first year of the New Deal. The unemployment figure had not been substantially reduced, nor had industrial production, prices, and profits made strong forward progress. Confidence could not be measured according to the usual business yardsticks, but it was ever present in 1933— in the form of fireside chats, the Blue Eagle parades and movies, and in the projected phonograph service center scheme of the Michigan businessman. Whether it would continue or be enough to sustain businessmen in subsequent years appeared to be forgotten for the moment.

The business-government cooperation in the NIRA might be considered Act II in the great drama of the 1930s. Scene 1, Act I finds a large crowd of businessmen—from small entrepreneurs to corporate managers—expressing doubts about the inevitability of the return of prosperity in the late summer of 1932. Many admire the dictatorial stance and resultant actions of Benito Mussolini, and a few go so far as to call for the conferring of dictatorial powers on President Hoover. As the scene comes to a close, the businessmen appear baffled, leading an insightful adman to dub Gimbels' 1932 Christmas doll with the name Baffie. The curtain falls as Baffie suggests escapist themes in a baby-talk soliloquy. Scene 2, Act I is short and sweet. Businessmen have rallied around the new Democratic president, who has been the recipient of many of their votes. In fact, 2,000 noted businessmen joined the Roosevelt bandwagon as early as April 1932 when the Roosevelt Business and Professional League was organized through the efforts of Jesse Isidor Straus, president of R. H. Macy and Company. The passage of the National Industrial Recovery Act in 1933 ushered in Act II, which, as noted, represented the continuation of good times between business and FDR. Somewhat given to superstition, Roosevelt may well have seen some ominous signs as 1934 and Act III of the Depression drama unfold. New Year's Day in London is accompanied by the densest fog that the city had experienced in many a year. London bus conductors are forced to walk along the curbs shouting loudly and hopefully guiding drivers who could not see more than a distance of two feet. Four days later, the Loch Ness monster is spotted.

For Roosevelt and his relations with business, 1934 is to be a very bad year: two of his intimate advisers resign—banker Paul Warburg and budget director Lewis Douglas, both popular among businessmen. The passage of the Securities Exchange Act, rifts between business and labor over the implementation of the NIRA, and the attempt to strengthen labor's position in a permanent law outside the NIRA rubric—all bring forth frustration if not hostility from businessmen. Severe criticism of the New Deal dominates the Chamber of Commerce's annual meeting, and some of the members in the autumn declare open season on FDR by founding the American Liberty

League. Act III never seemed to end, especially as the New Deal changed directions in 1935. The planning, cooperative emphasis of the NIRA gave way to the Populist ideals of trust-busting, high taxes, and regulation. And the business crusade against Senator Wagner's labor bill, ultimately passed as the National Labor Relations Act, assumed almost fanatical proportions, with the National Association of Manufacturers' campaign described as "the greatest ever conducted by industry regarding any congressional measure." An undeclared war loomed between FDR and the Chamber of Commerce in 1935, the former breaking precedent by refusing to send a message of greeting to the organization located within shouting distance of the White House, the latter taking advantage of the territorial propinquity by shouting invectives. In a poll of its 1,500 members in September 1935, the Chamber found an anti-New Deal bias by a margin of 35 to 1. The president's overwhelming reelection in 1936 provided only a brief pause in the business–New Deal war. The fate of the Supreme Court-packing plan, the attempted but unsuccessful purge of anti-New Dealers in Congress, the criticism regarding the Works Progress Administration (work relief program), and the long fight over the passage of the Fair Labor Standards Act (minimum wage, maximum hours) revealed that the strength of business conservatives had ebbed the tide if not the flow of New Deal legislation. The drama of business and FDR had a tragic ending. What had started as a happy wedding and productive honeymoon soon became a separation and bitter divorce, a most atypical movie theme for the 1930s.

Yet there was nothing mysterious to the deteriorating state of relations between the business community and the Roosevelt administration after 1934. The most important reason for the widening breach was that businessmen were the first to benefit from the New Deal. Within a year of Roosevelt's inauguration, commercial and industrial failures declined and exports increased. The volume of industrial production and the price of business commodities recorded recognizable increases. With the economy showing signs of health at the top, some business groups naturally reverted to the old-time business creed: government should balance the budget, eliminate regulatory experimentation, cease tampering with the currency, and put its faith in private enterprise to implement the trickle-down theory. Then, too, the president was thin-skinned when it came to criticism from business. Obviously savoring the widespread support from the public at large, FDR shunned meetings with business leaders at critical times. He took their criticism personally rather than from a political perspective (many businessmen were Republicans). After their experience with the Republican administrations of the 1920s, businessmen had come to expect that the chief executive of the land would consult them—no matter whether they were progressives or conservatives—to solicit their advice on economic issues. Given the experimental, unpredictable nature of the New Deal, consultation was not too much to expect. One businessman summed up the feeling of many of his colleagues when he wrote the president: "Last week I wrote to an industrialist in Wisconsin and in my letter I asked, 'Where are we at,' to which he replied, 'You ask "where we are at." I am reminded that some time ago where a group of Democrats were comparing Roosevelt to Washington and Lincoln that they were interrupted by a Republican who said he thought Roosevelt could be more aptly compared to Christopher Columbus, because when he started he did not know where he was going, when he got there he did not know where he was, and when he got back, he did not know where he had been.' "

Of course, Roosevelt was no fool. He believed that businessmen in their national organizations (Chamber of Commerce, NAM), were not representative of Main Street, as illustrated by a press conference in January 1938:

Question: Can you tell us something in advance of your meeting with the businessmen?

The President: I don't know a thing.

Question: Mr. President, speaking of business, do you care to name the minority of businesses that you spoke about in your message?

The President: No, that is a silly question, Fred [Storm].

(Laughter)

Question: Have you identified them in your own mind?

The President: By individuals? No. That is spot news. I am talking about a generic group. Get away from spot news stuff. This is a conception: it is not a question of whether it is 59, 60 or 61 or 160 or 260. But it is a handful compared with the total.

The vast majority of letters sent to Roosevelt voiced support. "You stay right in there, Mr. President," hammered a hardware store owner from Kansas City, "and drive straight to your stake." A lumber company official counseled, "Go on with [the] New Deal—Some may 'cuss' it, but nobody has anything else to offer that is better." "Keep up your courage," advised a Fresno businessman, "and do not compromise with Congress on needed legislation." A good many letters were almost certain to lead the president to stand firm in his relations with the Chamber and NAM. A shoe store owner hoped that his "little letter will in a small way cheer you on and make you feel that your efforts are appreciated." The managing director of a small-town chamber of commerce in Texas who took issue with the "money and selfish" interests of the national organization concluded his missive with a rural postscript: "Just a few lines to let you know the people at the forks of the creek are still with you."

Finally, there was the missive from a tire dealer in Kansas who knew few of the fine points of spelling and grammar but wrote from the heart: "Mr. President, do you know that we never had such a man as you are. For the poor people. Never no never—I never did vote for a Democratic ticket in my life and have been voting for forty nine years. But believe me if I live I will vote for F D Roosevelt, and not only vote for him but will work I am for you from A to Z."

18

WORLD WAR II

American business not only helped to win World War II, but its contribution was more than the sum total of big tanks and bombers. Indeed, the history of that crisis is replete with unheralded advances in new products and inventions that we take for granted today. And even on the home front, business served the public well, utilizing scarce resources and imaginative ideas in such a way as to keep home folk contented. World War II was not only a major war but one of those rarities, a relatively good one, devoid of significant conflicts, thanks to the efforts of private enterprise.

When Adolf Hitler and his Nazi army invaded Poland on September 1, 1939, signaling the start of World War II, two American business products—nylon and aluminum—would help to ensure that Hitler's aggression, as well as that of the Japanese, would ultimately be unsuccessful. Both products seemed unlikely threats to militarism: after thirteen years of research and $27 million, E. I. du Pont de Nemours had 4,000 pairs of nylon stockings as evidence of its hard work by October 1939. Put on sale in six apparel stores in Wilmington, Delaware, every single stocking had been sold by one o'clock, and hundreds of women in long lines were involuntary nonpurchasers. Of course, they could still buy rayon and silk stockings, but these fabrics had little elasticity and were not as soft and long-wearing. Silk, moreover, wrinkled and was expensive. Nor was silk American. It was Japan's main export, with some 90 million pounds, 85 percent of Japan's production, consumed annually in the United States for stockings alone. As diplomatic relations between the two countries deteriorated by the 1930s, the price of silk fluctuated widely, from lows of about $1.50 a pound to nearly $3. After nylon hosiery was introduced, Japanese silk sold for $2.79 a pound as compared with $4.27 for nylon. However, nylon got more competitive as the United States became enmeshed in squabbles with Tokyo.

To be sure, nylon was not perfect for hosiery. It was originally dubbed no-run (no-run spelled backward was nuron, which became nylon). But it was not no-run. Sometimes women who wore nylons in 1939 broke out in a rash, presumably because of a dye. Nylons, like other hosiery of the time, also had a tendency to sag. But nylon seemed to be absolutely perfect for some items, as illustrated by a listing *Business Week* made in 1940: clothing (dress fabrics, raincoats, underwear); webbing; wire insulation; filters; umbrellas; shower curtains; sewing thread; toilet brushes; tennis strings; and surgical sutures. When the nation entered World War II in 1941, nylon found an even better use: first in parachutes which otherwise required Japanese silk. Used nylon hosiery could be sold as scrap to the government, which estimated that one parachute could be made from thirty-six pairs of hose. Betty Grable sold a pair for $40,000 to launch a War Bond campaign. Nylon was also used for "flak vests" that successfully served as shields against shell fragments. Nylon-reinforced tires permitted heavy bombers to land on nonexistent airstrips, and the product made dollar bills last a bit longer during the war, its fibers of silk replaced with nylon by the Treasury in 1941. Most of all, nylon, originally made from water, coal, and air, could be derived even from corncobs, as *Newsweek* reported by war's end. In sum, a nylon product was strong, elastic, mildew-resistant, easy to wash, and quick to dry. It was unattractive to bacteria, fungi, rodents, and insects. And oil and grease were turned off by nylon. All these qualities made it perfect for battlefield conditions.

The same could not be said for aluminum, which had a much harder time finding a place for itself in America. Of course, it was a much older product than nylon, with its history largely identified with one man, Arthur Vining Davis. Born in Sharon, Massachusetts, two years after the end of the Civil War, Davis's early life was undistinguished, although his father served the Boston area as a Congregational minister for over sixty years and his great aunt had been a resident of Boston at the time of the Battle of Bunker Hill. After attending school at Hyde Park, Massachusetts, and Roxbury Latin School in Boston, Davis entered Amherst College, graduating Phi Beta Kappa in 1888. His first postcollege employment in that year, which turned out to be his last, was secured as a result of his father's friendship with a former parishioner, one Alfred E. Hunt, who had moved to Pittsburgh where, in collaboration with other businessmen, he had founded the Pittsburgh Reduction Company for the making of aluminum. Although aluminum's favorable characteristics as an industrial metal had been known in the early nineteenth century, it was expensive to manufacture, with the largest piece (117½ ounces) used as a capstone for the Washington Monument in 1884. The Pittsburgh Reduction Company hoped to capitalize on the experiments of Charles Martin Hall, an Oberlin College chemical graduate, to produce the metal at low cost. Young Davis thus joined a firm that was boldly adventurous and unproven, requiring a handyman's disposition, workman's overalls, and a twelve-hour day given the fact that the manufacturing process was a continuous one. Davis and Hall became close associates during these early days and on Thanksgiving Day, 1888, poured the first commercial aluminum.

Yet the great breakthrough created another problem: there was no demand for aluminum. The fifty pounds that the firm was capable of producing each day was locked up in a safe, soon creating an enormous surplus. The price of the metal was reduced from $8 to $5, then $4. Even when it fell to $2 a pound, aluminum was still a bust, with manufacturers preferring to buy other metals. Davis became general manager of the firm, a stockholder in 1891, and director the next year. He continued as general manager when the firm became known as the Aluminum Company of America in 1907; three years later, he became president. Although by this time aluminum was more widely known than it had been in 1888, it was by no means a household word, in spite of the fact that numerous firms arose to make the metal. Davis's major responsibility as general manager and president was to promote the making and selling of quality aluminum products: Alcoa's Wear-Ever line of cookware was the first big break, sold by college students during their summer breaks; aluminum wire as an inexpensive electrical conductor was made by the company when copper-wire producers were opposed to doing so; and aluminum covers for jars and bottles, aluminum horseshoes, and aluminum bicycles would join canteens as evidence of the metal's versatility and Davis's salesmanship and leadership. The most significant use of aluminum, however, was unheralded, as Davis would later recount:

> There is one use of aluminum which occurred in 1890 which very few people know about. Orville and Wilbur Wright built of aluminum the engine which made the flight at Kitty Hawk which was the original flight of heavier-than-air machines. From this flight, as we all know, has sprung the enormous airplane industry of today. When the Wright brothers were building or designing the engine which made this initial flight, they were pleased to find instead of the engine developing 8 horsepower, as they had anticipated, it really developed 12 horsepower and, as Mr. Wilbur Wright said quite recently, from the time they found that the engine produced 12 horsepower, they never had any doubt about their ability to fly. This achievement is something which always meant a great deal to me because no doubt we made the aluminum they used.

But these years of Davis's tenure were not smooth flying, highlighted as they were by confrontations with the government over antitrust issues. In 1912 the Justice Department charged Alcoa with three counts of violation of the antitrust laws; within a few weeks the matter was ended when the company assented to a consent decree. In 1922 the company underwent investigation by the Federal Trade Commission, which ultimately resulted in dismissal of the case in 1930. Again in 1937 the Justice Department began an extensive antitrust case against Alcoa, which was conspicuous for its duration (thirteen years) and Davis's extraordinary performance in a trial lasting some twenty-six months. Having been elevated to chairman of the board in 1928, Davis was the star witness, on the stand for six weeks and contributing over 2,000 pages of testimony. In dismissing the lengthy petition of the Justice Department, the trial judge praised the seventy-two-year-old Davis, who also drew accolades from his Alcoa colleagues for having personally won the company's case. World War II would likewise exonerate Davis and Alcoa in terms of their contribution to the war effort. The production of aluminum, vital for airplanes, tripled by 1944, with nearly 300,000 planes built, three times the number of ships and tanks. By 1942 Alcoa developed four new alloys to make planes stronger. Combining aluminum with such metals as beryllium, magnesium, copper and zinc, and with silicon, the company ensured that metal fatigue was largely overcome, as was deterioration from high temperatures (the alloys could withstand temperatures up to 600 degrees Fahrenheit). Alcoa also came up with an aluminum mat for use in the construction of advance airfields. It weighed half as much as a steel mat, was composed of a large number of sections that fit together with a slide lock, and could be carried airborne or by small cargo vessels. And on the August day in 1945 that the Japanese surrendered, Alcoa announced success in developing a body armor similar to that worn by Crusaders in the Middle Ages, except that it was made of lightweight aluminum and nylon. Tested on soldiers in the South Pacific, the armored vests, especially worn by fliers, were resistant to the type of small shell fragments that caused the most casualties. At about the same time, the firm devised a process for recycling the aluminum in old airplanes through a type of caustic soda bath that dissolved the aluminum while leaving the other plane materials unaffected. Of course, with all this attention to war materials, Alcoa lost out to a competitor in bringing forth a revolutionary household form of aluminum, as illustrated by a small story in *The New York Times* on October 31, 1944:

> Yesterday at the Waldorf-Astoria, the Reynolds Metals Company introduced to home economists and food editors a new role for one of its familiar pre-war products. Aluminum foil, a sheer metal substance, formerly used in packaging cigarettes and processed cheeses, has now been designed for use in wrapping food for home-refrigeration and pantry storage. The foil, which will be packaged in rolls so that as much as is needed may be pulled out and ripped off, will be on the market for general distribution within the next two or three months.

No matter. Alcoa's Arthur Vining Davis would have the last word of sorts: he was awarded the Presidential Certificate of Merit for his work in ensuring that the government had adequate supplies of aluminum for the building of airplanes.

No industry was more important to winning World War II than the rubber manufacturers. A typical B-17 Flying Fortress consumed 1,000 pounds of rubber, a tank double that, and a battleship needed seventy-five tons of rubber to make it an effective threat on the high seas. Whereas World War I took thirty-two pounds of rubber for every person in arms, World War II took six times that amount. The problem in 1941, however, was that the Japanese controlled the areas in Southeast Asia from which the United States had gotten 90 percent of its supplies. By mid-1940 the federal government set up a Rubber Reserve Company to build up a large stockpile of natural rubber in the event of war, but by the end of 1941 the reserve amounted to less than a year's supply according to the 1940 domestic usage. Initially, the Roosevelt administration urged Americans to turn in their used rubber in what was hoped to be a massive drive to whip the Japanese after Pearl Harbor. But used rubber only had so much bounce; it could be recycled at most three times and then was as flat as an old doormat. About 335,000 tons of scrap rubber was collected from Americans in 1942, a drop in the bucket in terms of pressing war needs. Gas rationing was introduced a year later and while it reduced domestic driving as well as traffic accidents, the savings in rubber were still not adequate. All sorts of substitutes for rubber—ranging from wood to certain types of cloth—were proposed by various inventors, but none caught the fancy, at least not for very long, of government officials.

The Germans had pioneered the synthetic rubber industry during World War I. The disadvantages of the product outweighed the benefits, however: vehicles parked for any length of time had flat tires as a result of synthetic rubber. After 1933, the Nazis renewed their research with the help of a heavy import duty on natural rubber; by 1938, their synthetic rubber appeared to be quite satisfactory and was even sent to United States manufacturers for observation. Yet the synthetic rubber research conducted by various American companies appeared to be less than satisfactory by 1940. It was three times more expensive than natural rubber, and the word *synthetic* to many Americans meant lesser quality. B. F. Goodrich marketed the first American synthetic tires in 1940 under the name Ameripol. In an advertisement in October of that year entitled "Synthetic Rubber for Freedom," the company foresaw the necessity for reliance on its new product:

> Because rubber is obtained from trees which must see seven years of development before bearing, the establishment of plantations in the Western hemisphere to fill our rubber requirements can hardly be advanced as a practical solution.
>
> Is synthetic rubber the answer?

Providentially, in this hour of national need, our scientists, after working 14 years on the problem, realized the goal of American-made synthetic rubber, capable of being used in the manufacture of tires and thousands of other rubber products.

Last June The B. F. Goodrich Company announced its synthetic rubber, Ameripol, and through the intervening months we have manufactured and sold to American car owners tires in which Ameripol replaces rubber by over 50%. Although synthetic rubber at present costs three times as much as natural rubber and the price of these tires is therefore one-third higher, many public-spirited Americans have purchased them and Ameripol tires are now giving satisfactory service on the highways. . . .

Just as insurance in the form of battleships and airplanes is now being created under the national defense program, insurance in the form of synthetic rubber productive capacity is justified as a national defense measure in the interest of 130,000,000 Americans whose daily life depends upon unfailing supplies of rubber.

After Pearl Harbor, the federal government appeared unwilling to make a full-fledged commitment to synthetic rubber. Roosevelt appointed a Rubber Survey Committee in August 1942, comprised of leading Americans, including Bernard M. Baruch, who spearheaded the War Industries Board of World War I, Dr. James B. Conant, president of Harvard University, and Dr. Karl M. Compton, president of the Massachusetts Institute of Technology. In about a month, the committee made its report with a sense of crisis—the existing situation, it said, was "so dangerous that unless corrective measures are taken immediately this country will face both a military and civilian collapse." The report went on: "Let there be no doubt that only actual needs, not fancied wants, can, or should be satisfied. To dissipate our stocks of rubber is to destroy one of our chief weapons of war. We have the choice. . . . We cannot base military offensives on rubber we do not have. All our lives and freedoms are at stake in this war. . . . In rubber, the United States must be listed as a 'have not' Nation." Within weeks after the Baruch committee reported, the government raced to provide funding for government plants to produce synthetic rubber that were leased to private rubber, chemical, and petroleum companies on a cost-plus-fee basis. Some fifty-one plants were built between 1942 and 1944, with one at Institute, West Virginia, run by the United States Rubber Company, capable of producing 90,000 tons of synthetic rubber annually. By 1944 production from all plants totaled 800,000 tons, adequate to sustain war and critical domestic needs. Rubber director William Jeffers, president of the Union Pacific Railroad, supervised the operation, and Americans became rubber and synthetic-rubber conscious as a result of B. F. Goodrich's slogan, "Hitler Smiles When You Waste Miles."

The rubber industry made other contributions to the war effort. One of the biggest was in the development of self-sealing fuel tanks for combat airplanes. A flying projectile could bring about total loss of fuel, which led the United States Rubber Company to devise a type of sandwich liner that automatically sealed any puncture. Additional work by the company during the course of the war led to the development of a V-board, a nonmetallic casing, as a fuel tank liner that provided enormous tensile strength. No less important was the work of the Goodyear Tire and Rubber Company in building blimps that were critical in patrols along United States coastal waters. Over 130 blimps were constructed by Goodyear for the Navy, which used them as aerial escorts for convoys, thereby reducing the likelihood of attacks by enemy submarines. Only one blimp was downed as a result of enemy gunfire, and production was halted a year in advance of war's end because of the blimps' excellent record in patrolling. Goodyear was also the firm that built, along with some other companies, the phantom fleet designed to confuse the Nazis before the D day invasion of France in June 1944. One of the main builders of rubber balloon figures for New York's annual Thanksgiving parades, Goodyear built inflatable reproductions of American planes, tanks, and boats that were sent to England and employed at various places at different times in the weeks before the Normandy invasion. The usual ploy was to deflate them at night, rush them to new coastal locations by dawn, and then inflate them so that German reconnaissance planes could view them by day. Of course, Goodyear's workers had no idea about the use of their toy weapons, but their attitude reflected that of their president, Edwin J. Thomas, who would later write about the war effort. "Our attitude," said Thomas, "was, 'Tell us, Government, what you need most to win the war, and that's what we will do.' "

Because Americans could not buy most consumer goods as a result of war, they gave much business to the media. Movies, the radio industry, newspapers, and magazines adapted nicely to the war exigency, meeting at the same time the expectations of consumers. Of course, shortages affected the film industry—from paint to razors to film stars who entered the armed services—but Hollywood soon took very seriously President Roosevelt's view that "the American motion picture is one of our most effective mediums in informing and entertaining our citizens." Film stars toured the country urging that Americans buy war bonds to the total of $775 million. Actually, moviegoers bested that record in 1942 by nearly $64 million, often by buying a bond and thereby gaining free admission to the theater. The industry provided an almost perfect mix of movies for viewers who turned out in record numbers: to be sure, there were plenty of war stories such as *Wake Island* (1942) and *Casablanca* (1942), but before Pearl Harbor was a year old, there were lighter touches in the form of *Yankee Doodle Dandy, The Pride of the Yankees,* and *The Man Who Came to Dinner.* By 1944 the blend between war and peace continued as illustrated by the popular film *Going My Way* (starring Bing Crosby as a priest), and the equally popular *Thirty Seconds over Tokyo* and *A Wing and a Prayer.* The industry gave free films to the armed forces for overseas viewing by servicemen, and the Hollywood Victory Committee, representing actors and technical staff alike, saw to it that 3,865 members of the industry contributed to a grand total of 47,330 free appearances in over 6,800 events ranging from overseas tours to bond rallies in the United States. What is more, the industry provided education in current events through the *March of Time* series and Pathé's *This Is America* releases which were periodically featured with the main movie. Of course, sometimes this news feature together with a double feature of films meant that a moviegoer was confined to the theater for four hours or longer, but in retrospect, this type of imprisonment was most attractive to teenagers—who could do much more harm to society in their idle hours outside a movie house.

Movies made money with their attractive film fare. So too did radio networks and stations, who capitalized on the fact that theirs was the most disseminated and inexpensive form of entertainment. The income for a typical radio station doubled from 1942 to 1944, from $36,488 to $82,402, all attributable to higher advertising income. The industry blended three emphases in their programming during the war: first, there was news and news programs; then there was the mystery show; perhaps the most popular was the comedy series, such as "Fibber McGee and Molly." And then there were the serial shows for youngsters that filled the late afternoon hours as they returned from school. Because Americans listened to the radio for an average of 4½ hours each day, they made heroes and heroines out of the radio stars, such as Kate Smith, and became conscious of the jingles used by advertisers that would help to sell their products after the war. Even news commentators, whose views were wide-ranging in terms of political ideology (such as H. V. Kaltenborn, Edward R. Murrow, and Gabriel Heatter), became identified with specific business sponsors. Not surprisingly, there were some congressmen who worried about the increasing commercialization of radio, but few could deny that the industry was providing enormous public service in the form of instant news and news commentaries, which accounted for nearly 40 percent of NBC's programming by 1945. And a

Roper poll during the war indicated that Americans, by an almost two-to-one margin, believed that the war news received over the radio was more accurate than that delivered by newspapers.

Like radio, newspapers had no appreciable government censorship during the war and thrived in terms of their bottom lines. Circulation of newspapers rose from 42 million in 1941 to 46 million three years later; Sunday circulation gained nearly 5 million readers in these same years and this in spite of a decrease in both daily and Sunday papers, from 1,857 to 1,744 and 510 to 481, respectively. Newspapers spent a lot of money to bring their readers in-depth news about the war; the D day invasion alone was covered by more than 450 correspondents. The total bill for the three main press associations in providing four years of war news was $30 million. Combined with actual photographs of men at war, firsthand accounts were often moving historical portraits that would not be improved upon by subsequent writers. What is more, newspapers and their reporters were conspicuous for a record unblemished by leaks that could have mushroomed circulation. As the director of censorship said,

> The plain and sober truth is that in no war in history and in no country in the world has the common man been given access to such detailed and comprehensive reports of warfare as those that are placed hourly before readers of American newspapers and listeners beside American radios. The correspondents on the fighting line and the newspapers and broadcasters at home have done a fabulously successful job of protecting the national security.

Even when there was good reason for newspapers to use a story as a means to increase circulation, there was unusually good taste illustrated, as in the case of General George Patton, who slapped down a bedridden soldier in Sicily because his malady appeared to be combat neurosis. Instead of printing the incident, a reporter wrote General Eisenhower, providing complete details, including the fact that the soldier was actually hospitalized with malaria. Eisenhower made an investigation, reprimanded and removed Patton, and the incident, although well-known to reporters, was closed. When Drew Pearson subsequently relayed it over the radio, journalists were critical of Pearson for using bad judgment. Like the movies, newspapers balanced war news with an expanding fare of comics: Bill Mauldin's "Up Front" along with "Kerry Drake" and "Johnny Hazard" joined such old standbys as "Bringing Up Father" and "Gumps." By 1945 Hearst newspapers were making more than half their income from their comics syndication, and some 70 million Americans followed daily the exploits of such home-spun characters as "Joe Palooka" (40 million readers); "Blon-die" (35 million); "Li'l Abner" (32 million); "Orphan Annie" (32 million); "Terry and the Pirates" (31 million); "Dick Tracy" (30 million); "Moon Mullins" (28 million); and "Gasoline Alley" (27 million). Most comic strip characters were not drafted into the military, providing a sense of continuity to a nation that had known more peace than war; those that were had the advantage of making it through the crisis and continuing their sagas afterward.

Magazines had a longer shelf life than newspapers and showed some of their best days during World War II, in spite of paper shortages. More than 6,500 magazines circulated in America and most took advantage of the fact readers had money to spend. Because so many women were the main readers, new magazines came to the fore during the war, such as *Mademoiselle, Glamour,* and *Seventeen.* Advertisers increased their advertising in magazines by $100 million between 1942 and 1944, even though few copies were printed and only the early morning purchaser was assured an ample variety to choose from. War news, of course, was big news for the magazines as it was for the media in general; magazines, however, had more time and colors to gussy it up. *Life* magazine alone had some thirty painters, and photographers abounded among most magazines. In fact, the selling point of magazines was their pictorial appeal—to cut through the narratives one would have to combat even in a *Reader's Digest* and receive a continuous story through pictures and brief captions. At the same time, magazines recognized that contemporary events had more reader appeal than the fiction on which they had traditionally relied; magazine writers became more research oriented; and the likelihood of only good fiction finding space improved the overall quality of the final product. The same was true for the book trade, which provided numerous nonfiction angles to the war but in greater length than either newspapers or magazines. William L. Shirer's *Berlin Diary* was the nonfiction best-seller in 1941; it would be followed by Ambassador Joseph Davies's *Mission to Moscow.* And no book sold better than presidential candidate Wendell L. Willkie's *One World,* released in 1943. A result of his tour around the world in 1942, Willkie's book was a clarion affirmation of America's destiny in world affairs. Sixteen weeks on the best-seller first position, *One World* sold 2 million copies within two years. Its publisher, Simon and Schuster, thought that it would do well if it had 250,000 buyers. Although there were a few fiction best-sellers, the war provided another alternative—contemporary accounts and history—that would not be lost on book publishers after 1945.

If the media illustrated ingenuity in adapting to what President Roosevelt called "the greatest war this nation has ever faced," no less could be said for the American inventor who was absolutely certain that the end of the crisis would necessitate better goods to sustain the typical American and his family. For that reason all sorts of domestic-oriented inventions received patents during the war, with *The New York Times* periodically noting some of the most unusual, such as four that surfaced during the last week of June 1942: among the 827 awarded during the seven-day period, there was one for a pincer to extract an olive from a tall, narrow bottle; another for shaded eyeglasses that fell into slats over the main frame; and a third for a bottle that fed milk into a baby's mouth without any oozing out elsewhere. Finally, there was a patent for a sterilizer for the mouthpiece of a cradle telephone. When the phone was deposited on the cradle, the mouthpiece slipped into the sterilizer tray.

19

THE FABULOUS FIFTIES

During the Prohibition era, a New York journalist believed that he could capsule the entire history of the United States in eleven words: "Columbus, Washington, Lincoln, Volstead, two flights up and ask for Gus." The business history of the 1950s could be summarized in even fewer words: "TV, youth, leisure, plastics, and 'I like Ike.'"

Television was the most unexpected business winner, in large part because radio was so well ingrained in America by World War II. More than 27 million families had radios by 1939, with nearly 11 million sets produced in the same year. Radio broadcasting was simple for both broadcaster and receiver, whereas television transmission required enormous outlays for station and viewer. For that reason, radio would outdistance television until the late 1940s, having by that time carved out a programming menu that was well received, consisting of music, news, drama, comedy, and quiz shows. Although television had been demonstrated in the 1920s and employed experimentally in theaters in the next decade, it had a lot of technical kinks to overcome, including a fuzzy picture. Why should anyone pay good money to go to a movie theater and watch instantaneously relayed events that were difficult to see? Films were much better, even when they broke in midstream, for they could be readily repaired. One of TV's greatest promoters for using the receiver in the home was Allen B. DuMont, who began manufacturing sets in 1938. NBC and CBS, having opened experimental stations even earlier, began transmitting special events, such as the New York World's Fair in 1939, and tried to tackle some of the technical problems. Then came World War II, which put television on the media's back burner. DuMont's television set production came to an end, and transmission and receiving equipment was converted to war use. Still, all was not quiet on the viewing front: DuMont set up its own network in 1942; together with CBS and NBC, the three stations broadcast a few hours each week—not for profit so much as for toying with an idea that the Encyclopedia Britannica had panned a few years earlier.

Production of sets resumed in 1946, but at a snail's pace as a result of other return-to-peacetime priorities. It soon became obvious that a television set attracted viewers like flypaper attracted airborne insects, even when the broadcast dealt with serious subjects, such as a meeting of the United Nations Security Council. Such crowds around the tube in store windows induced manufacturers like DuMont to speed up production: 179,000 sets were made in 1947; nearly 1 million a year later. They were expensive and tiny, about 5¾ inches by 4½ inches and retailing for about $10 a square inch or over $200. No matter. Television soon became a symbol of the American family's upward mobility; the symbol was strengthened by the reality that it was an entertaining medium outdistancing any other. Even though Milton Berle took a pay cut from his radio salary to serve as master of ceremonies on "The Texaco Star Theatre" in 1948, his salary mushroomed the next year. So did the popularity of other shows that were introduced in TV's first big year: Arthur Godfrey's "Talent Scouts," Ted Mack's "Original Amateur Hour," and Ed Sullivan's "Toast of the Town."

The race for station licenses as a result of TV's big reception in 1948 led the Federal Communications Commission to put a freeze on all new licensing. In 1952 the ban was lifted; the number of stations doubled a year later, then doubled again by 1954. In that same year 26 million American families owned television sets; by 1960 nearly 90 percent of the nation's 53 million households boasted a tube. Also, in 1954 the TV dinner was born, but the most significant advance was in technology. By 1957, videotape transformed the industry. Developed by Bing Crosby Enterprises and two other firms, the tape made it possible for entertainers to perform only one show instead of the two required by the different time zones between the East and West coasts. Taping also meant that shows could be readily syndicated and shown for years after the fact, especially as some series, such as "I Love Lucy" inaugurated in 1951, appeared to be timeless in their quality. From a business standpoint, video-tape permitted economies in production: television studios could be built that combined all processes under one roof in a task-on-task format that mimicked factory production of goods. And, of course, the nonlive show gave actors the opportunity to give their best performance—at least that was Ronald Reagan's view of the situation from his experience as host and star of the "General Electric Theater":

Watch those live shows—the pants don't change. This is what made for the slower pace; very often one camera would focus on a steaming cup of coffee, or the curling smoke from a cigarette on an ashtray. Twenty seconds would be wasted on this scenic nothing, while actors scrambled into a new getup. . . . Nancy and I did a live half-hour for GE and she played the first ten minutes wearing two dresses. At one point she left a romantic scene with me, running like crazy for another set, while a wardrobe woman unzipped and removed the outer dress (pull one zipper too many and we'd be off the air). Her next scene called for her to be worried to the point of distraction. Now, what emotion did she sustain?

Television sets got bigger and better in these early years. In 1951 Arvin claimed it was the first to offer a built-in UHF tuner, with screen sizes ranging from 8½ inches to 21 inches and prices starting at $129.95. Arvin's controls were strong enough to "rebuff 'air-plane flutter' and other interference." A year later Crosley advertised its installment purchase plan, making it possible to purchase a seventeen-inch TV at $2.05 per week, and Sylvania touted its HaloLight, "the frame of soft restful light for greater viewing comfort." Magnavox provided a twenty-one-inch screen slanted to divert reflections, and Motorola could not say enough nice things about its new picture tube that "brings the action right into the room . . . closer than ever before" or about its "sabre jet" tuner that whirled at the flick of a finger. Commercials that paid for TV's programs also got bigger but not necessarily better—and more expensive, with one show bringing forth a $300,000 commercial price tag by the mid-1950s. Fortunately for the viewer, they came pretty much at predictable times, providing the opportunity to make visits to the kitchen or bathroom, the latter ritual sometimes requiring an adaptation by local water companies regarding adequate supplies and pressures. To critics television was a wasteland that richly deserved obscurity, to the FCC it was a haven for commercialization and, what was worse, violence and crime; and to sociologists it was the force that contributed to the breakdown of communication within families. But TV had more assets than liabilities: while it sometimes brought the worst of American entertainment into the home, it also brought some of the best. Opera, virtually unappreciated by millions of Americans, received a new lease on life when NBC broadcast Gian-Carlo Menotti's "Amahl and the Night Visitors" on Christmas eve, 1951; the "See It Now" series of Edward R. Murrow introduced viewers to the television documentary that could at once be informative and entertaining; every generation of youngsters could see *The Wizard of Oz,* beginning in 1956, and even old witches and wizards could look forward to its annual presentation; and the major events of each day in the nation and world could be summarized in thirty minutes at suppertime or bedtime. Equally important was the fact that television in America, unlike that of some other nations, would be a private enterprise, with enormous freedom to do its own thing. And it homogenized America by disseminating a value system that would be strong enough to weather such crises as Vietnam and Watergate with minimal adverse effects.

Young people had a big impact on business in the 1950s. There were plenty of them, for one reason. The baby boom began in 1946, peaked in 1954, and ebbed only slightly in the next ten years. Between 1946 and 1964 more than 76 million babies were born in America. They made for a "really big shew" in economic terms. Money spent on diapers increased from $32 million in 1947 to $50 million by 1957; toys and children's clothes soon became boom industries; the sales of hot dogs alone tripled in the decade. As for manufacturers of clothes endorsed by the heroes of children's TV, they wallowed in dollars. Nearly $300 million was spent on fabric replicas of such idols as Hopalong Cassidy, Roy Rogers, Wyatt Earp, and the Cisco Kid. In five months in 1955, a whopping $100 million was spent on Davy Crockett coonskin caps alone. But it was the teenager who really spent the moola in the decade: by 1959 *Life* magazine estimated that teenagers spent $10 billion a year, more than the total sales of General Motors. About 38 percent of the total was spent on transportation and related items; in fact, teenagers helped to increase car registrations by 25 million. They owned a million and a half automobiles. Another 22 percent of teenage spending each year was on food. Because they ate more than adults (by at least 20 percent), they gave new life to the dairy industry, gulping down 3½ billion quarts of milk, four times the amount consumed by infants under the age of one, and some 145 million gallons of ice cream. About 16 percent of the teenager's dollar was spent on entertainment. That $1.5 billion total included $75 million on single records. Teenagers bought records and record players in astonishing numbers, with record sales doubling in one 3-year period, accounting for nearly half of all such purchases. They owned 10 million phonographs and 13 million cameras and bought 22 million records of Bill Haley and the Comets in a two-year span. Their entertainment heroes were much bigger business stars than the cowboy idols of younger folk: Dick Clark and his "American Bandstand," Elvis Presley, and Pat Boone and numerous other musical figures brought forth a following of millions. Presley's first major record, "Heartbreak Hotel," sold 3 million copies in 1956. In the next two years he grossed $100 million, not including income from Elvis jeans, lipstick, buttons —and yes, even toilet paper. The entertainment heroes of teenagers were not monolithic, however, as illustrated by James Dean and Marlon Brando who in their silence and mumbling created a new type of youth-oriented product.

Another 24 percent of teenage spending went to clothing and sports. Females spent $20 million dollars annually on lipsticks, $9 million on home permanents. Both sexes shelled out $25 million for deodorants, and male teenagers owned 2 million electric razors. Breck shampoo increased its sales to teenagers by a million dollars from 1956 to 1959. It was not at all unusual for teenagers to begin hope chests at age fifteen, for one third of eighteen-to-nineteen-year-old girls were married, providing a big boost to the furniture and silver industries. Teenagers were the typical people who patronized the movies and soft drink industry, and armed with aluminum-supported backpacks and American Express Travelers Checks, they began to invade European cities and towns seeking out the inexpensive youth hostel. If they had any problems, it was with their complexion —acne remedies proliferated as manufacturers tried various compounds to eliminate the unsightly pimples. Not surprisingly, Dick Clark's "American Bandstand" was sponsored by Clearasil. As for an end to the teenage spending binge, *Life* magazine said to forget it: "If parents have any idea of organized revolt, it is already too late. Teen-age spending is so important that such action would send quivers through the entire national economy."

About one sixth of the nation's spending in the 1950s went for leisure products. For the first time in the twentieth century, Americans had just about the right mix of work and play: in the first decades they worked too long, in the Great Depression they worked too little, during World War II overtime was the patriotic thing to do; by the 1950s work settled into the five-day routine that would typify subsequent decades. White-collar workers would outdistance blue-collar employees by mid-decade, and 40 percent of all women would be in the work force by 1959—both trends increasing the likelihood of more money and time for leisure. The automobile was the major medium for pleasure spending; over 12 million families by 1958 had two or more cars, and the total number of vehicles exceeded the number of households. The actual miles traveled increased from 458 billion in 1950 to nearly 800 billion by decade's end. Two out of every three Americans drove to work, and auto sales were brisk in every year of the 50s:

Passenger Car Factory Sales

Year	In Millions
1950	6.7
1951	5.3
1952	4.3
1953	6.1
1954	5.6
1955	7.9
1956	5.8
1957	6.1
1958	4.3
1959	5.6
1960	6.7

The motel business boomed, with some 56,000 units taking in $850 million in 1958. So did drive-ins and distant traveling to the West Coast and Florida, where tourism became democratized, no longer the monopoly of the rich. Air travel, which accounted for only 5 percent of people on the move before

World War II, took its place with competitors, rising from 8 million passenger miles in 1950 to 30 million by 1960. Americans inundated European countries during the summer months, often by ship and increasingly by air, with the passenger miles of overseas airlines more than tripling in the decade.

Leisure time also meant the opportunity to read books and go to the movies; book sales more than doubled during the 50s as a result of the paperback revolution. By June 1954, Mickey Spillane's tales of detective Mike Hammer had sold 24 million copies. Hammer was a distinctively American hero: there was no mystery a la Agatha Christie's books; instead, the reader was absolutely certain that Hammer would triumph over evil, even if his methods were heavy-handed and outside the law. Women were sexually attracted to him, and his big physical frame was in no way impaired by his heavy drinking and smoking. A sort of sleazy urban Superman, Hammer found a niche among Americans who in an urbanized and impersonal society were finding it difficult to express their individuality directly and therefore vented it vicariously. Hollywood did not provide any Mike Hammers as a means of increasing its leisure business, but it experimented with a variety of films to compete with TV. To be sure, the industry had little choice: TV was booming, with CBS earning a profit of $8.9 million in 1953, $22.2 million in 1957. "Don't be a 'Living Room Captive,' " read one movie industry ad in 1952. "Step out and see a great movie!" A great movie was first defined in some technological gimmick, such as 3-D and wide-screen films under such names as CinemaScope or Panavision. Then it was defined in extravaganzas consisting of thousands of actors, animals, and sets, as illustrated by *Quo Vadis* (1951) and *The Ten Commandments* (1956). And it was also defined in some mysteries fashioned by Alfred Hitchcock under such titles as *Dial M for Murder* and *To Catch a Thief.* But the industry really found its niche simply by producing good movies and cooperating fully with television. Some of the biggest box-office hits were Oscar winners, such as *The Greatest Show on Earth* (1952), *From Here to Eternity* (1953), *Around the World in 80 Days* (1956), and *The Bridge on the River Kwai* (1957). And the industry made money by decade's end by producing movies and various series for the TV networks and by taking a good hard look at the foreign films that were trickling into movie houses with their scenes of nudity and overt sexuality, an educational lesson that would not be lost on American filmmakers in the 1960s.

Even religion was a form of profitable recreation for Americans in the 1950s. Among the ten big songs in 1953 were Les Paul and Mary Ford's "Vaya con Dios" and Frankie Laine's "I Believe." Reverend Norman Vincent Peale not only sold books in record numbers—*A Guide to Confident Living* (1948) and *The Power of Positive Thinking* (1952)—but he founded his own magazine, *Guideposts,* which soon had a circulation of 800,000. Because Peale combined religion with the business gospel of self-help and stick-to-itiveness, he fit in nicely with the decade's economic tempo; in fact, in 1954 one survey put him among the twelve best salesmen in the United States. Another religious salesman who operated according to modern business techniques was Billy Graham, whose Evangelistic Association was incorporated in 1950 and soon had a hefty $2 million budget. Graham wrote books, a newspaper column that attracted 28 million readers every day, appeared on television and radio, and, most of all, hosted crusades throughout the nation and world. His public relations man associated Graham with the "Cadillac" of preachers, and like GM's most expensive car, Graham and his staff ran smoothly over each crusade city months before the actual event—a planning technique that ensured a successful turnout. Graham even used computers to ascertain the tempo of individual conversions at the crusades.

Contributing enormously to the leisure pace of Americans in the 1950s was the chemical industry, perhaps best identified with its plastics, the product that Dustin Hoffman in *The Graduate* was urged to get into as a sure means of good employment and advancement. Plastics made for consumer goods that were easy to care for and virtually unbreakable, thereby releasing the consumer from household drudgery. Take vinyl flooring, for example. In the mid-1950s, a plant making this product required a three-hour cycle from start to finish, with an estimated 16 to 18¢ of investment for every dollar of sales revenue. By contrast, the linoleum flooring that vinyl replaced required about $1.35 for each dollar of sales revenue. What was worse, the production cycle was similar to that of a brewery; made of linseed oil and other chemicals, the initial product had to cure for several weeks before being mixed with other materials, then it had to be baked. Total time cycle: thirty to ninety days. Then there was the toy industry which was transformed by plastics. Originally relying on wood and metals, the industry eventually took to the products of such firms as Dow Chemical, which boasted its "super impact styron 475," meaning "toys with long life built in." According to Dow, its plastic had "five times the impact strength of general-purpose polystyrene. It is capable of taking stresses and strains without shattering, chipping or cracking." By 1967 the biggest use of plastics in toys was for dolls, followed by nonriding transportation toys. Plastics invaded the kitchen with dishware that was unbreakable, redecorated other rooms with inexpensive wall tile, even with curtains and drapes selling for as little as $1, and got the homeowner secure on a vacation, thanks to Fiberglas-reinforced plastic luggage touted by Arthur Godfrey on nationwide TV. "You can drop it," read the ad. "You can kick it around. Fiberglas luggage won't scuff, warp, dent or puncture. It'll take the roughest travel battering in the world and never lose its streamlined shape." There were also plastic containers and parts of major home appliances, such as refrigerators, easy to care for as a result of polystyrene crisper trays and door shelves.

The fact that plastics were long-lasting, lightweight, resistant to chemicals, and inexpensive ensured their rapid expansion—a twelvefold increase—from 1946 to 1968. Because leather hides were insufficient to shoe increasing numbers of Americans, plastics made for another footwear alternative. They also affected the actual construction of houses, as illustrated by the following product estimates for 1960 (in millions of pounds):

Flooring	240
Paints and coating	300
Pipe and fitting	90
Adhesive and caulking	140
Decorative laminate	70
Panel, siding, roof	35
Wood composite	140
Wire cover	260
Vapor barrier and insulation	40
Furniture	400

And plastic usage in motor vehicles grew from 104 million pounds in 1950 to 229 million in 1960.

The chemical firms that produced plastics were in their heyday in the 1950s. All major firms grew phenomenally, engaging in research yet still maintaining ample funds for dividends, wages, modernization, and expansion. Productivity was raised while prices were held steady. Little wonder that *Fortune* magazine in 1950 called it "the premier industry in the United States." In addition to plastics, the industry created new products such as Orlon and other synthetic fibers, detergents, fertilizers, aerosols, pesticides, antifreeze, additives, and drugs. It was the leading industry in terms of direct investment in other countries with $742 million poured into Canada, $440 million into Europe, and $360 million in Latin America. Some firms, like Du Pont and Dow, became household words in at least three of the four corners of the globe.

The same could not be said for William J. Levitt, although, to be sure, his name would be known to numerous Americans. Born in Brooklyn in 1907, Levitt appeared in his early years to be destined to deserved obscurity. He quit New York University in his third year and looked around for some fast ways for making a lot of money. Along with his brother and father,

Levitt built houses in the northeast, at sums ranging from $9,000 to $18,000, with most falling on the higher end of the price scale. Then came World War II and the great demand by the government for fast, low-cost housing at critical military areas. The Levitts gave this priority their best shot in Norfolk where 757 houses were built for the Navy. Bill Levitt got a brainstorm from this experience, calculating that good, low-cost housing built in volume could make him a lot of money. Enter the first Levittown on Long Island, impressive enough to put him on the cover of *Time* magazine in 1950. Comprised of 40,000 residents, with one-fifth children and very few over thirty-five, Levittown "cannot be mistaken for castles," observed *Time*. At the same time, it was spanking clean, even antiseptic, with flat, wide streets and new homes that were affordable at $7,990. In fact, each house had an angled roof, one picture window, a 12 by 16 living room with fireplace, one bath, and kitchen. The attic could be expanded into two more bedrooms and a bath. A veteran need pay nary a cent down to get into a Levittown home, with a monthly payment of $56 for thirty years; nonveterans had to shell out a 5-percent down payment. Levitt liked to call himself the General Motors of the housing industry, the builder of "the best house in the U. S." And if the demand for his houses were any indication of the truth of his claims, then he was everything he said he was. His community also had a lot of pluses: every home had a Bendix washer and Admiral TV at no extra cost; there were swimming pools and play areas that would ensure good recreation for the kids; there were even rules and regulations for keeping Levittown attractive. No fences or clotheslines; nap time was from 12 to 2 P.M., and lawns had to be mowed at least once a week. No, it was not heaven at Levittown, but the idea was worth mimicking by other builders. So was Levitt's twenty-six stages of building houses quickly, using prefabricated materials, kicking the featherbedding out of the construction workers, and adopting such shortcuts as spray painting. "The countless new housing projects," *Time* wrote, "made possible by this financial easy street are changing the way of life of millions of U. S. citizens, who are realizing for the first time the great American dream of owning their own home." Instead of having to save for years to buy a home, young Americans could realize their dream immediately and upgrade it over the years by selling one house and using the equity and house inflation to buy a bigger and better one. The result was not only to make Levitt the biggest builder of houses but to make construction one of the solid growth areas of the economy. Levitt's example moved the industry to move faster than its peak year of 1949 when 104,000 units were underway. By 1960 one fourth of all existing residential housing had been built in the 1950s. Never had so much, to rework Winston Churchill's famous phrase, been done for so many at such little cost.

The same might also be said for Dwight David Eisenhower, the decade's most famous person. To be sure, intellectuals and the media would disagree with such a conclusion, but they were the odd men out. Americans liked Ike—and for so many good reasons. A military man, Ike never fought his political opponents or got in bed with them. Senator Joseph McCarthy was basically ignored after Ike got into the White House and fashioned his own political noose ("I will not get in the gutter with that guy," Ike said to an aide). The Korean War came to an end under Eisenhower, and the Cold War lessened, with American troops sent abroad in only one instance, in Lebanon, during the entire decade. For businessmen, Ike was enormously attractive, although some would not appreciate that fact for some time. The first Republican president since the 1920s, Ike could have attempted to turn back the clock to that pre-Depression decade when conservative GOP doctrines prevailed, emphasizing among other things the superiority of corporate executives, the evils of popular government, the primacy of economic goals (including a balanced budget and reduction of the national debt), and the absolute minimum in the scope and function of government. Limited government to businessmen in the 1920s meant the protection of life and property through the establishment of military, diplomatic, police, and judicial institutions, as well as the power to tax to provide for such security. It meant therefore the acceptance of the self-regulating economy of the nineteenth century that was supposed to follow natural economic laws that were "right" but not necessarily benign.

Such political thinking, largely espoused by Senator Robert A. Taft, whom Ike defeated for the GOP nomination, not only turned its back on the Progressive reforms of the early twentieth century but was certainly at war with the New Deal. It also took exception to the Democratic-fashioned foreign policy that made containment and detente, rather than victory, its guiding lights. Instead of following this right-wing Republican philosophy, Ike headed for the wide middle road. His Modern Republicanism set the standard for successful chief executives who would follow, geared as it was to acceptance and cautious expansion of the Progressive-New Deal reforms and to adherence to prudent fiscal policies. Public works and social welfare programs expanded under Ike—in Social Security and minimum wage coverage and benefits, education assistance, public housing, and the federal highway program. At the same time, the administration tried to keep its ear to the fiscal ground in terms of excessive federal outlays, but when recession came as in 1953–54 and 1957–58, Ike responded by priming the spending pump. The result of Ike's middle way was a 20 percent rise in real wages for a typical American family, a low inflation rate, few labor disputes, a solid American dollar abroad, and thus an excellent environment for American business. "In our Nation work and wealth abound," said Ike in his second inaugural address. "Our population grows. Commerce crowds our rivers and rails, our skies, harbors, and highways. Our soil is fertile, our agriculture productive. The air rings with the song of our industry—rolling mills and blast furnaces, dynamos, dams, and assembly lines—the chorus of America the bountiful." Of course, if business violated the important regulatory rules, there would be hell to pay. For that reason, the Eisenhower administration illustrated a vigorous enforcement of antitrust laws, culminating in the massive case against electrical manufacturers, resulting in penalties of nearly $2 million and jail terms for seven executives. And the cases were initiated in the election year of 1960.

Modern Republicanism would have another name when the other party was in power: Modern Democracy. The prudent middle road of the Progressive movement, expanded but badly emotionalized during the New Deal years in the 1930s, was restored by Dwight David Eisenhower. And in terms of the alternative economic routes that other times and nations had fashioned, it was clearly the best highway for American business.

20
FINE POINTS

The history of business in the quarter century after 1960 has been the least exciting of its lengthy past in America. The reason is that both business and society in general are mature institutions, with a similar mindset about politics and economics. Unlike John Winthrop in Puritan times, political and business leaders do not have to sweat the details about survival of the American capitalistic system or about its inherent morality. Unlike the era of the American Revolution, there are no social or political revolutions with which business has to contend. Unlike the nineteenth century, popular economic ideas hostile to big business are reserved for extremists who have no political clout. Unlike the brouhaha between business and Franklin D. Roosevelt that emerged during the middle phase of the New Deal, business and government today engage only in modest rhetorical forays, with radical legislation unlikely to be the end result. Today, business gets excited or worries about fine points, which are rarely the stuff of good history—whether they involve foreign policy, multinational firms, maintenance technology, business education and ethics, or politics. Even American business's reaction to Japanese industrial practices has been evolutionary rather than revolutionary, with little strident opposition or rush to emulate. Little wonder that businessmen who exceed these parameters, such as Lee Iacocca, achieve the status of American heroes.

The history of fine points in the business environment may well have begun in 1962 with the confrontation between President John F. Kennedy and U.S. Steel executive Roger Blough. When Kennedy took office in January 1961, he found a slumping national economy. During the following months he attempted to revitalize the recession-plagued nation with measures designed to ease the adverse balance of payments, increase industrial production, and to reduce unemployment. The bulwark of this antirecession policy was to maintain price stability through the moderation of wage demands, especially in the bellwether industry, steel. In a letter addressed to the executives of the twelve leading steel companies in the summer of 1961, the president urged that prices be held down, and he committed his administration to similar efforts in regard to union wage goals. In March 1962 the steelworkers signed a contract that reflected adherence to the president's guidelines; however, the following month Blough visited the White House, announcing a 3.5 percent increase in the company's prices, an action soon to be duplicated by five other firms. In his press conference the following day, Kennedy referred to the "tiny handful of steel executives whose pursuit of private power and profit exceeds their sense of public responsibility," and before U.S. Steel had rescinded its price increases on Friday, April 13, the president had marshaled the full force of the federal government against Blough and his cohorts. Justice Department and FBI officials began amassing evidence of collusion, Congress contemplated price legislation, and Secretary of Defense Robert McNamara shifted defense orders to firms that held the line on prices. Much ado about nothing, or a small price hike, was the way the event appeared a few weeks after the so-called crisis. The press divided on the matter in terms of whether Kennedy with his excessive use of government power or Blough with his bad timing was the villain. It was a draw on a low-key matter, the first of many in the following twenty-five years that would be recorded mostly as one-day or one-week stands in newspaper pages.

Even on seemingly important issues in recent decades American business differed little from the public at large. Contrary to radical theory that suggests that imperialism and war are the last stages of capitalism, the Vietnam War evoked the same agony and ecstasy in businessmen as it did in the general population. The hawks appeared numerous when the going looked good, the doves when the military bottom lines seemed excessively mired in the red blood of American lives. By the spring of 1967, *Business Week* felt that the increasing outlays—in American lives, money, and resources—and small returns could "weaken rather than strengthen the nation in its ability to defend its vital interests around the world and to deal with pressing domestic problems." Its recommendation: the pursuit of a limited policy that would confine American troops to defensible and important pieces of South Vietnamese real estate. *Fortune* magazine, on the other hand, defended the Vietnamese involvement in the critical years from 1964 to 1967. In April 1965 it argued that the effectiveness of the strategy of escalation had been demonstrated in Lebanon, Berlin, and Cuba and therefore its use in Vietnam was well grounded. In an eloquent defense of "The American Empire," *Fortune* saw the foreign policies of many presidents continued in current history: "We are bound by our past deeds to a deep involvement in the fate of many nations, and we can be certain this involvement will continue for many years, probably decades, into the future." This optimistic tone characterized other editorials, in particular their titles, "The Overlooked Victory in Troubled Vietnam," "The Emerging Victory in Asia" (two-part editorial), and "New Building Blocs in Asia." In a special issue devoted to the war in April 1967, the *Fortune* editors concluded there was no alternative except the "long, difficult road to victory," the effects of which would permeate all Asia. The most typical business response to the Vietnam War was serpentine, illustrating, like most Americans, varying degrees of support, opposition, and/or indifference. At one time the image of America in the Vietnamese jungle was historically sanctioned if not morally imperative; at another time the specter of commitment in so insignificant a land seemed a poor investment of American lives and resources; and at still other times the meaning of the war was indirect, in the form of inflation, shortages, or "unbusinesslike" planning. But to few businessmen was the dollar sign the basis of content or discontent. America and its capitalistic system, now at middle age, were more than the sum total of economic gain or loss.

To be sure, some analysts would disagree, especially with respect to the large American multinational firms that appeared to dominate vast areas of the world in the 1970s. But the book *Global Reach: The Power of Multinational Corporations* (1974) attracted primarily academic circles and the media; within a few years, the ballyhoo died down, as reality suggested that MNCs were neither bad guys nor good guys so much as they were economic institutions involved in complex situations, inundated with fine points. Most multinational investment, for example, has been in developed areas such as Canada and Europe, with less than 5 percent of the total directed to the Third World. Historically, American firms in Canada and Europe have caused little stir because of the economic, political, and cultural affinity of the three areas. Not so in developing countries where the individuals who are most likely to direct the course of MNCs have myopic economic vision: grown wealthy from agricultural endeavors, these politically influential people hope to effect profits by having multinationals mechanize agriculture. However, this mechanization displaces enormous numbers of farm workers, thereby increasing unemployment. Consequently, in recent years, only about 4 million of the 680 million people living in less-developed nations have found jobs that are attributable to MNC presence. The ideal pattern for prudent industrialization by such nations is to have MNCs build factories that are highly productive; these factories create jobs that are attractive to low-paid farm workers who rush to fill them; a labor shortage then arises on farms and wages rise; farm managers therefore move in the direction of mechanization. Because few developing nations have pursued this wise course, the MNCs get blamed for not creating jobs, a fine point that is unlikely to undergo radical change for the better. The same might be said about the necessity for multinationals to work with all types of political regimes in the Third World. If the governments are corrupt and undemocratic, the MNC is perceived as consorting with crooks; if the regimes are not, there is the ever present likelihood that their tenure will be short-lived and that the American firm must be a friend to all factions and foes. In an attempt to deal with these unstable conditions, some American firms have resorted to methods that are illegal at home (bribes, payoffs, gifts, commissions) and proscribed as of 1977 in the Foreign Corrupt Practices Act. Because American law has no jurisdiction over Third World nations, their practices are unlikely to change, and MNCs are caught between a rock and a hard, fine point.

Then there are critiques of MNCs in less-developed countries that focus on their adverse effects on people at home and abroad. American laborers, under this view, are hurt when MNCs leave the higher-wage domestic economy for the lower-wage developing nation. Unemployment is created at home and unions are weakened. Less-developed nations, on the other hand, are unlikely to possess unions that will resist unfair labor policies. Advocates of this critique, in another context, might criticize American corporate management for failure to pursue cost-effective strategies; however, when it does so by investing abroad, it is condemned. The Catch-22 continues: workers for MNCs in Third World countries are unlikely to rise to top management. Consigned to mundane tasks, with low pay and long hours, the implication is that they would have been better off had there been no multinational development. For technology pollutes their air, capitalism their motivation, and the search for wealth lessens their lifelines. A fine point mostly confined to academe, the critique has in no material way dictated the course of American multinationals in developing areas.

The concern of a mature society for fine points is also manifest in its policies regarding productivity. A century ago, one of the worst fears was technology's effect on the worker's health, for the number one cause of poverty was industrial accidents. Machines would be inherently dangerous, it was assumed at the time; therefore, workers should be assured of some sort of remuneration in the event of incapacity. The result was workmen's compensation insurance. With these two matters—worker safety and injury-related unemployment—resolved the issue of technology and its relation to the larger environment arose. By the 1960s, no longer fearful that industrial machines would kill or maim workers, Americans turned their attention to whether technology would destroy their physical environment, in particular, plant, animal, and human life. This area of concern, unlike the other two, would be debatable, geared to a whole lot of fine points. When a machine ripped off a worker's arm, it was not mind-boggling to establish a cause-and-effect relation. But when machines emitted vapors or materials in the air and water, the relation of such acts to adverse results was rarely clear and short-term. Nevertheless, not a little of America's technological genius in recent years has been geared to a "maintenance" objective—to ward off the alleged deleterious effect of technology. To be sure, maintenance technology has little drama in its history. One good example is the jet age in terms of airplanes that have changed little in real technology since the 1960s. The supersonic jet is confined to other nations, what with its seemingly adverse environmental effects, and the American models are only variations of a general theme established a quarter century ago. What is worse, this concern about the environment gets even murkier when related to the complaints of white-collar workers using high-tech machinery.

Some employees experience vision problems as a result of looking at the green computer screens all day; others contend that
the highest state-of-the-art lighting appears incompatible with
a congenial mindset; and not surprisingly, at least one super-
market checker has won a worker's compensation case for a
tennis elbow-type malady linked to forearming and backhand-
ing grocery items across a computer scanner—all hardly the
ingredients of a great story. Yet, this concern for fine points by
American society has meant that business productivity must be
geared to meet more than the one objective of earlier times.

Even the study of business in recent decades has undergone
a transformation into fine points that turn out students more
likely to be conscientious caretakers than creative entrepreneurs. A business education in the old days consisted of
courses in economics and accounting, with the rest in the field
of liberal arts. Since the 1950s, however, business schools have
rushed to offer specialized instruction that comprise an ever-
increasing proportion of the student's total hours. Conceivably
motivated by the objective of making business tantamount to
medicine and law in professional training, business schools have
increased their offerings to include such fine points as Collective
Bargaining in the Private Sector, Decision Sciences for Management, Personnel Resource Planning, International Finance
(as opposed to International Banking), Financial Statement
Analysis, Partnership Taxation, Managerial Cost Accounting,
and Managerial Accounting and Business Policy. The American Assembly of Collegiate Schools of Business, which accred-
its b-schools, uses language in its standards and guidelines that
illustrates that it is serious (although not clear) about these fine
points of a business education: the curriculum should "provide
students with the common body of knowledge in business administration," and "programs shall include in their course of
instruction the equivalent of at least one year of work compris-
ing the following areas: . . . (e) a study of administrative processes under conditions of uncertainty including integrating
analysis and policy determination at the overall management

level." Of course, the problem with this educational concern for fine points is that the narrow focus might prevent the broad sweeps of innovation and strategy that marked earlier business history and that may still be necessary in the future.

And the study of business ethics has taken on the imprimatur of a mature American society. Textbooks have increasingly used the term *social responsibility* instead of *ethics.* Most delineate the various categories of issues relating to social responsibility (philanthropy, employee relations, community affairs), with some even broaching the idea of using quantitative techniques to measure corporate performance, although in the view of some corporate executives that management science is still a long way from full bloom. According to George Weissman, chairman and chief executive officer of Philip Morris, Inc.,

> I can't precisely measure the effectiveness of our social decisions and programs, but I also can't precisely measure the effectiveness of a Marlboro ad in *Time* or a $400,000 Miller commercial during the Super Bowl. What I do know is what's happened to Philip Morris in the 35 years I have been with the company. . . . So while I can't tell you that being actively responsible has helped me, I sure can tell you that it hasn't hurt.

Business philanthropy in recent years has been played very close to the corporate chest, in part because of a court case dealing with a New Jersey firm. In 1953 after the company made a contribution to Princeton University, one of its stockholders sued on the grounds that management had no right to donate property belonging to stockholders. The court upheld the contribution because in the particular instance private education was a "cause intimately tied to the preservation of American business and the American way of life." Although the court confirmed one example of corporate philanthropy, it did not negate the rights of stockholders or endorse the idea of leaving such things to chance or whim. For this reason, corporations have focused on safe bets in their philanthropy. They gave over $1 billion to educational institutions in 1980; in fact, 90 percent of corporations with assets in excess of $50 million (excluding those with separate foundations) contributed to education, mostly in forms of scientific philanthropy (refereed, audited grants and the like). Rarely do corporate foundations take the risky yet exciting path of the Chicago-based John D. and Catherine D. MacArthur Foundation which in recent years has been awarding "genius" grants. Instead of talented academics having to apply for the awards, the foundation chooses recipients on criteria known only to its staff. Moreover, the grants—up to $300,000 spread over a five-year term—are tax free and can be used for whatever purpose the recipient chooses. Eschewing the meticulous fine points of most corporate philanthrophy, the MacArthur Foundation has received no little publicity, as well as enormous controversy, for its daring and deviant program.

Business's recent role in politics has been limited to fine points. In the post-Civil War era, industrial titans used money to turn the wheels of local government, state legislatures, and even Congress in their direction. Beginning in 1907, restrictions on the business influences in Congress were imposed and expanded over the years, especially in the wake of the Watergate scandal in the 1970s. By that time, American society blossomed in pluralism, thereby permitting every interest group the opportunity to influence politics according to the designated rules of the game. One strategy permitted by the rules was the political action committee (PAC), a sort of halfway house (between direct influence and none at all) that could solicit, receive, and distribute funds in behalf of legislation and candidates. Business PACs would be legal, as would PACs established by labor unions, the American Medical Association, or the National Education Association. The good point about PACs is that they serve as funnels for numerous special-interest groups to attempt to make their political impact; the bad point is that the relation between a PAC's existence, funding amounts, and success is rarely obvious. Put another way, the raison d'être of PACs might be viewed as analogous to that of the arms race. The United States government continues to invest in nuclear arms because if it did not, the Soviet Union might surpass it, thereby threatening the nation's independent existence. Whether, in fact, this equality of deterrence effects stability is debatable. The same with the political scene: corporate PACs exist, in large part, because other PACs seemingly antithetical to business concerns exist. Whether any of them really accomplish anything significant is moot—except perhaps to insure against a first and radical strike via congressional legislation. Little wonder, then, that the history of PACs has occasioned so little real gain, engendering mostly emotional debate over fine points.

In a mature business society, there have been some daring attempts by corporations to break out of the ho-hum state of economic affairs. The conglomerate movement has accelerated for that reason. Because the start-up costs for establishing new industries are enormous, conglomerate mergers provide the opportunity for corporate growth although, to be sure, sometimes the expectations exceed abilities, as illustrated by the bankruptcy in 1982 of Baldwin-United Corporation, a piano manufacturer that hit sour notes in its bid to become a diversified firm. Even more daring have been takeover efforts whose targeted companies have been forced to pay greenmail, that is, to buy out their suitors at above-market prices of stock. Then there have been the marketing ploys to break out of the corporate routine: Wendy's and Burger King would make advertising war on McDonald's, Coca-Cola would change its traditional formula only to drop it within days because of consumer opposition; Procter & Gamble would host a big news conference to announce the transformation of one of its oldest products, Tide detergent, into a liquid form. And PepsiCo's takeover of Pizza-Hut would attempt to make pizza a truly fast-food item by cutting down the cooking time to five minutes—give or take a few nanoseconds.

Popular attention would be focused less on takeover bids, marketing tactics, and the seamy side of business (such as John DeLorean's *On A Clear Day You Can See General Motors)* and more on the Sylvester "Rocky" Stallone of corporate America: Lido (Lee) Iacocca, who would beat all the odds in taking on a sick automobile company and making its turnaround story the bestselling book in America. No doubt, there will be other Horatio Alger stories like Iacocca's, but American business in the future will not be as dependent on these as it has been in the past. For although much has been said in criticism of the humdrum nature of a sophisticated business civilization, even more can be said in its defense. The likelihood of the federal government making war on corporate business through the frequent and strict use of punitive legislation, such as the Sherman Antitrust Act, is lessened; instead of reducing the size of firms, federal policy has expanded the market, by reducing protectionist barriers and permitting entry of foreign products that are strong inducements for improvement of American products; the case-by-case deregulation of business, begun in recent years, will no doubt continue, and self-regulation, already employed in industries such as meat packing, will take the place of government supervision; application of the profit principle might well be expanded to traditional nonprofit institutions such as hospitals or even prisons, providing savings and better service; the tendency of business to be better prepared for the next demographic wave—the graying of America—than it was for the baby boomers is already being illustrated through the development of new goods and services; and, perhaps most important, a mature society means a wider appreciation, thanks to an increasingly educated and affluent population, of the positive, incremental gains of business in technology and strategies. That is only a variation of what de Tocqueville in 1835 believed to be the essence of the United States. Americans, he noted,

> have all a lively faith in the perfectability of man, they judge that the diffusion of knowledge must necessarily be advantageous, and

the consequences of ignorance fatal; they all consider society as a body in a state of improvement, humanity as a changing scene, in which nothing is, or ought to be, permanent; and they admit that what appears to them today to be good, may be superseded by something better tomorrow.

SELECT
BIBLIOGRAPHY

BEASLEY, NORMAN. *Main Street Merchant: The Story of J. C. Penney Company.* New York: Whittlesey Press, 1948.

BODE, CARL, ed. *American Life in the 1840s.* Garden City, N.Y.: Anchor Books, 1967.

BROOKS, JOHN, ed. *The Autobiography of American Business: The Story Told by Those Who Made It.* Garden City, N.Y.: Anchor Books, 1975.

BRUCHEY, STUART, comp. and ed. *The Colonial Merchant: Sources and Readings.* New York: Harcourt, Brace & World, 1966.

BURLINGAME, ROGER. *March of the Iron Men: A Social History of Union Through Invention.* New York: Grosset & Dunlap, 1938.

DIAMOND, SIGMUND. *The Reputation of the American Businessman.* Gloucester, Mass.: Peter Smith, 1970.

DOEZEMA, MARIANNE. *American Realism and the Industrial Age.* Cleveland: Cleveland Museum of Art, 1980.

EMMET, BORIS, and JOHN E. JEUCK. *Catalogs and Counters: A History of Sears Roebuck and Company.* Chicago: University of Chicago Press, 1950.

FLINK, JAMES J. *The Car Culture.* Cambridge, Mass.: The MIT Press, 1975.

FRESE, JOSEPH R., and JACOB JUDD, eds. *An Emerging Independent American Economy 1815–1875.* Tarrytown, N.Y.: The Sleepy Hollow Press, 1980.

GLOVER, JOHN GEORGE, and WILLIAM BOUCK CORNELL. *The Development of American Industries.* New York: Prentice-Hall, 1941.

GOODMAN, NATHAN G., ed. *A Benjamin Franklin Reader.* New York: Thomas Y. Crowell Company, 1971.

GRAS, N. S. B., and HENRIETTA M. LARSON. *Casebook in American Business History.* New York: Appleton-Century-Crofts, 1939.

HAMMOND, BRAY. *Banks and Politics in America, from the Revolution to the Civil War.* Princeton, N.J.: Princeton University Press, 1957.

JENSEN, MERRILL. *The New Nation: A History of the United States During the Confederation 1781–1789.* New York: Vintage Books, 1950.

KIRKLAND, EDWARD CHASE. *Industry Comes of Age: Business, Labor and Public Policy, 1860–1897.* Chicago: Quadrangle Books, 1967.

LEWIS, PETER. *The Fifties.* Philadelphia: Lippincott, 1978.

LINGEMAN, RICHARD R. *Don't You Know There's a War on? The American Home Front, 1941–1945.* New York: Paperback Library, 1971.

MITCHELL, BROADUS. *Alexander Hamilton,* 2 vols. New York: Macmillan Company, 1957–62.

MORGAN, EDMUND S. *The Puritan Dilemma: The Story of John Winthrop.* Boston: Little, Brown and Company, 1958.

O'REILLY, MAURICE. *The Goodyear Story.* Ed. by James T. Keating. Elmsford, N.Y.: Benjamin Company, 1983.

ROSATO, DOMINICK V., and others. *Markets for Plastics.* New York: Van Nostrand Reinhold Company, 1969.

SCHLESINGER, ARTHUR MEIER. *The Colonial Merchants and the American Revolution, 1763–1776.* New York: F. Ungar Publishing Company, 1957.

SETTEL, IRVING. *A Pictorial History of Television.* New York: Ungar Publishing Company, 1983.

STRUIK, DIRK J. *Yankee Science in the Making.* New York: Collier Books, 1962.

SWARD, KEITH. *The Legend of Henry Ford.* New York: Atheneum Publishers, 1968.

WIEBE, ROBERT H. *The Search for Order 1870–1920.* New York: Hill and Wang, 1967.

WISH, HARVEY, ed. *William Bradford's Of Plymouth Plantation.* New York: Capricorn Books, 1962.

WRIGHT, LOUIS B. *Life in Colonial America.* New York: Capricorn Books, 1971.

WRIGHT, LOUIS B., and MARION TINLING, eds. *The Great American Gentleman: The Secret Diary of William Byrd of Westover in Virginia, 1709–1712.* New York: Capricorn Books, 1963.

YOUNG, ELEANOR. *Forgotten Patriot: Robert Morris.* New York: Macmillan Company, 1950.

YOUNG, JAMES HARVEY. *The Toadstool Millionaires: A Social History of Patent Medicines in America Before Federal Regulation.* Princeton, N.J.: Princeton University Press, 1961.

INDEX

INDEX

assembly line, 66, 176, 178, 180, 182
  See also mass production
Astrop, Robert Francis, 122
automobile, 150, 171, 174–87, 224, 242,
    254, 256, 260, 275
  economy, 175–79, 182
  luxury, 175, 182, 258
  used, 183–84
  See also individual companies

Bacon, Sir Francis, 209
Baer, George F., 202–3
Baldwin-United Corporation, 274
Baltimore, Maryland, 76, 82, 90, 93,
    94, 101–2, 108, 190–92
Bank of England, 70
Bank of North America, 56–58
Bank of Philadelphia, 56
Bank of the Manhattan Company
    (Chase Manhattan), 71
Bank of the United States, 63, 70, 72,
    74, 88
bankruptcy, 54, 71, 131–32, 144, 145,
    274
Bankruptcy Act of 1800, 58
banks, 71, 72, 88, 113, 115, 117, 140,
    179, 185, 194
  national, 52, 56–58, 63, 70, 72, 73,
    74, 113, 144, 200
bargaining, collective. *See* unions
barter, 115
Baruch, Bernard M., 242
bathtub, 212–13
Beecher, Catherine, 131
Belcher, Andrew, 11
Bellamy, Edward, 137, 138
benefits, 166, 197, 199–200, 202,
    225–26, 263, 270, 271
  See also insurance; pension funds
Bessemer process, 154, 156
Best Stove and Stamping Company, 209
bicycles, 165, 238
Bill of Rights, 51–52
Bing Crosby Enterprises, 252
Birmingham, Alabama, 107–8, 117, 119
Blacks, 26–27, 109, 112, 114–15, 116
blinds, venetian, 205, 215–16
Bloomer, Amelia, 120, 131
Blough, Roger, 266–67
Blue Eagle, 227, 230
boards of trade, 198

Bolgiano Manufacturing Company, 206
bonds, 142, 153, 236, 244
Bonsack machine, 118
book publishing, 9, 21, 60, 95, 248, 257
Boston, Massachusetts, 8, 9, 11, 12, 13,
    15, 24, 40–41, 44, 70, 95, 105, 209,
    237
  transportation to, 78, 80, 82
  violence in, 42, 43
Bowen, Francis, 126–27
boycotts, 40, 41–42, 44–45, 73–74, 194
Boyle, Charles, Earl of Orrery, 33, 35
Bradford, William, 2–6, 12, 13
Breck, 255
Brook Farm, 124
Brown, Moses, 97
Bryan, William Jennings, 195
Buick, 182, 184
Bunker Hill, Battle of, 45, 190, 237
Bureau of Corporations, 200–201
burglar alarm, 102
Burr, Aaron, 71, 72, 73, 108
Burrill, George, 12
business. *See* capitalism; entrepreneurs;
    management; *and individual
    industries*
Business Advisory Council, 227
Business and Professional League, 231
Butterfield, John, 79
buttons, 103–4, 214
Byrd, William II, 26–37, 107

Cadillac, 182, 258
Calhoun, John C., 113
California, 79, 90, 139, 205, 234
Canada, 46, 260, 268
canals, 9, 81–84, 85
  Erie, 82–83, 84, 111
canning, 105, 205
capitalism, 63, 88, 126, 137, 157, 159,
    198, 265, 267, 268, 270
  colonial, 2, 4, 6, 8, 13, 16, 109–10
Caribbean. *See* West Indies
Carnegie, Andrew, 143–44, 146,
    152–59, 182, 185
Carnegie Company, 156, 193
Carroll, John Lee, 191
cartels, 224
Carver, John, 1, 2
cash register, 102–3
cattle, 8, 9, 78

280

INDEX